SMITHSONIAN HANDBOOKS

DINOSAURS
AND PREHISTORIC LIFE

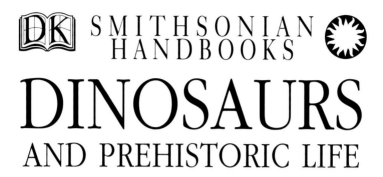

DK SMITHSONIAN HANDBOOKS

DINOSAURS
AND PREHISTORIC LIFE

HAZEL RICHARDSON

Consultant
DR DAVID NORMAN

A Dorling Kindersley Book

LONDON, NEW YORK, MUNICH,
MELBOURNE, and DELHI

Project Editor Cathy Meeus
Art Editor Lee Riches
Designers Tracy Miles, Rebecca Milner
Picture Researcher Mariana Sonnenberg
DTP Designer Rajen Shah
Senior Editor Angeles Gavira
Senior Art Editor Ina Stradins
Production Controller Melanie Dowland
Managing Editor Liz Wheeler
Managing Art Editor Phil Ormerod

Consultants Dr. David Norman,
M. K. Brett-Surman Ph.D., Douglas H. Erwin,
Matthew Carrano

2/3D Digital illustrations Jon Hughes
Additional 3D content Russell Gooday

First American Edition, 2003
03 04 05 06 07 10 9 8 7 6 5 4 3 2 1

Published in the United States by
DK Publishing, Inc.
375 Hudson Street
New York, New York 10014

A Cataloging-in-Publication record for this book
is available from the Library of Congress.

ISBN 0-7894-9361-6

Reproduced by Media Development Printing,
Great Britain
Printed and bound in Slovakia by TBB

see our complete product line at
www.dk.com

CONTENTS

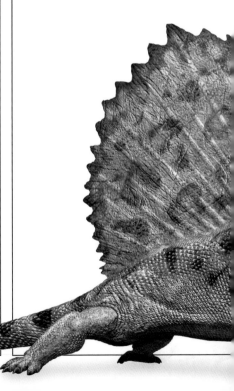

HOW THIS BOOK WORKS

This book opens with an introductory section that describes the evolution of early animals, followed by a summary of the environment on Earth during its early history. The main part of the book contains profiles of the major prehistoric animals from the Mesozoic and Cenozoic Eras.

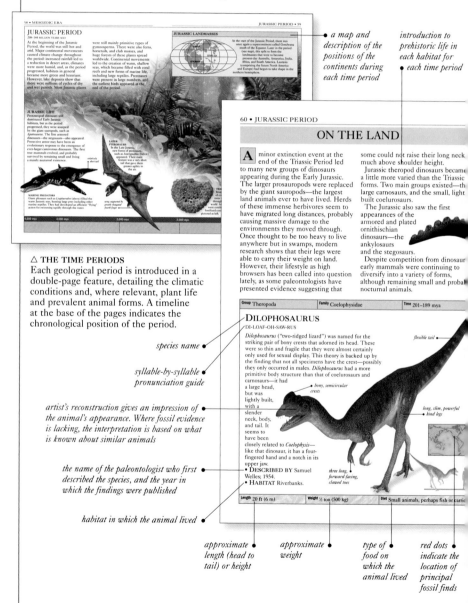

- a map and description of the positions of the continents during each time period

- introduction to prehistoric life in each habitat for each time period

△ **THE TIME PERIODS**
Each geological period is introduced in a double-page feature, detailing the climatic conditions and, where relevant, plant life and prevalent animal forms. A timeline at the base of the pages indicates the chronological position of the period.

60 • JURASSIC PERIOD

ON THE LAND

A minor extinction event at the end of the Triassic Period led to many new groups of dinosaurs appearing during the Early Jurassic. The larger prosauropods were replaced by the giant sauropods—the largest land animals ever to have lived. Herds of these immense herbivores seem to have migrated long distances, probably causing massive damage to the environments they moved through. Once thought to be too heavy to live anywhere but in swamps, modern research shows that their legs were able to carry their weight on land. However, their lifestyle as high browsers has been called into question lately, as some paleontologists have presented evidence suggesting that some could not raise their long neck much above shoulder height.

Jurassic theropod dinosaurs became a little more varied than the Triassic forms. Two main groups existed—the large carnosaurs, and the small, light built coelurosaurs.

The Jurassic also saw the first appearances of the armored and plated ornithischian dinosaurs—the ankylosaurs and the stegosaurs.

Despite competition from dinosaurs early mammals were continuing to diversify into a variety of forms, although remaining small and probably nocturnal animals.

Group Theropoda	Family Coelophysidae	Time 201–189 mya

DILOPHOSAURUS
DI-LOAF-OH-SAW-RUS

Dilophosaurus ("two-ridged lizard") was named for the striking pair of bony crests that adorned its head. These were so thin and fragile that they were almost certainly only used for sexual display. This theory is backed up by the finding that not all specimens have the crest—possibly they only occurred in males. *Dilophosaurus* had a more primitive body structure than that of coelurosaurs and carnosaurs—it had a large head, but was lightly built, with a slender neck, body, and tail. It seems to have been closely related to *Coelophysis*—like that dinosaur, it has a four-fingered hand and a notch in its upper jaw.
• **DESCRIBED BY** Samuel Welles; 1954.
• **HABITAT** Riverbanks.

flexible tail

bony, semicircular crests

long, slim, powerful hind legs

three long, forward-facing, clawed toes

Length 20 ft (6 m)	Weight ½ ton (500 kg)	Diet Small animals, perhaps fish or carrion

- species name

- syllable-by-syllable pronunciation guide

- artist's reconstruction gives an impression of the animal's appearance. Where fossil evidence is lacking, the interpretation is based on what is known about similar animals

- the name of the paleontologist who first described the species, and the year in which the findings were published

- habitat in which the animal lived

- approximate length (head to tail) or height

- approximate weight

- type of food on which the animal lived

- red dots indicate the location of principal fossil finds

▽ ANIMAL PROFILES
Arranged by time period, habitat (land, water, or air), and by group, each major animal is described in detail. The text includes information about the animal's physical features, diet, and lifestyle. Colored bands summarize key information about classification, dates, dimensions, and diet. Each animal is illustrated by an artist's reconstruction and/or fossil remains. Key features are annotated. In each case, a map identifies the approximate location of main fossil finds of that creature.

scientific name of main group

scientific name of family

time when the animal existed in millions of years ago (mya) or years ago (ya)

COLOR KEY
The bands at the top of each entry are color-coded to identify the time period to which it belongs. The bands at the base of each entry are colored according to the habitat in which the animal lived.

TIME-PERIOD COLORS

Precambrian

Cambrian

Ordovician

Silurian

Devonian

Carboniferous

Permian

Triassic

Jurassic

Cretaceous

Early Tertiary

Late Tertiary

Quaternary

HABITAT COLORS

Land

Water

Air

▽ FEATURE SPREAD
Animals of special interest are featured in a double-page entry. These show the animal in the type of landscape in which it is believed to have lived. Additional photographs and information boxes expand on the standard information for each featured animal.

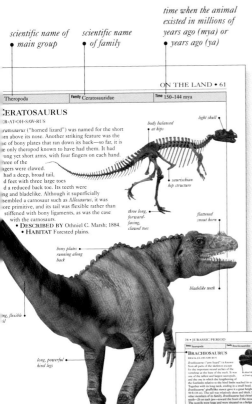

ON THE LAND • 61

| Theropoda | Family Ceratosauridae | Time 150–144 mya |

CERATOSAURUS
ER-AT-OH-SAW-RUS

eratosaurus ("horned lizard") was named for the short rn above its nose. Another striking feature was the e of bony plates that ran down its back—so far, it is e only theropod known to have had them. It had ong yet short arms, with four fingers on each hand. hree of the gers were clawed. had a deep, broad tail, d feet with three large toes d a reduced back toe. Its teeth were ng and bladelike. Although it superficially sembled a carnosaur such as *Allosaurus*, it was ore primitive, and its tail was flexible rather than stiffened with bony ligaments, as was the case with the carnosaurs.
• DESCRIBED BY Othniel C. Marsh; 1884.
• HABITAT Forested plains.

light skull
body balanced at hips
saurischian hip structure
three long, forward-facing, clawed toes
flattened snout horn
bony plates running along back
bladelike teeth
ng, flexible il
long, powerful hind legs
long foot
reduced back toe

15–20 ft (4.5–6 m) | Weight 1 ton (1 metric ton) | Diet Herbivorous di

the length or height of each animal is indicated in comparison to human dimensions

8 in (20 cm)

6 ft (1.8 m)

78 • JURASSIC PERIOD

ON THE LAND • 79

BRACHIOSAURUS
BRACK-EE-OH-SAW-RUS

Brachiosaurus ("arm lizard") is known from all parts of the skeleton except for the important neural arches of the vertebrae at the base of the neck. It was one of the tallest and largest sauropods, and the one in which the lengthening of the forelimbs relative to the hind limbs reached its extreme. Together with its long neck, ending in a small head, *Brachiosaurus*' girafflike stance gave it a great height: up to 30 ft (16 m). The tail was relatively short and thick. Like other members of its family, *Brachiosaurus* had chisel-like teeth—26 on each jaw—toward the front of the mouth. The nostrils were large and were situated on a bulge on the top of the head. The legs were pillarlike, and the feet all had five toes with fleshy pads behind. The first toe of each front foot bore a claw, as did the first three toes of the hind feet. Like other sauropods, it probably swallowed its food. *Brachiosaurus* was adapted for feeding off vegetation from the tops of trees. The length of its neck means that it would have had to have an extremely large, powerful heart, and very high blood pressure to pump blood up to its head. *Brachiosaurus* is thought to have laid its eggs while walking, leaving the young to fend for themselves.
• DESCRIBED BY Elmer S. Riggs; 1903.
• HABITAT Plains

nostrils on bulge on top of head
chisel-like teeth at front of mouth
long neck made up of 13 (14-m) long vertebrae
body sloping downward from shoulder to hip
relatively thin, pillarlike legs

MASSIVE BONES
The femur (thigh bone) of *Brachiosaurus* was over 6 ft (1.8 m) long and massively thick to support the dinosaur's weight. One of the first bones discovered by Elmer S. Riggs in 1900, was the humerus (upper arm bone). It was over 7 ft (2.1 m) long, which was so much greater than that of any known humerus that Riggs thought it was a crushed femur of an *Apatosaurus* (p.76).

80 ft (26 m) | Weight 55 tons (50 metric tons) | Diet Plants

CLASSIFICATION OF LIFE

An accurate understanding of living things and how they have evolved relies on their being classified into groups according to their similarity. Animals are classified in groups of decreasing diversity. The diagram outlines the evolution of the major groups of vertebrates through time, from the primitive jawless fish to mammals. This is based on an analysis of features shared between species and their ancestors.

THE CLADISTIC SYSTEM

Cladistic analysis shows the closeness of a relationship between a species and its most recent ancestor by a branching diagram called a cladogram. This is constructed by assessing characteristics that are shared between species and the order in which these arise.

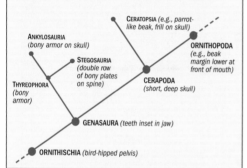

CERATOPSIA (e.g., parrot-like beak, frill on skull)

ANKYLOSAURIA (bony armor on skull)

ORNITHOPODA (e.g., beak margin lower at front of mouth)

STEGOSAURIA (double row of bony plates on spine)

THYREOPHORA (bony armor)

CERAPODA (short, deep skull)

GENASAURA (teeth inset in jaw)

ORNITHISCHIA (bird-hipped pelvis)

THE LINNAEAN SYSTEM

Devised by Karl von Linné (Carolus Linnaeus), this system subdivides all living things into ever more specific groups down to species level. Many paleontologists prefer to use cladistic analysis to describe the relationships between species, but the Linnaean system of Latin species names remains standard throughout the scientific community. The Linnaean classification of *Tyrannosaurus rex* is shown below.

KINGDOM :	Animalia
PHYLUM :	Chordata
CLASS :	Reptilia
ORDER :	Saurischia
FAMILY :	Tyrannosauridae
GENUS :	*Tyrannosaurus*
SPECIES :	*Tyrannosaurus rex*

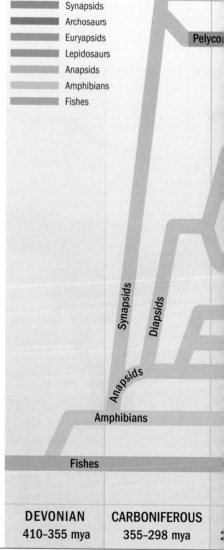

KEY TO FOSSIL EVIDENCE

Synapsids
Archosaurs
Euryapsids
Lepidosaurs
Anapsids
Amphibians
Fishes

Pelyco

Synapsids

Diapsids

Anapsids

Amphibians

Fishes

DEVONIAN	CARBONIFEROUS
410–355 mya	355–298 mya

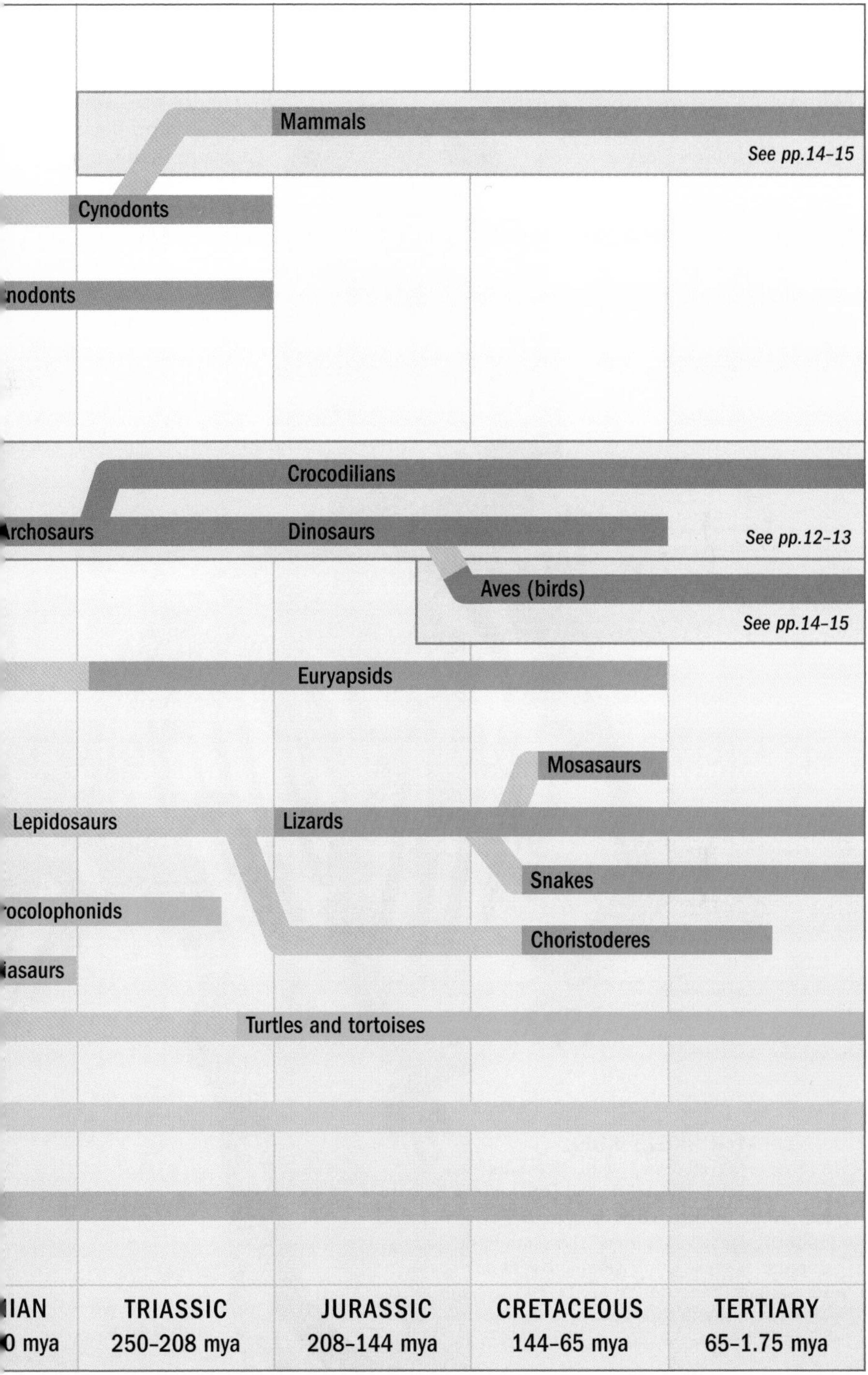

Mammals

See pp.14–15

Cynodonts

nodonts

Crocodilians

rchosaurs

Dinosaurs

See pp.12–13

Aves (birds)

See pp.14–15

Euryapsids

Mosasaurs

Lepidosaurs

Lizards

Snakes

ocolophonids

Choristoderes

asaurs

Turtles and tortoises

IAN 0 mya	TRIASSIC 250–208 mya	JURASSIC 208–144 mya	CRETACEOUS 144–65 mya	TERTIARY 65–1.75 mya

WHAT WERE DINOSAURS?

Dinosaurs dominated the Earth's ecosystems for 165 million years. Although they evolved from a group of reptiles called the archosaurs, they possessed certain un-reptilian features, as did other non-dinosaur groups such as the pterosaurs. Dinosaurs are defined as a group that shares certain characteristics. These include: upright limb posture (see facing page), three or fewer phalanges in the fifth finger of the hand, an elongate deltopectoral crest on the humerus, three or more sacral vertebrae, a ball-like head on the femur, and a fully open acetabulum (hip-socket in the pelvis).

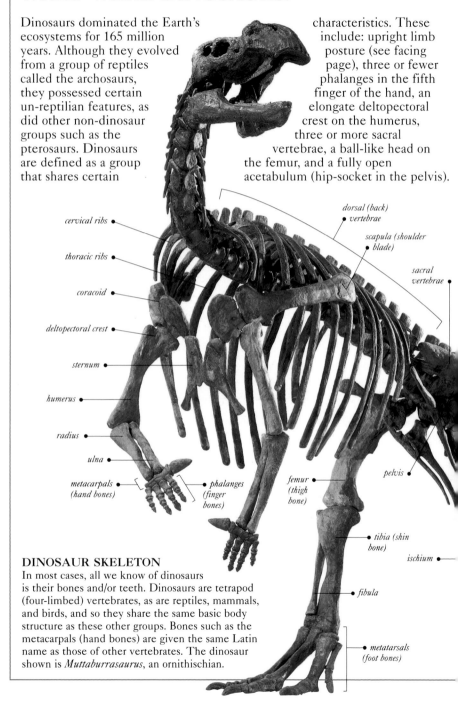

cervical ribs

thoracic ribs

coracoid

deltopectoral crest

sternum

humerus

radius

ulna

metacarpals
(hand bones)

phalanges
(finger
bones)

dorsal (back)
vertebrae

scapula (shoulder
blade)

sacral
vertebrae

femur
(thigh
bone)

pelvis

tibia (shin
bone)

ischium

fibula

metatarsals
(foot bones)

DINOSAUR SKELETON
In most cases, all we know of dinosaurs is their bones and/or teeth. Dinosaurs are tetrapod (four-limbed) vertebrates, as are reptiles, mammals, and birds, and so they share the same basic body structure as these other groups. Bones such as the metacarpals (hand bones) are given the same Latin name as those of other vertebrates. The dinosaur shown is *Muttaburrasaurus*, an ornithischian.

UPRIGHT POSTURE

All living reptiles have a sprawling gait, with their knees and elbows held out at an angle from their bodies. One of the factors that led to the success of dinosaurs was their upright stance. This provides great advantages over the normal reptilian posture: it allows for longer strides and therefore faster movement. Early meat-eating archosaurs and dinosaurs were often fast and agile hunters. The upright posture of the dinosaurs also allowed the evolution of bipedal (two-legged) walking.

UPRIGHT DINOSAUR STANCE

TYPICAL SPRAWLING
LIZARD STANCE

WARM-BLOODED?

The traditional view of sluggish, cold-blooded dinosaurs has largely given way to the theory that they were warm-blooded. Some were feathered, many were fast runners, and some lived in cold climates that would have been unsuitable for cold-blooded reptiles.

close similarities to
warm-blooded birds,
• including feathers

• moderately
large brain
would need
warm-blooded
metabolism

VELOCIRAPTOR

DINOSAUR HIPS

In 1887, the English anatomist Harry Seeley recognized that there were two different types of dinosaur pelvises. Some dinosaurs had a typical lizard-like pelvic structure: Seeley called these saurischian ("lizard-hipped"). Another group had a pelvis that looked like that of modern birds. He called these ornithischian ("bird-hipped"). It is not clear whether the two groups evolved independently or from a common saurischian ancestor.

caudal (tail)
• vertebrae

tarsus (ankle) •

• phalanges (toe bones)

SAURISCHIAN PELVIS
The pelvis is made up of the ilium, pubis, and ischium. In most saurischians, the ischium points backward and the pubis points forward.

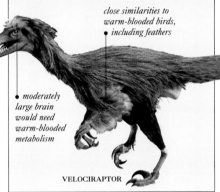

ilium

acetabulum •

ischium •

pubis •

ORNITHISCHIAN PELVIS
In ornithischian dinosaurs, and some rare saurischian groups, the pubis lies against the ischium.

ilium •

acetabulum •

• pubis

• ischium

EVOLUTION OF THE DINOSAURS

The dinosaurs and their closest relatives were the dominant animals throughout the Mesozoic Era. The first step in the evolution of the dinosaurs occurred in the Permian Period. A new line of reptiles evolved, called the archosaurs ("ruling reptiles"). Some of these developed the ability to walk upright in two feet. The dinosaurs, crocodiles, and the pterosaurs all evolved from these early archosaurs during the Triassic Period. There are two main groups of dinosaurs: the saurischian ("lizard-hipped") group and the ornithischian ("bird-hipped") dinosaurs. Birds are believed to have evolved from the theropod group of saurischian dinosaurs toward the end of the Jurassic Period. Together with the crocodiles, they are the only surviving archosaurs.

ARCHOSAURS
The first true archosaurs appeared late in the Permian. Many had rows of bony armor along the back. Some groups took to a marine way of life, and in the Triassic the first true crocodiles appeared. A wide variety of land-based archosaurs evolved, including lightly built bipedal runners, such as *Lagosuchus* (see p.42). It seems probable that the first dinosaurs evolved from these small archosaurs. The origins of the pterosaur group of flying archosaurs are still debated. They share many characteristics with early dinosaurs, and some paleontologists believe they evolved from a *Lagosuchus*-type archosaur. Others feel that pterosaurs evolved from an earlier diapsid reptile.

SAURISCHIANS
The theropods, which were the first saurischians to appear, were bipedal. The two main groups were the ceratosaurs and tetanurans. The more primitive ceratosaurs had many of the bones in their hips and feet fused. The tetanurans had a stiff tail and three fingers on each hand and included large, heavily built predators, such as the carnosaurs and the tyrannosaurs, as well as more lightly built animals with small heads and long arms, such as the oviraptorids. Advanced theropods, such as dromaeosaurs, had many birdlike features, and it is likely that birds evolved from this group of dinosaurs. Among the saurischians were also the sauropodomorphs, a group of often enormous, quadrupedal herbivorous dinosaurs that included the prosauropods and sauropods.

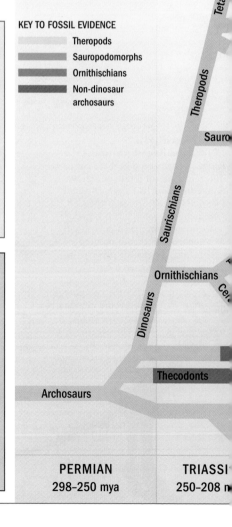

KEY TO FOSSIL EVIDENCE

- Theropods
- Sauropodomorphs
- Ornithischians
- Non-dinosaur archosaurs

Tetanurans

Theropods

Sauro

Saurischians

Ornithischians

Ce

Dinosaurs

Thecodonts

Archosaurs

PERMIAN
298–250 mya

TRIASSI
250–208 m

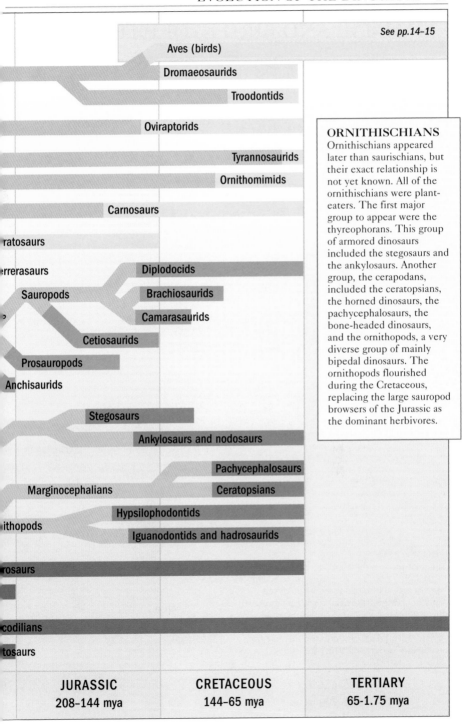

See pp.14–15

Aves (birds)

Dromaeosaurids

Troodontids

Oviraptorids

Tyrannosaurids

Ornithomimids

Carnosaurs

ratosaurs

rrerasaurs

Sauropods

Diplodocids

Brachiosaurids

Camarasaurids

Cetiosaurids

Prosauropods

Anchisaurids

Stegosaurs

Ankylosaurs and nodosaurs

Pachycephalosaurs

Marginocephalians

Ceratopsians

Hypsilophodontids

ithopods

Iguanodontids and hadrosaurids

rosaurs

codilians

tosaurs

ORNITHISCHIANS
Ornithischians appeared later than saurischians, but their exact relationship is not yet known. All of the ornithischians were plant-eaters. The first major group to appear were the thyreophorans. This group of armored dinosaurs included the stegosaurs and the ankylosaurs. Another group, the cerapodans, included the ceratopsians, the horned dinosaurs, the pachycephalosaurs, the bone-headed dinosaurs, and the ornithopods, a very diverse group of mainly bipedal dinosaurs. The ornithopods flourished during the Cretaceous, replacing the large sauropod browsers of the Jurassic as the dominant herbivores.

JURASSIC	CRETACEOUS	TERTIARY
208–144 mya	144–65 mya	65–1.75 mya

MAMMAL AND BIRD EVOLUTION

Modern theories of the evolution of mammals hold that the advanced group of synapsids called cynodonts were the direct ancestors of modern mammals. The origin and evolution of birds is still a matter of debate among paleontologists. *Archaeopteryx* is widely regarded as the first true bird, and provides a link between theropod dinosaurs and modern birds. However, the fossil record of the ancestors of birds between *Archaeopteryx* and modern bird species is patchy and inconclusive.

MAMMALS

The synapsids were a group of reptiles that dominated the land throughout the Permian and through much of the Triassic. These had a pair of openings in the skull behind each eye socket, giving them a more powerful bite. This group also evolved different types of teeth: molars, canines, and incisors. The earliest synapsids were the pelycosaurs (see p.8). These were followed by the dicynodonts. True mammals probably evolved from a later group of advanced synapsids, the cynodonts. After the mass extinction event at the end of the Cretaceous, primitive mammal groups underwent a massive evolutionary spurt and diversified into many forms, including marsupials and placental mammals. By the Tertiary, most modern mammal groups were well established.

BIRDS

Although the first birds probably arose in the Jurassic, up until the Cretaceous there is only a sparse record of birds. It seems that their evolution first provided them with shorter tails, then further feather and skeletal adaptations. By the time of the appearance of the Carinates, birds were powerful fliers. Teeth were only lost from the jaws in modern birds (the Euornithes).

KEY TO FOSSIL EVIDENCE (Birds)
- Ratites
- Euornithes
- Ichthyornithiforms
- Hesperornithiforms
- Enantiornithes
- Primitive birds

KEY TO FOSSIL EVIDENCE (Mammals)
- Placentals
- Marsupials
- Primitive mammals
- Monotremes
- Morganucodontoids

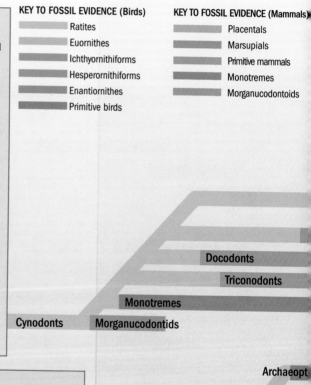

Docodonts

Triconodonts

Monotremes

Cynodonts

Morganucodontids

Archaeopt

Ornithothorac

Aves

Theropods

TRIASSIC
250–208 mya

JURASSIC
208–144 mya

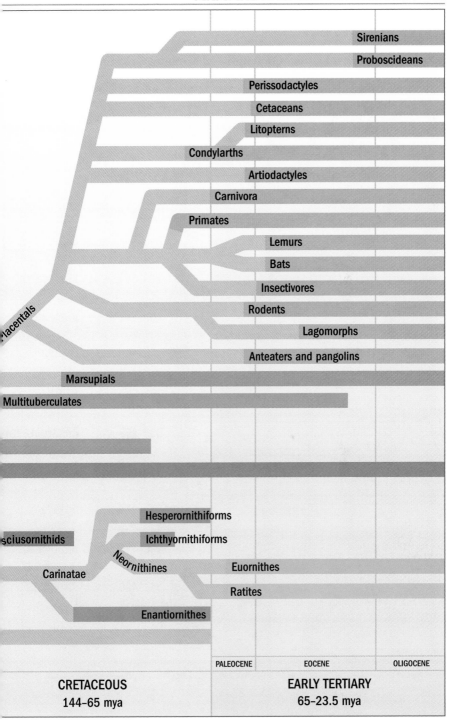

GEOLOGICAL TIME

Geologists subdivide the history of the Earth into very long time intervals called eons. Eons are, in turn, subdivided into eras, eras into periods, and periods into epochs.

The oldest rocks that have survived to be excavated were formed about four billion years ago, in the Archean Eon. The earliest fossils come from rocks of about this age.

ROCKS OF AGES

Where rock strata have remained undisturbed, a vertical section through the layers can reveal the rock types laid down during each time period. From these, it is possible to identify the environment (such as desert) and sometimes the age of fossils embedded in that rock, as shown below for rock strata in the Grand Canyon.

ROCK	ENVIRONMENT	PERIOD
Shale, siltstone, mudstone	Tidal flat	Triassic
Limestone	Marine	Permian
Sandstone	Desert	
Shale	Savanna	
Mixed strata–shales, sandstones, limestones	Flood plain	Permian and Late Carboniferous
Limestone	Marine	Early Carboniferous
Limestone	Marine	Devonian
Limestone		Cambrian
Shale	Marine	
Sandstone	Marine	
Complex mixed strata	Marine and volcanic	Precambrian

CENOZOIC ERA	1.75 mya–present	QUATERNARY
	23.5–1.75 mya	LATE TERTIARY
	65–23.5 mya	EARLY TERTIARY
MESOZOIC ERA	144–65 mya	CRETACEOUS
	208–144 mya	JURASSIC
	250–208 mya	TRIASSIC
PALEOZOIC ERA	298–250 mya	PERMIAN
	355–298 mya	CARBONIFEROU
	410–355 mya	DEVONIAN
	435–410 mya	SILURIAN
	490–435 mya	ORDOVICIAN
	542–490 mya	CAMBRIAN
	4,600–542 mya	PRECAMBRIAN

4,600 mya	4,000 mya	3,000 mya

GRAND CANYON
Arizona's Grand Canyon provides the world's most impressive display of sedimentary deposition of rocks. It is over 6,000 ft (2,000 m) deep, and shows a clear progression over 300 million years. Layers include sandy limestone, petrified sand dunes, and shale.

MACRAUCHENIA

The ice ages of the Quaternary Period led to the evolution of many mammals adapted to cold climates, such as mammoths. Modern humans evolved.

TITANIS

In the Late Tertiary, large expanses of grassland spread, inhabited by grazing mammals and predatory giant birds. The first humans evolved from primate ancestors.

AMBULOCETUS

After the end-Cretaceous mass extinctions, mammals evolved into large forms. Some took to a marine way of life. Giant flightless birds evolved.

BAROSAURUS

The Cretaceous was a time of flowering plants, browsing duckbilled dinosaurs, immense tyrannosaurid predators, armored ankylosaurs, and horned ceratopsians.

ALPHADON

In Jurassic times, the land was dominated by huge sauropods and large predators. A wide variety of pterosaurs evolved. Mammals remained small.

The Triassic marked the dawning of the age of dinosaurs. Advanced synapsids died out after giving rise to mammals.

HERRERASAURUS

DIMETRODON

Synapsids became the dominant land animals during the Permian. The period ended with the largest mass extinction event ever.

GRAEOPHONUS

Tropical forests flourished and oxygen levels were very high during this period. The first four-limbed animals and, later, the first reptiles moved onto the land.

The Devonian Period was a time of rapid evolution. Ammonoids and bony fish evolved and diversified. Trees appeared on land, as did insects.

EASTMANOSTEUS

Invertebrate species recovered rapidly during the Silurian, and the first jawed fish appeared. Primitive lycopods and myriapods became the first true land organisms.

SAGENOCRINITES

ESTONIOCERAS

Ordovician seas teemed with primitive fish, trilobites, corals, and shellfish. Plants made their first approaches onto land. The period ended with mass extinctions.

The first animals with skeletons evolved during the Cambrian "explosion of life." The oceans teemed with trilobites, brachiopods, and the first jawless fish.

XYSTRIDURA

CHARNIODISCUS

During the Precambrian, life arose in the oceans—first as single-celled bacteria and algae, then evolving into soft-bodied, multicellular animals, such as jellyfish and worms.

| 2,000 mya | 1,000 mya | 500 mya | 250 mya | 0 |

FOSSIL EVIDENCE

Evidence of prehistoric life comes from remains (such as bones) that over time have become mineralized to form fossils. Most animal fossils are of creatures that died in or near water. After death, if the hard remains, such as teeth and bones, quickly become covered in mud or sand, dissolved minerals in water are able to seep into the bone pores, initiating a process called permineralization. This reinforces the bones and makes them harder. Sometimes minerals replace the bone completely, petrifying it, or minerals dissolve the bone away, leaving a bone-shaped hollow called a mold.

dinosaurs congregate near water source

dinosaur dies and decomposes in riverbed

river sediments cover skeleton

compressed layers of sand and mud form rock strata

DISCOVERY AND EXCAVATION

Only certain rock types are rich in dinosaur fossils. These include sedimentary sandstones, shales, and mudstones formed in deserts, swamps, and lakes. Most fossil discoveries come from areas where severe erosion exposes deep layers of rock, such as cliffs and mountain slopes, or from places such as quarries and coal mines. Excavating dinosaurs from hard rock may necessitate the use of power tools or explosives. Fossils in desert areas can sometimes be exposed by carefully brushing away the sand covering them.

skeleton becomes mineralized, enabling it to withstand weight of rock forming overhead

EXCAVATION
Paleontologists dig around bones to estimate the fossil's state of preservation and size. Delicate scraping and chiseling is needed to reveal delicate structures without causing damage.

TRACE FOSSILS

Besides fossil remains such as bones, skin impressions, and teeth, dinosaurs left other clues to their existence and lifestyle. Trace fossils include fossil footprint trackways made in mud that dried out in the sun (below right). Coprolites (fossilized droppings) give further clues about a dinosaur's anatomy and lifestyle. Piles of gizzard stones (stones that were swallowed to aid digestion) are also often found.

FOSSIL OF THE FUTURE?
Dinosaur fossils found in the Sahara Desert were formed when the area was a swamp. This recent camel skeleton may become fossilized if it is buried by the sand.

remains of more recent animals and plants form a separate—"younger"— fossil layer

TRACKS
Fossilized dinosaur tracks, also called ichnites, can provide information about foot structure, speed, and in what position the tail was held. Importantly, they can also show whether the animal walked on two or four feet. The tracks pictured at left are those of a theropod dinosaur.

excavation or natural erosion of rocks reveals fossil- bearing strata

THE FOSSILIZATION PROCESS
Fossilization depends on the rapid covering of remains by sediments that exclude air and water and thereby arrest the normal processes of decay. In time, minerals from the covering sediments permeate the bone or other tissues, replacing the original material. The soft tissues usually decompose before the process of fossilization begins, so soft-bodied animals, such as jellyfish and worms, are generally poorly preserved.

PRECAMBRIAN TIME

UP TO 542 MILLION YEARS AGO

Current estimates put the age of the Earth at 4,600 million (i.e., 4.6 billion) years. The years from that date up until about 542 million years ago (mya) are grouped in one large division of geological time—the Precambrian. This was the time when life first evolved, although evidence of living creatures is sparse. During the first million years of its existence, the world was hot, molten, and totally inhospitable to life. As the earth cooled, volcanic gases and water vapor formed a crude atmosphere, and the oceans began to form. Before about 3,000 mya, most of the Earth's surface was volcanic rock, with craters and many unstable regions of volcanic activity. Stable continental areas then began to form. Fossil evidence of life is first seen in rocks dated at 3,800 million years old. The earliest life forms on Earth were simple cells and bacteria. More complex cells and algae first evolved about 1,000 mya. Multicelled plants and animals did not appear until near the end of the Precambrian—about 550 mya.

VENDIAN LIFE

impression of early jellyfish burrow or • track of simple worm

Extraordinary fossils found in in Precambrian rocks of the Vendian Period date from 600 mya, and are thought to be the remains of the earliest multicellular animals. The *Mawsonites* fossil (above) has been interpreted as a jellyfish or traces of a primitive worm.

4,600 mya   4,000 mya   3,000 mya

PRECAMBRIAN LANDMASSES

NORTHERN RODINIA

SOUTHERN RODINIA

Landmasses began to form about 3,000 mya. About 900 mya they joined to form the first supercontinent, Rodinia. By 750 mya, Rodinia was sitting across the Equator, but it then started to move southward. This triggered the Verangian Ice Age. Between 750 and 650 mya, Rodinia split into two halves (see map), but by the end of the Precambrian, Rodinia again formed a single continent.

PRECAMBRIAN LIFE

The first living cells were microscopic organisms possibly living in hot springs. By about 3,500 mya, photosynthesizing algae may have formed layered structures called stromatolites. As oxygen built up in the atmosphere, multicellular animals evolved.

STROMATOLITES
These layered silica or limestone structures were created by colony-forming algae and provide evidence of early life. *Collenia* (left) was a type of Precambrian stromatolite.

FIRST ANIMALS
Late in the Precambrian, the first true animals and plants appeared. *Spriggina* (above) was a strange, long, tapering animal, with V-shaped segments running along the length of its body.

FILTER FEEDER
The feather-shaped fossil of *Charniodiscus* is thought to represent an early filter-feeding animal that lived on the sea floor late in the Precambrian.

| 2,000 mya | 1,000 mya | 500 mya | 250 mya | 0 |

CAMBRIAN PERIOD

542–490 MILLION YEARS AGO

The beginning of the Cambrian Period marks the start of the Phanerozoic Era, known as the "Era of Abundant Life." The Cambrian is remarkable for the amazing increase in the number of marine animals and plants. However, the land remained barren. The evolutionary spurt was probably helped by the relatively warm climate. Rapid continental movements led to high sea levels, and large expanses of shallow water covered large parts of the continents. These shallow seas were warm worldwide, since there were no ice caps at either pole.

BURGESS SHALE

A huge variety of fossil animals, called the Burgess Shale fauna, have been found in shale rocks of the Cambrian Period in British Columbia, Canada. Over 120 species of invertebrates have been discovered there. Chordates (creatures with a primitive backbone called a notochord), such as *Pikaia* (right), are also preserved in the Burgess Shale.

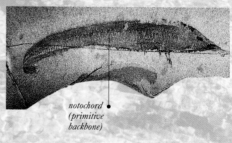

notochord (primitive backbone)

4,600 mya	4,000 mya	3,000 mya

CAMBRIAN LANDMASSES

Continental drift was remarkably rapid during the Cambrian. The Rodinia supercontinent broke up, and the continents moved apart (see map). This caused a rise in sea levels. By 500 mya, the continents of Laurentia, Baltica, and Siberia were lined up along the Equator, with the supercontinent Gondwana (present-day South America, Africa, Antarctica, Australia, and Asia) extending into temperate regions.

CAMBRIAN LIFE

Almost all of the present-day major groupings of animals started to appear during this 50-million-year period, including worms, crabs, shellfish, and sponges. Many of the new animals had a hard external skeleton. This provided protection within which multicellular organisms could grow.

TRILOBITES

This group of early animals were remarkable for being the first organisms with eyes—compound eyes rather like those of insects. *Xystridura* (left), like other trilobites, lived on the seabed, and had a skeleton composed of a head shield, a jointed thorax, and a tail shield.

jointed bony thorax with many legs

many small protective plates

WIWAXIA

Many mollusk- and wormlike animals evolved. *Wiwaxia* (right), a mollusklike creature covered with hard spines, lived on the ocean floor.

2,000 mya   1,000 mya   500 mya   250 mya   0

ORDOVICIAN PERIOD

490–435 MILLION YEARS AGO

The Ordovician Period saw the first movement of life from the oceans onto the land. Before about 450 mya, the land was barren, apart from mats of algae close to shores. After this time, early forms of liverwort-type plants evolved, possibly from larger algae. They quickly colonized boggy regions and areas around lakes and ponds. In the oceans, the earliest jawless fish (agnathans) appeared; they were mainly tear-drop-shaped animals covered in bony plates. An extreme Ice Age occurred at the end of the period. Fluctuations in the climate and sea levels caused by the advance and retreat of glaciers may have led to a second mass extinction. Warm-water coral reefs died out, and three-quarters of all marine species became extinct within less than a million years.

BRACHIOPODS
Mainly living attached to reefs, these were the most abundant two-shelled organisms in the oceans. *Strophomena* (left) was a medium-sized brachiopod.

4,600 mya	4,000 mya	3,000 mya

ORDOVICIAN LANDMASSES

At the beginning of the Ordovician Period, the supercontinent Gondwana still lay in the southern hemisphere. The other continents were spread out along the Equator and were gradually pushed apart by the expansion of the Iapetus Ocean (see map). Later in the Ordovician Period, the movement of Gondwana toward the South Pole triggered another ice age. By 440 mya, present-day North Africa lay over the South Pole.

ORDOVICIAN LIFE

The warm equatorial seas that existed for much of the Ordovician were ideal for the evolution of marine life. Coral reefs appeared, and soon spread widely. The oceans were also filled with jellyfish, sea anemones, and other colony-forming organisms. A variety of shelled animals, such as brachiopods, lived on the seabed around the reefs.

• fanlike colonies held in branching, tubelike structures

GRAPTOLITES
Graptolites, such as *Rhabdinopora* (above), were unusual colony-forming organisms that floated through the water, feeding through minute tentacles.

segmented • body

NAUTILOIDS
Primitive shelled cephalopods (a group that includes modern cuttlefish) called nautiloids were abundant. Many, such as *Estonioceras* (left), were coiled. They moved by squirting water out of a tube in their body cavity.

TRILOBITES
The new coral reefs were an ideal habitat for trilobites. *Sphaerexochus* (above) was a typical Ordovician trilobite, with a body of 11 segments.

SILURIAN PERIOD

435–410 MILLION YEARS AGO

Before the Silurian Period, the land had been largely barren, apart from some mossy growth and liverworts close to water. The landscape was transformed by the appearance of the first true land plants. These were primitive and simple, but had branching stems, roots, and tubes for water transport. Such plants were able to grow to larger sizes than their more primitive antecedents. As areas around water began to be covered by vegetation, soil built up, and water became trapped in the land. These conditions allowed the first advances of animal life onto the land. By the end of the Silurian, there were many land arthropods, including primitive centipedes, and spider- and scorpion-like arachnids.

SILURIAN LIFE

After the mass extinctions at the end of the Ordovician, evolution progressed at a rapid rate. The earliest true jawed fish (acanthodians) appeared, and were followed in the Late Silurian by another major group of jawed fish, the placoderms. Many new aquatic invertebrates, such as sea urchins, also appeared. Trilobites and mollusks increased in diversity.

12 plated tail segments

small eye

large eye

large, powerful claw

SEA SCORPION
The largest Silurian marine invertebrates were the sea scorpions (eurypterids), such as *Pterygotus* (above). In some cases longer than a man, these were the dominant hunters of the early seas, and a few may have been able to crawl ashore.

4,600 mya	4,000 mya	3,000 mya

SILURIAN LANDMASSES

The end of the Ordovician Ice Age led to rising sea levels and flooding of some low-lying areas. The climate became warmer and less seasonal. The supercontinent Gondwana was still lying over the South Pole, with Laurentia sitting astride the Equator (see map). The collision of smaller landmasses formed new mountain ranges. By the end of the Silurian, all of the landmasses were grouped closely together.

SIBERIA

LAURENTIA BALTICA

GONDWANA

freely moving arms

EARLY PLANTS
The earliest plants, such as *Cooksonia* (left), had a simple branching form. They had water-conducting vessels, and reinforced stems.

CRINOIDS
Despite their plantlike appearance, crinoids (sea lilies) were animals. Many species populated Silurian seabeds. *Sagenocrinites* (above) was a small one, with a very compact head and many slender tentacles.

characteristic Y-shaped branching stems

BIRKENIA
Despite the evolution of the jawed fish, jawless fish (agnathans) were still thriving. *Birkenia* (right) was a freshwater fish that probably fed on the algae that it strained out of muddy lake- and riverbeds.

| 2,000 mya | | 1,000 mya | | 500 mya | 250 mya | 0 |

DEVONIAN PERIOD

410–355 MILLION YEARS AGO

During the Devonian, green plants of increasing size started to spread across the landscape. Later in the period, some plants evolved woody tissue and the first trees appeared. Toward the end of the Devonian, the climate became much warmer. Droughts were common and alternated with periods of heavy rain. Sea levels fell worldwide, and large deserts formed. A wide variety of fish evolved—the Devonian is often called "the Age of Fish." Swampy deltas and river estuaries provided an important habitat for the emergence of animal life onto land.

LIFE ON LAND

About 370 mya, the first four-legged amphibians, such as *Acanthostega* (right), ventured out of the water onto the land. They evolved from one of the groups of lobe-finned fish, whose living relatives are lungfish. The paired fleshy fins of these fish could have evolved into limbs.

sharp teeth suggest a diet of fish

4,600 mya   4,000 mya   3,000 mya

DEVONIAN LANDMASSES

At the start of the Devonian, the northern landmasses formed one large supercontinent called Laurasia, separated from Gondwana by the Tethys Sea (see map). Huge mountain ranges formed in the future eastern North America and western Europe. By the mid-Devonian, Gondwana and most of Laurasia had moved south of the Equator. The lands that would become China and Siberia were north of the Equator.

DEVONIAN LIFE

The most important evolutionary step during the Devonian was the development of four-limbed land animals. Arthropods also moved onto the land and the first insects appeared. The oceans teemed with armored jawless fish and the more modern jawed fish. Sharks and ammonoids (a group of mollusks) were common.

body armor

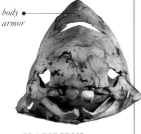

PLACODERMS
Abundant in Devonian seas, placoderms were jawed fish. Toward the end of the Devonian some of these creatures reached 33 ft (10 m) in length. *Eastmanosteus* (above), although less than 6½ ft (2 m) long, was a fearsome hunter.

pointed fins

LUNGFISH
Lungfish, such as *Dipterus* (above) have primitive lungs as well as gills, and survive during seasons of drought by breathing air in watertight burrows in the mud.

dorsal fin

EARLY SHARKS
The seas of the Late Devonian teemed with squid, small fish, and crustaceans, which were ideal prey for early sharks such as *Cladoselache* (right). This shark did not have scales on its body.

numerous sharp teeth

| 2,000 mya | 1,000 mya | 500 mya | 250 mya | 0 |

CARBONIFEROUS PERIOD

355–298 MILLION YEARS AGO

The Carboniferous Period opened with tropical conditions over much of the Earth. There were large coastal seas and vast swamps covering the coastal plains. Insects and amphibians found the swamps an ideal environment. Early amphibians looked rather like salamanders, but they soon evolved into many forms, including giant ones. In the warm, moist climate, huge forests of giant tree ferns flourished, producing an oxygen-rich environment. There were also giant horsetails, clubmosses, and seed-bearing plants. Large amounts of decaying vegetation led to the buildup of thick layers of peat, which would later become coal deposits.

CARBONIFEROUS LIFE

There were many types of amphibian tetrapods, ranging from newtlike animals to those the size of crocodiles. By the late Carboniferous, the first reptiles appeared, with the evolution of a shelled egg. The early reptiles were small, but they spread rapidly on land, moving into drier, upland areas.

diamond-shaped leaf bosses •

TREES
Huge forests of woody trees, such as *Lepidodendron* (a specimen of fossilized bark is shown at left), spread worldwide. This giant clubmoss had a column-like trunk with skeletal, spreading branches and could grow to heights of 115 ft (35 m), with a trunk diameter of over 6½ ft (2 m).

small, slim, yet
• sturdy body

FIRST REPTILE?
When first discovered, *Westlothiana lizziae* (right) was hailed as the first real reptile. It is now regarded as reptilelike rather than a true reptile. *Westlothiana* has features that indicate an evolutionary position between primitive tetrapods and true reptiles.

INSECTS AND ARTHROPODS
Already populous by the Carboniferous, insects and arthropods continued to diversify. *Graephonus* (above) was a whip scorpion, with six legs and a pair of pincers.

4,600 mya	4,000 mya	3,000 mya

CARBONIFEROUS LANDMASSES

At the beginning of the Carboniferous, most of the Earth's landmasses were arranged in two great supercontinents: Laurasia in the north and Gondwana in the south (see map). Later in the Carboniferous they moved closer together. Gondwana started to move over the South Pole again. The advance and retreat of the ensuing ice sheets led to at least two ice ages in the last half of the Carboniferous.

LAURASIA

GONDWANA

LIFE IN A SWAMP
The spread of the forests raised oxygen levels around the world, and this factor, combined with the increasingly humid conditions, may have allowed the evolution of very large amphibians and insects. Crocodile-like amphibians, such as *Eryops*, hunted at the bottom of the swamps. The largest Carboniferous dragonflies had wingspans of up to 6½ ft (2 m), and some early scorpions were more than 2 ft (60 cm) long.

early reptiles, such as Hylonomus, *migrated* • *to drier areas*

the dragonfly Meganeura, *one of the largest flying* • *insects*

Eryops, *a large, amphibian aquatic hunter* •

2,000 mya   1,000 mya   500 mya   250 mya   0

PERMIAN PERIOD

298–250 MILLION YEARS AGO

The Permian was a time of dramatic climatic changes. At the start of the Permian, Gondwana was still in the grip of an ice age. It gradually warmed over the next few million years, as it moved northward. Large parts of Laurasia became very hot and dry, and massive expanses of desert formed. This had a damaging effect on amphibian populations: they were confined to the fewer damp areas and many species became extinct. This provided the opportunity for reptiles to spread more widely and diversify. Continental upheavals and further extreme climate changes at the end of the Permian led to the largest mass-extinction event ever. More than half of all animal families became extinct.

PERMIAN LIFE

Reptiles continued to spread rapidly. Among the dominant land animals of the time were the synapsids (mammal-like reptiles). By the mid Permian, these had diversified into the therapsids. Later in the period, a mammal-like group of therapsids called the cynodonts ("dog teeth") evolved.

bony spike

PAREIASAURS

These were large, primitive, herbivorous reptiles. *Elginia* (a fossil skull is shown at left) was one of the smaller pareiasaurs and one of the last of the group.

broad vertebrae at base of spine

EARLY ANAPSID

Procolophodon (right) was a small, primitive member of the anapsid group of reptiles. It may have eaten insects. Later members of its family were larger, and had teeth designed for eating plants.

ribs enclosing rounded body

| 4,600 mya | 4,000 mya | 3,000 mya |

PERMIAN LANDMASSES

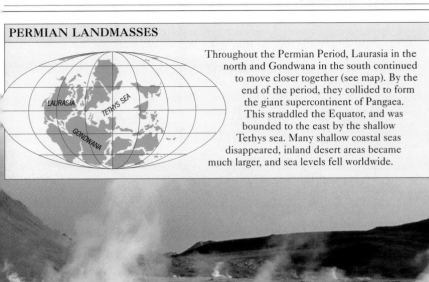

Throughout the Permian Period, Laurasia in the north and Gondwana in the south continued to move closer together (see map). By the end of the period, they collided to form the giant supercontinent of Pangaea. This straddled the Equator, and was bounded to the east by the shallow Tethys sea. Many shallow coastal seas disappeared, inland desert areas became much larger, and sea levels fell worldwide.

PELYCOSAURS

One of the best-known of this group of early Permian synapsid predators, *Dimetrodon* (left) had a distinctive sail on its back, which was supported by bony rods. This is thought to have been for heat exchange or sexual display.

large, sharp teeth indicate carnivorous lifestyle

2,000 mya   1,000 mya   500 mya   250 mya   0

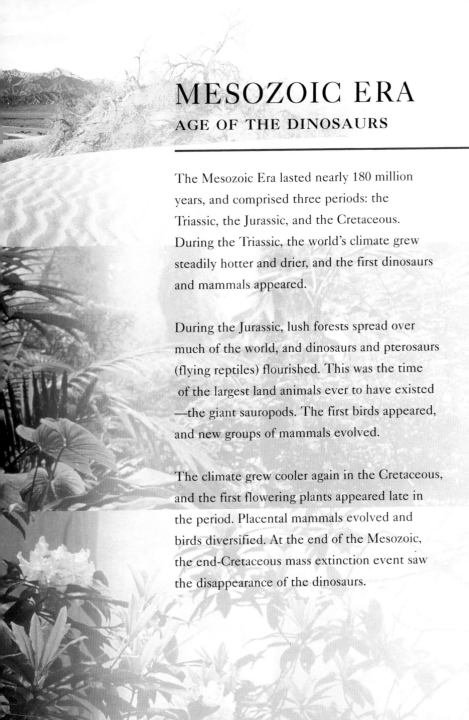

MESOZOIC ERA
AGE OF THE DINOSAURS

The Mesozoic Era lasted nearly 180 million years, and comprised three periods: the Triassic, the Jurassic, and the Cretaceous. During the Triassic, the world's climate grew steadily hotter and drier, and the first dinosaurs and mammals appeared.

During the Jurassic, lush forests spread over much of the world, and dinosaurs and pterosaurs (flying reptiles) flourished. This was the time of the largest land animals ever to have existed —the giant sauropods. The first birds appeared, and new groups of mammals evolved.

The climate grew cooler again in the Cretaceous, and the first flowering plants appeared late in the period. Placental mammals evolved and birds diversified. At the end of the Mesozoic, the end-Cretaceous mass extinction event saw the disappearance of the dinosaurs.

TRIASSIC PERIOD

250–208 MILLION YEARS AGO

After the mass extinctions at the end of the Permian, the oceans and land were left startlingly empty of life. It took about 10 million years for the Earth's ecosystems to recover. During the Triassic, the surviving reptile groups spread widely, and the first true dinosaurs appeared. A large area of the world's landmasses lay in the equatorial belt, and interior regions were subject to alternating seasons of heavy monsoonal rains and drought. The climate was generally warm, and there were no polar ice caps. These conditions favored certain types of plants, such as seed ferns and conifers, that could cope with arid conditions, and horsetails in damper areas. The climate grew even drier at the end of the Triassic.

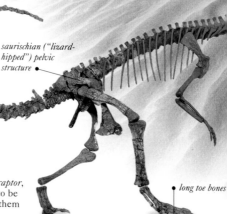

TRIASSIC LIFE

Most of the synapsids, which had dominated the land in Permian times, did not survive into the Triassic. The surviving groups radiated again, but lost a number of their ecological niches to new reptile groups—the archosaurs ("ruling reptiles") and the rhynchosaurs (a short-lived group of diapsid reptiles). Several lines of aquatic reptiles also evolved. These were the nothosaurs, placodonts, and ichthyosaurs. The Late Triassic saw the arrival of the dinosaurs, crocodilians, pterosaurs, turtles, and primitive mammals.

saurischian ("lizard-hipped") pelvic structure •

CYNODONTS

The cynodonts (doglike mammal ancestors) were a group that survived into the Triassic. *Cynognathus* (above) was a large Triassic carnivorous cynodont.

FIRST DINOSAURS

The earliest dinosaurs evolved about 230 mya. *Herrerasaurus* (right) and *Eoraptor*, both found in Argentina, are thought to be among the earliest dinosaurs. Both of them were agile, bipedal hunters.

• long toe bones

4,600 mya	4,000 mya		3,000 mya

TRIASSIC LANDMASSES

The supercontinent Pangaea reached its maximum state of fusion in the mid Triassic about 230 mya. Parts of present-day Asia may have formed islands, but most of the landmasses of the Earth were in contact. Pangaea straddled the Equator, reaching from pole to pole. The temperature gradient between the Equator and the poles was far less extreme than it is in modern times, and there were no polar ice caps.

FLYING REPTILES

The earliest known flying reptiles are pterosaurs, found in Late Triassic deposits. They were accomplished flyers with wings made of skin attached to an elongated fourth finger. *Peteinosaurus* (above) was a rhamphorynchoid pterosaur (a primitive form) with a short neck, and a long bony tail.

TRIASSIC VEGETATION

Many plants of the Paleozoic Era relied on high rainfall and damp conditions. *Dicroidium* (right) was a seed fern the size of a small tree. It thrived in swampy areas of the Triassic southern hemisphere. In many areas, however, such tropical vegetation was gradually replaced by plants, such as cycads, ginkgos, and evergreen trees, which were better suited to the prevailing arid conditions.

• *opposing pairs of leaflets*

•*"Y"-forked leaf*

| 2,000 mya | 1,000 mya | 500 mya | 250 mya | 0 |

ON THE LAND

As the first period in the Mesozoic Era, the Triassic was the start of what is popularly called "The Age of Reptiles." Several groups of mammal-like reptiles (synapsids) survived the end-Permian extinction event. One of these groups, the herbivorous dicynodonts, radiated worldwide, reaching large sizes toward the end of the Triassic before dying out. The cynodonts, a group of advanced synapsids, were also important. Some of them, such as *Thrinaxodon*, were very successful predators, and are thought to have been "warm-blooded" and covered with fur. The first true mammals evolved at the end of the Triassic. These were tiny, shrewlike animals, and were probably nocturnal.

The first archosaurs ("ruling reptiles") appeared in the Early Triassic. They branched into two main groups—one led to the crocodilians, and the other to dinosaurs. The Late Triassic saw the appearance of the first true dinosaurs, which evolved from bipedal archosaurs, such as *Lagosuchus*.

The early dinosaurs were bipedal, small carnivorous theropods, such as *Eoraptor*. However, by the end of the Triassic Period, the quadrupedal prosauropods had evolved. They were all small, lightly built animals, with long necks and tails. Their blunt, rounded teeth suggest a mixed diet of plants and animals.

Group Prolacertiformes	Family Tanystropheidae	Time 215 mya

TANYSTROPHEUS

TAN-EE-STRO-FEE-US

This reptile is one of the strangest to have ever existed. Its incredibly long neck was composed of only ten vertebrae, which were so elongated that they were first thought to be leg bones. The neck length has led to much speculation about this animal's lifestyle, since it was not well-adapted for either walking or swimming. Current opinion is that it used its neck to fish from sea or lake shores or from shallow water.

• **DESCRIBED BY**
Hermann von Meyer; 1855.
• **HABITAT**
Shorelines.

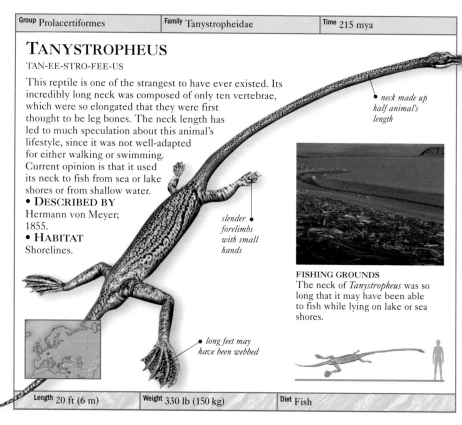

neck made up half animal's length

slender forelimbs with small hands

long feet may have been webbed

FISHING GROUNDS
The neck of *Tanystropheus* was so long that it may have been able to fish while lying on lake or sea shores.

Length 20 ft (6 m)	Weight 330 lb (150 kg)	Diet Fish

Group Rhynchosauria	Family Rhynchosauridae	Time 230 mya

SCAPHONYX

SCA-FON-IKS

Scaphonyx ("canoe-claw") was an early rhynchosaur. Like other members of the group, it was a heavy-bodied, four-legged plant eater. Its body was pig-shaped and its head was large and deep. At the front of the mouth was a curved beak, and the mouth also bore two short tusks.
• **DESCRIBED BY** Arthur Smith Woodward; 1908.
• **HABITAT** Woodland.

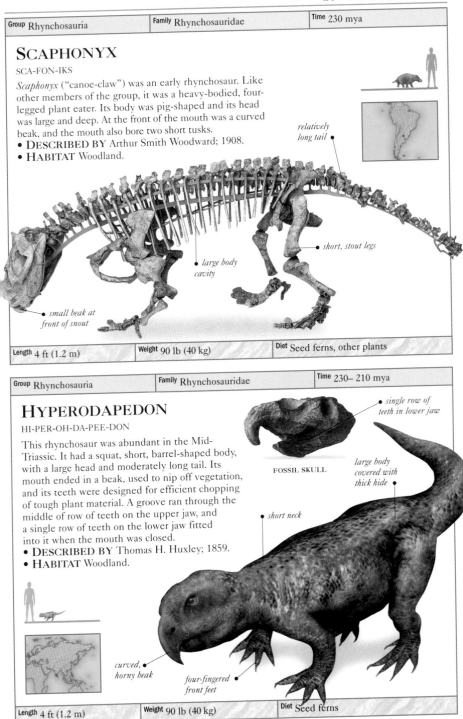

relatively long tail

large body cavity

short, stout legs

small beak at front of snout

Length 4 ft (1.2 m)	Weight 90 lb (40 kg)	Diet Seed ferns, other plants

Group Rhynchosauria	Family Rhynchosauridae	Time 230– 210 mya

HYPERODAPEDON

HI-PER-OH-DA-PEE-DON

This rhynchosaur was abundant in the Mid-Triassic. It had a squat, short, barrel-shaped body, with a large head and moderately long tail. Its mouth ended in a beak, used to nip off vegetation, and its teeth were designed for efficient chopping of tough plant material. A groove ran through the middle of row of teeth on the upper jaw, and a single row of teeth on the lower jaw fitted into it when the mouth was closed.
• **DESCRIBED BY** Thomas H. Huxley; 1859.
• **HABITAT** Woodland.

single row of teeth in lower jaw

large body covered with thick hide

FOSSIL SKULL

short neck

curved, horny beak

four-fingered front feet

Length 4 ft (1.2 m)	Weight 90 lb (40 kg)	Diet Seed ferns

Group Archosauria	Family Proterosuchidae	Time 250 mya

CHASMATOSAURUS

KAZ-MAT-OH-SAW-RUS

Formerly known as *Proterosuchus*, *Chasmatosaurus* was one of the earliest known archosaurs. It had a large, heavy body, and its legs were angled out from the body, resulting in a sprawling, lizardlike gait. It probably lived a lifestyle similar to that of crocodiles, spending most of its time hunting in rivers. Its teeth were sharp and curved backward, and there were also primitive teeth on the palate. Some reconstructions show this animal with a pointed snout.
- **DESCRIBED BY** Thomas H. Huxley; 1865.
- **HABITAT** Riverbanks.

large head with long snout

long, heavy tail

sprawling, sturdy limbs

Length 6½ ft (2 m)	Weight Unknown	Diet Fish, herbivorous dicynodonts

Group Phytosauridae	Family Mystriosuchinae	Time 235–223 mya

PARASUCHUS

PAR-A-SOOK-US

Parasuchus, whose name means "near crocodile," looked remarkably like a modern crocodile. Its throat and back were protected by heavy armored plates (or scutes), and the belly was strengthened by a dense arrangement of abdominal ribs. The skull was long, with a slender snout. The jaws were lined with conical teeth. Nostrils positioned on top of the head allowed *Parasuchus* to breathe while underwater.
- **DESCRIBED BY** Richard Lyddeker; 1885.
- **HABITAT** Riverbanks and marshy areas.

back protected by heavy scutes

nostrils on top of snout

Length 8¼ ft (2.5 m)	Weight Unknown	Diet Fish

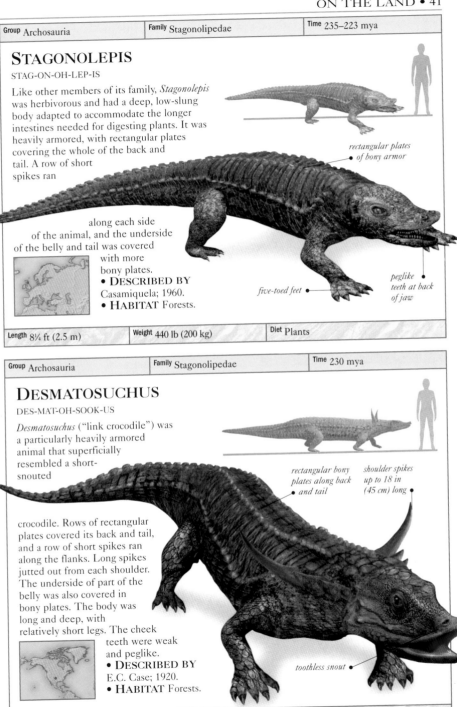

| Group Archosauria | Family Stagonolipedae | Time 235–223 mya |

STAGONOLEPIS

STAG-ON-OH-LEP-IS

Like other members of its family, *Stagonolepis* was herbivorous and had a deep, low-slung body adapted to accommodate the longer intestines needed for digesting plants. It was heavily armored, with rectangular plates covering the whole of the back and tail. A row of short spikes ran

rectangular plates of bony armor

along each side of the animal, and the underside of the belly and tail was covered with more bony plates.
• **DESCRIBED BY** Casamiquela; 1960.
• **HABITAT** Forests.

five-toed feet

peglike teeth at back of jaw

| Length 8¼ ft (2.5 m) | Weight 440 lb (200 kg) | Diet Plants |

| Group Archosauria | Family Stagonolipedae | Time 230 mya |

DESMATOSUCHUS

DES-MAT-OH-SOOK-US

Desmatosuchus ("link crocodile") was a particularly heavily armored animal that superficially resembled a short-snouted

rectangular bony plates along back and tail

shoulder spikes up to 18 in (45 cm) long

crocodile. Rows of rectangular plates covered its back and tail, and a row of short spikes ran along the flanks. Long spikes jutted out from each shoulder. The underside of part of the belly was also covered in bony plates. The body was long and deep, with relatively short legs. The cheek teeth were weak and peglike.
• **DESCRIBED BY** E.C. Case; 1920.
• **HABITAT** Forests.

toothless snout

| Length 16 ft (5 m) | Weight 660 lb (300 kg) | Diet Plants |

Group Archosauria	Family Ornithosuchidae	Time 235 mya

EUPARKERIA

EWE-PARK-ER-EE-A

Euparkeria was an early archosaur, and was unusual among its contemporaries in that the relative length of its hind legs to its forelegs was greater than that of contemporary reptiles. It probably spent most of its time on all fours, but was capable of rising onto its hind legs to run. Its tail made up about half its body weight, and was held outstretched for balance as it ran. The body was small and slim, with thin bony plates covering the middle of the back and

ridge of light bony plates running along back

lightly built head despite large size

tail. The head was large but light, and the many teeth were sharp, serrated, and curved backward, indicating a carnivorous way of life.
- **DESCRIBED BY** E. D. Cope; 1869.
- **HABITAT** Woodland.

four-fingered hands

Length 24 in (60 cm)	Weight 30 lb (13.5 kg)	Diet Meat

Group Archosauria	Family Ornithosuchidae	Time 230 mya

LAGOSUCHUS

LAY-GO-SOOK-US

long, slim snout

It was once thought that the small "rabbit crocodile" *Lagosuchus* was the most likely ancestor of the

dinosaurs. It was indeed strikingly similar in appearance to small, early theropod dinosaurs. Its body was slim and lightly built, the tail was long and flexible, and the hind legs were long and thin, with shin bones much longer than the thighs. *Lagosuchus* ran on its hind legs. Although a valid genus, one of its species has been reassigned to a new genus, *Marasuchus*.
- **DESCRIBED BY** Romer; 1972.
- **HABITAT** Forest.

thighs shorter than shins

long feet

Length 12 in (30 cm)	Weight 3¼ oz (90 g)	Diet Meat

Group Theropoda	Family Herrerasauridae	Time 228 mya

HERRERASAURUS

HERR-RAY-RAH-SAW-RUS

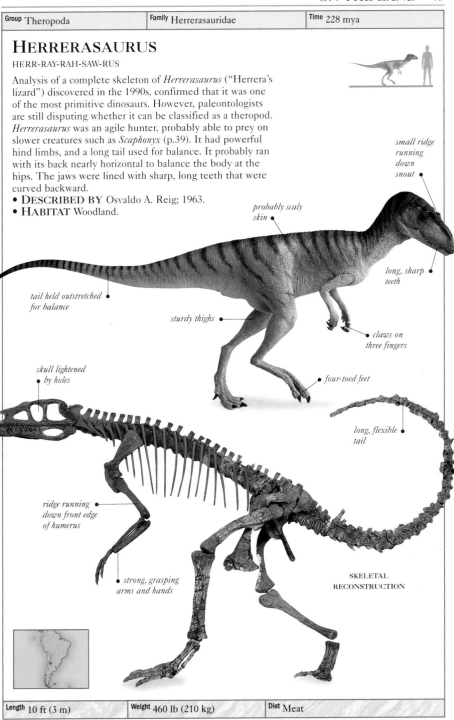

Analysis of a complete skeleton of *Herrerasaurus* ("Herrera's lizard") discovered in the 1990s, confirmed that it was one of the most primitive dinosaurs. However, paleontologists are still disputing whether it can be classified as a theropod. *Herrerasaurus* was an agile hunter, probably able to prey on slower creatures such as *Scaphonyx* (p.39). It had powerful hind limbs, and a long tail used for balance. It probably ran with its back nearly horizontal to balance the body at the hips. The jaws were lined with sharp, long teeth that were curved backward.

• **DESCRIBED BY** Osvaldo A. Reig; 1963.
• **HABITAT** Woodland.

small ridge
running
down
snout

probably scaly
skin

long, sharp
teeth

tail held outstretched
for balance

sturdy thighs

claws on
three fingers

four-toed feet

skull lightened
by holes

long, flexible
tail

ridge running
down front edge
of humerus

strong, grasping
arms and hands

SKELETAL
RECONSTRUCTION

Length 10 ft (3 m)	Weight 460 lb (210 kg)	Diet Meat

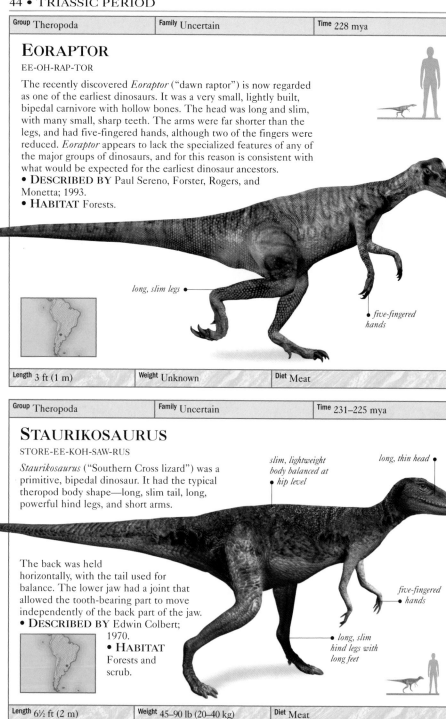

Group Theropoda	Family Uncertain	Time 228 mya

EORAPTOR

EE-OH-RAP-TOR

The recently discovered *Eoraptor* ("dawn raptor") is now regarded as one of the earliest dinosaurs. It was a very small, lightly built, bipedal carnivore with hollow bones. The head was long and slim, with many small, sharp teeth. The arms were far shorter than the legs, and had five-fingered hands, although two of the fingers were reduced. *Eoraptor* appears to lack the specialized features of any of the major groups of dinosaurs, and for this reason is consistent with what would be expected for the earliest dinosaur ancestors.
• **DESCRIBED BY** Paul Sereno, Forster, Rogers, and Monetta; 1993.
• **HABITAT** Forests.

long, slim legs •

• five-fingered hands

Length 3 ft (1 m)	Weight Unknown	Diet Meat

Group Theropoda	Family Uncertain	Time 231–225 mya

STAURIKOSAURUS

STORE-EE-KOH-SAW-RUS

Staurikosaurus ("Southern Cross lizard") was a primitive, bipedal dinosaur. It had the typical theropod body shape—long, slim tail, long, powerful hind legs, and short arms.

slim, lightweight body balanced at • hip level

long, thin head •

The back was held horizontally, with the tail used for balance. The lower jaw had a joint that allowed the tooth-bearing part to move independently of the back part of the jaw.
• **DESCRIBED BY** Edwin Colbert; 1970.
    • **HABITAT** Forests and scrub.

five-fingered • hands

long, slim hind legs with long feet

Length 6½ ft (2 m)	Weight 45–90 lb (20–40 kg)	Diet Meat

Group Theropoda	Family Coelophysidae	Time 208–200 mya

COELOPHYSIS

SEE-LOW-FIE-SIS

Coelophysis ("hollow face") was a small, lightly built, early dinosaur with open skull bones (hence its name). The body was long and slim, and the head was pointed, with many small, serrated teeth. *Coelophysis* is one of the best-known dinosaurs due to the excavation of dozens of skeletons from New Mexico (see right). Many of these fossils contained bones of young *Coelophysis* in their abdominal regions, suggesting that in some circumstances this dinosaur may have eaten its own young. Two types of *Coelophysis* have been described: robust and gracile. These probably represent male and female forms.
- **DESCRIBED BY** Edward Drinker Cope; 1889.
- **HABITAT** Desert plains.

GHOST RANCH, NEW MEXICO
Many fossil skeletons of *Coelophysis* have been found at this site.

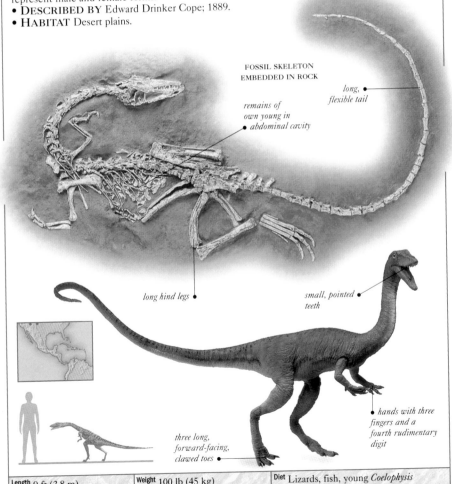

FOSSIL SKELETON
EMBEDDED IN ROCK

long, flexible tail

remains of own young in abdominal cavity

long hind legs

small, pointed teeth

hands with three fingers and a fourth rudimentary digit

three long, forward-facing, clawed toes

Length 9 ft (2.8 m)	Weight 100 lb (45 kg)	Diet Lizards, fish, young *Coelophysis*

Group Prosauropoda	Family Anchisauridae	Time 220–209 mya

SELLOSAURUS

SEL-OH-SAW-RUS

This early prosauropod, is believed by some paleontologists to be a separate species named *Efraasia* (see Additional Dinosaurs). It was lightly built, with a small head, fairly long neck, bulky body, and long tail. Its legs were longer than its arms, and its five-fingered hands had a large thumb claw. It may have walked on all fours to browse, rising onto its hind legs to run.
• **DESCRIBED BY** Eberhard Fraas; 1909.
• **HABITAT** Dry upland plains.

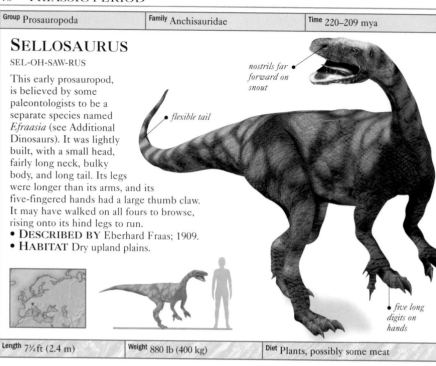

nostrils far forward on snout

flexible tail

five long digits on hands

Length 7¾ ft (2.4 m)	Weight 880 lb (400 kg)	Diet Plants, possibly some meat

Group Prosauropoda	Family Plateosauridae	Time 219–210 mya

PLATEOSAURUS

PLAT-EE-OH-SAW-RUS

This "flat lizard" was one of the most common dinosaurs of the Late Triassic Period. The large number of fossil finds suggest that *Plateosaurus* may have lived in herds and migrated to avoid seasonal droughts. It walked on all fours, rearing up on its hind legs to browse on high vegetation. The thumbs on its hands were partially opposable, allowing it to grasp food. Its small skull was deeper than in most other prosauropods, and its fairly short neck. *Plateosaurus* had many small, leaf-shaped teeth, and the hinge of the lower jaw was low-slung to give greater leverage. These factors indicate a diet primarily composed of plants. This dinosaur also had a very large nasal chamber, but the reason for this is as yet unknown.
• **DESCRIBED BY** Hermann von Meyer; 1837.
• **HABITAT** Dry plains, desert.

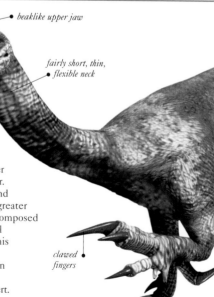

beaklike upper jaw

fairly short, thin, flexible neck

clawed fingers

Length 26 ft (8 m)	Weight 1⅔ tons (1.5 metric tons)	Diet Leaves, small amounts of meat

Group Prosauropoda	Family Anchisauridae	Time 223–209 mya

THECODONTOSAURUS

THEE-COH-DONT-OH-SAW-RUS

This dinosaur was the first prosauropod to be discovered, and is one of the most primitive known. Its name ("socket-toothed lizard") was given because its saw-edged teeth looked like those of a monitor lizard, but were embedded in the sockets in the jaw bones. *Thecodontosaurus* had a relatively small head and a long tail. Mainly bipedal, it seems to have had some ability to walk on all fours.

- **DESCRIBED BY** H. Riley and S. Stutchbury; 1836.
- **HABITAT** Desert plains, dry upland areas.

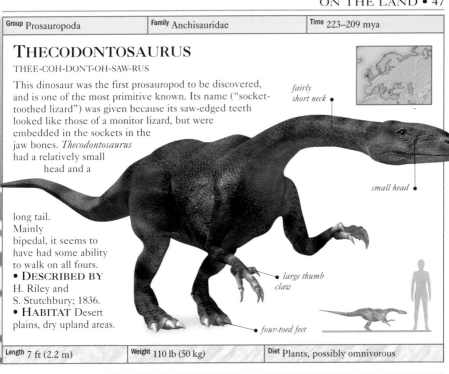

fairly short neck

small head

large thumb claw

four-toed feet

Length 7 ft (2.2 m)	Weight 110 lb (50 kg)	Diet Plants, possibly omnivorous

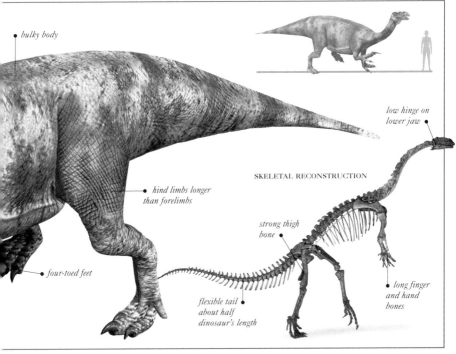

bulky body

low hinge on lower jaw

SKELETAL RECONSTRUCTION

hind limbs longer than forelimbs

strong thigh bone

four-toed feet

long finger and hand bones

flexible tail about half dinosaur's length

Group Dicynodontia	Family Lystrosauridae	Time 240 mya

LYSTROSAURUS

LIS-TRO-SAW-RUS

Lystrosaurus, whose name means "shovel lizard," was a heavily built, early dicynodont with a short, stubby tail. It had two tusklike fangs made of horn. It used to be thought of as a type of reptilian hippopotamus because of its long, downturned snout and the placement of its nasal openings high on the snout. However, new analysis suggests *Lystrosaurus* led terrestrial lifestyle: the skull and jaw features were adaptations to a fibrous diet, the pelvis was well-developed, and the hind limbs were semi-erect.

• **DESCRIBED BY** E.D. Cope; 1870.

• **HABITAT** Dry floodplains.

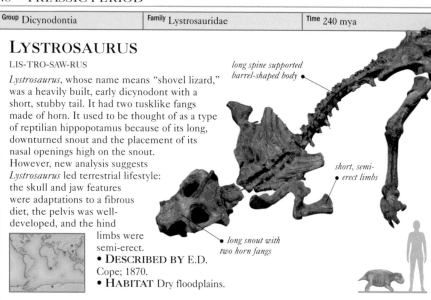

long spine supported barrel-shaped body

short, semi-erect limbs

long snout with two horn fangs

Length 3 ft (1 m)	Weight 200 lb (92 kg)	Diet Plants

Group Dicynodontia	Family Kannemeyeriidae	Time 235 mya

SINOKANNEMEYERIA

SY-NOH-KAN-EH-MEY-REE-A

This long-snouted member of the dicynodont ("two-dog teeth") group of synapsids was well adapted for a lifestyle as a terrestrial herbivore. Its head was massive, with large openings for the eyes, nostrils, and jaw muscles. These reduced the weight of the skull. A hinge between the lower jaw and the skull allowed the jaws to move backward and forward with a shearing action. Although the jaws were toothless, this motion would have ground up the toughest vegetation. The front of the jaw had a small horn-covered beak, and there were two small tusks growing from bulbous projections on the upper jaw. These tusks could have been used to dig up roots. *Sinokannemeyeria* had relatively short, stumpy legs, which were held in a slightly sprawling gait to the sides of its body. The limb girdles were formed into large, heavy plates of bone to support the weight of the wide, heavily built body. *Sinokannemeyeria* was probably not a fast or agile mover.

• **DESCRIBED BY** N. King; 1990.

• **HABITAT** Plains and woodland.

large attachment points for jaw muscles

large eye sockets

turtlelike horny beak at front of mouth

broad toes on flat feet

Length 6 ft (1.8 m)	Weight 220 lb (100 kg)	Diet Tough vegetation, roots

Group Dicynodontia	Family Kannemeyeriidae	Time 222–215 mya

PLACERIAS

PLAH-SEE-REE-AS

Placerias was a heavily built, powerful animal, with the characteristic dicynodont jaw structure. Its jaw margins were toothless, except for two horny tusks near the front of the mouth. The tip of the snout ended in a beak used for uprooting plants. *Placerias* was one of the last of the dicynodont species.

• **DESCRIBED BY** C.L. Camp, S.P. Welles; 1956.

• **HABITAT** Flood plains.

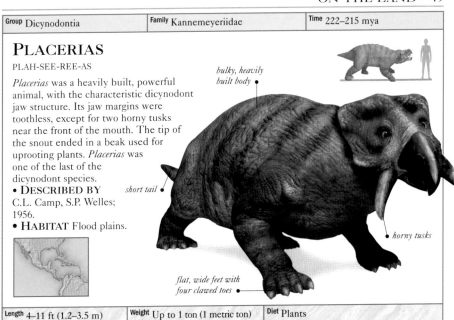

bulky, heavily built body

short tail

horny tusks

flat, wide feet with four clawed toes

Length 4–11 ft (1.2–3.5 m)	Weight Up to 1 ton (1 metric ton)	Diet Plants

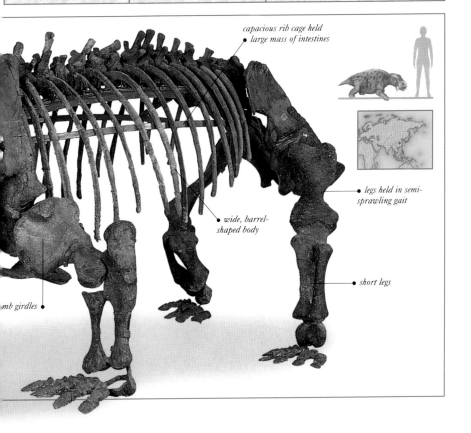

capacious rib cage held large mass of intestines

legs held in semi-sprawling gait

short legs

wide, barrel-shaped body

limb girdles

Group Cynodontia	Family Cynognathidae	Time 230–245 mya

CYNOGNATHUS
SY-NOG-NAY-THUS

This wolf-sized carnivore was a ferocious Triassic predator. It was one of the largest cynodonts ("dog-toothed" synapsids), and was heavily built, with strong legs positioned directly under its body, and a tail shorter than that of most other reptiles. Its head was more than 12 in (30 cm) long. It is thought that it was probably warm-blooded, that its skin may have been covered with hair, and that it may also have given birth to live young. *Cynognathus* ("dog jaw") had doglike teeth, with cutting incisors, long canines, and a shearing set of cheek teeth. The jaws had a wide gape and a very powerful bite.
• **DESCRIBED BY** H.G. Seeley; 1876.
• **HABITAT** Woodland.

large eye socket

long canine teeth

FOSSIL SKULL

Length 5 ft (1.5 m)	Weight 90–110 lb (40–50 kg)	Diet Herbivorous therapsids

Group Cynodontia	Family Thrinaxodontidae	Time 156–145 mya

THRINAXODON
THRIN-AX-OH-DON

This small, solidly built carnivore had a long body, which was distinctly divided into thoracic and lumbar regions (the first time this was seen among vertebrates). The division was marked by the ribs, which were borne only on the thoracic vertebrae. This suggests that *Thrinaxodon* ("trident tooth") probably had a diaphragm, as modern mammals do. One of the foot bones had evolved into a heel, so that the foot could be levered clear of the ground for more efficient running. The teeth were set into a single bone, which made the jaws stronger.
• **DESCRIBED BY** Seeley; 1894.
• **HABITAT** Woodland.

body may have been covered with hair

toes of equal length

teeth with three sharp cusps

Length 20 in (50 cm)	Weight Unknown	Diet Meat

Group Mammaliaformes	Family Morganucodontidae	Time 220–200 mya

EOZOSTRODON

EE-OH-ZOH-STROH-DON

This shrewlike animal was one of the earliest true mammals. It probably laid eggs, but is thought to have fed its young with milk produced by mammary glands. Its four short legs had a slightly sprawling gait and ended in five-toed feet with claws. Its tail was long and possibly hairy. Its snout was long, slim, and contained true mammalian teeth (the cheek teeth comprised simple premolars and molars with multiple sharp cusps, and were replaced only once during the animal's lifetime). The large eyes suggest that *Eozostrodon* was probably a nocturnal hunter, and the sharp teeth indicate a diet predominantly of insects and small animals. This genus is probably the same as the later-named genus *Morganucodon*.
• **DESCRIBED BY** F.R. Parrington; 1941.
• **HABITAT** Forest floors.

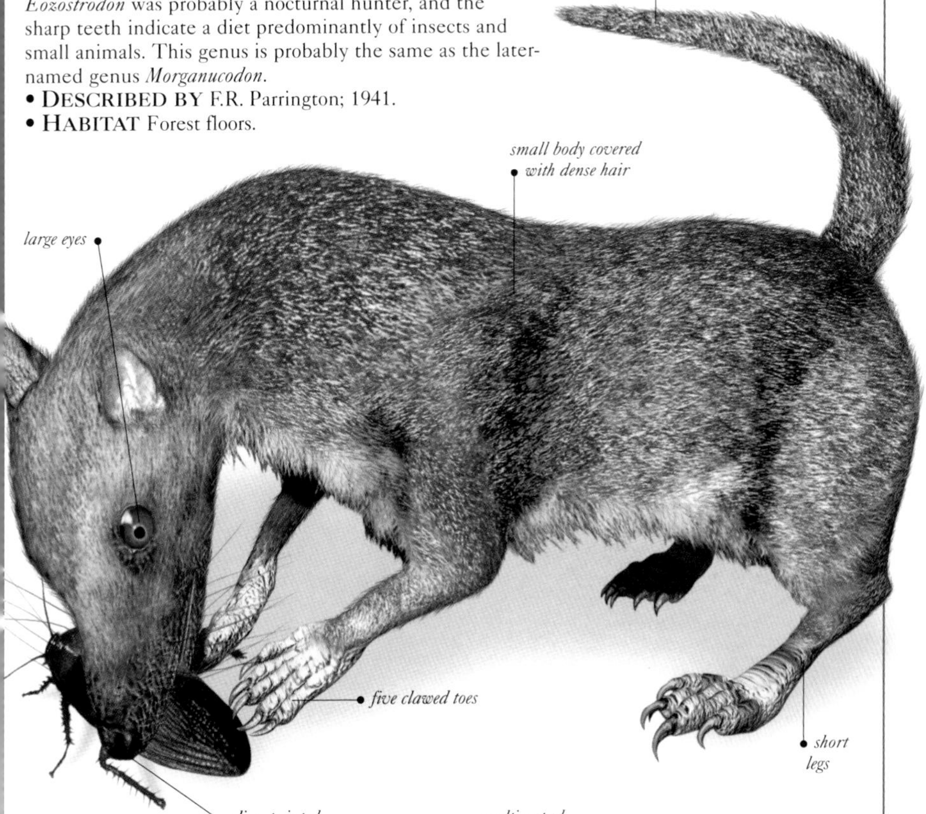

long, furry tail

small body covered with dense hair

large eyes

five clawed toes

short legs

slim, pointed snout may have had whiskers

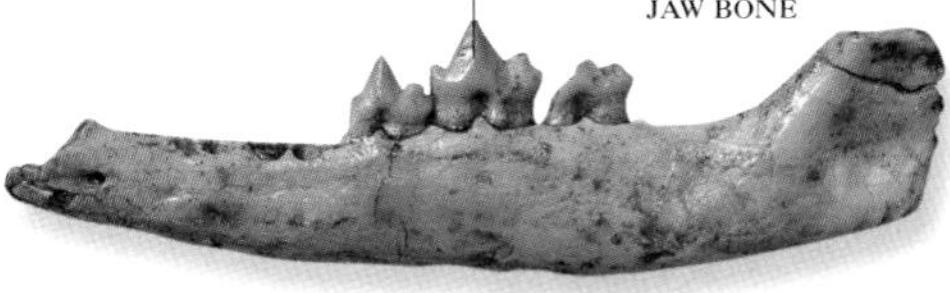

multicusped molars

JAW BONE

Length 4 in (10 cm)	Weight 5 oz (150 g)	Diet Insects, small animals

IN THE WATER

D uring the Mesozoic, many groups of reptiles became readapted to a marine or aquatic lifestyle. In the Triassic there were three main groups of marine reptiles—the placodonts, nothosaurs, and primitive ichthyosaurs.

Placodonts were the least specialized swimmers of the three, and they vanished at the end of the Triassic. Although many species evolved, they never invaded the open seas. Instead, they seem to have been restricted to the shallow, warm Tethys Sea. With the formation of coral reefs in the Triassic, many new mollusks had evolved, and the teeth and mouth of the placodonts show adaptations to a diet of shellfish and crustaceans. Some species spent equal amounts of time on land and in the water. Other groups became fully aquatic and developed turtlelike shells as protective armor.

Nothosaurs were marine animals with long, streamlined bodies. They had webbed feet, and their sharp teeth were well-adapted for eating fish. They seem to have lived a lifestyle rather like that of modern seals—hunting at sea and coming ashore to breed. Like placodonts, nothosaurs died out at the end of the Triassic.

Ichthyosaurs were the most specialized marine reptiles. They were fish-eaters shaped somewhat like a modern dolphin. Triassic forms (shastasaurs) swam in an eel-like way; later species became more fishlike. No longer able to come ashore, some species gave birth to live young at sea. Fossils have been found of female ichthyosaurs in the process of giving birth. Shastasaurs were so successful that they continued to diversify through the Jurassic and Cretaceous Periods.

Group Placodontia	Family Henodontidae	Time 235–223 mya

HENODUS

HEN-OH-DUS

Henodus ("single tooth") was an armored placodont shaped much like a modern turtle. It was as wide as it was long, and its back and belly were protected by bony, many-sided plates that made up a defensive shell. This in turn was completely covered with plates of tough horn. *Henodus* was unusual among placodonts in that it was able to live in fresh water. It had a strangely square snout and no teeth in the mouth. Instead, it is thought there was a horny beak at the front of the mouth, similar to that of modern turtles. This could be used to pluck shellfish off rocks and crush them efficiently. Its short, clawed feet may have been webbed.

• **DESCRIBED BY** Friedrich von Huene; 1936.
• **HABITAT** Lagoons.

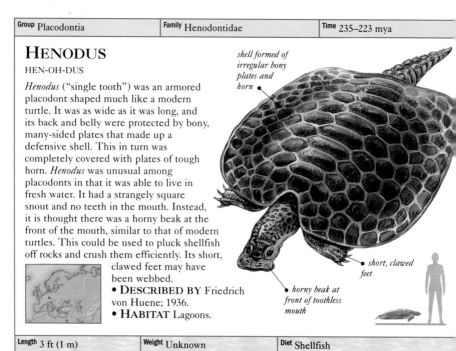

shell formed of irregular bony plates and horn

short, clawed feet

horny beak at front of toothless mouth

Length 3 ft (1 m)	Weight Unknown	Diet Shellfish

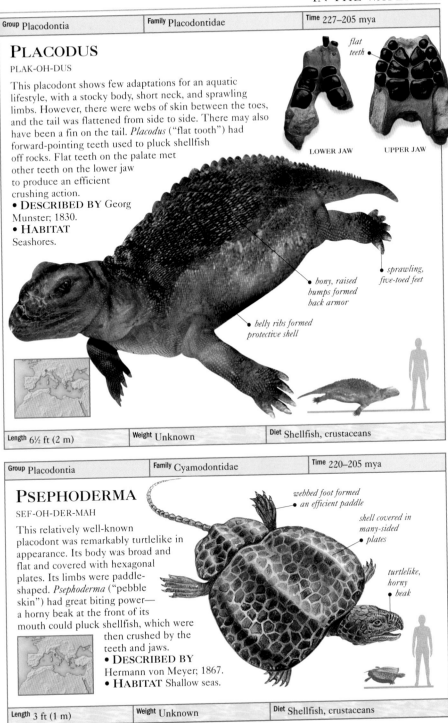

| Group Placodontia | Family Placodontidae | Time 227–205 mya |

PLACODUS

PLAK-OH-DUS

This placodont shows few adaptations for an aquatic lifestyle, with a stocky body, short neck, and sprawling limbs. However, there were webs of skin between the toes, and the tail was flattened from side to side. There may also have been a fin on the tail. *Placodus* ("flat tooth") had forward-pointing teeth used to pluck shellfish off rocks. Flat teeth on the palate met other teeth on the lower jaw to produce an efficient crushing action.
• **DESCRIBED BY** Georg Munster; 1830.
• **HABITAT** Seashores.

flat teeth

LOWER JAW   UPPER JAW

sprawling, five-toed feet

bony, raised bumps formed back armor

belly ribs formed protective shell

| Length 6½ ft (2 m) | Weight Unknown | Diet Shellfish, crustaceans |

| Group Placodontia | Family Cyamodontidae | Time 220–205 mya |

PSEPHODERMA

SEF-OH-DER-MAH

This relatively well-known placodont was remarkably turtlelike in appearance. Its body was broad and flat and covered with hexagonal plates. Its limbs were paddle-shaped. *Psephoderma* ("pebble skin") had great biting power—a horny beak at the front of its mouth could pluck shellfish, which were then crushed by the teeth and jaws.
• **DESCRIBED BY** Hermann von Meyer; 1867.
• **HABITAT** Shallow seas.

webbed foot formed an efficient paddle

shell covered in many-sided plates

turtlelike, horny beak

| Length 3 ft (1 m) | Weight Unknown | Diet Shellfish, crustaceans |

Group Nothosauria	Family Nothosauridae	Time 250 mya

CERESIOSAURUS

SER-EE-SEE-OH-SAW-RUS

Ceresiosaurus ("deadly lizard") had toes that were much longer than those of other nothosaurs due to hyperphalangy (an increased number of bones in each toe). The length of its feet, which may have been webbed, meant that efficient swimming flippers were formed. The forelegs were longer than the hind legs, suggesting that they were the ones used most for steering. *Ceresiosaurus* is thought to have swum by undulating its flexible body and tail from side to side.
• **DESCRIBED BY** Peyer; 1931.
• **HABITAT** Shallow seas.

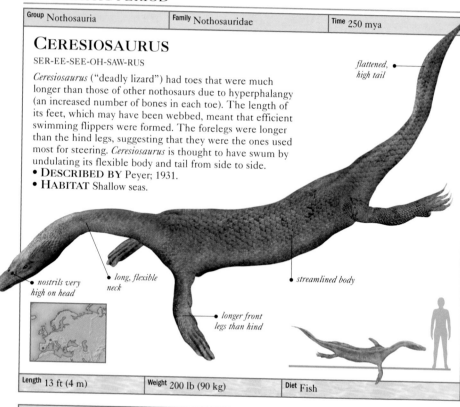

flattened, high tail

nostrils very high on head

long, flexible neck

streamlined body

longer front legs than hind

Length 13 ft (4 m)	Weight 200 lb (90 kg)	Diet Fish

Group Nothosauria	Family Nothosauridae	Time 248–206 mya

NOTHOSAURUS

NOH-THO-SAW-RUS

Nothosaurus ("false lizard") was a typical nothosaur. Its long body, neck, and tail were flexible and moderately streamlined. Some fossils have impressions of webbed skin between the five toes of the feet. The head was slim, and the jaws contained many sharp, thin teeth that interlocked when the mouth was closed. The nostrils were placed high on the head, close to the eyes.
• **DESCRIBED BY** Georg Munster; 1834.
• **HABITAT** Coastal regions.

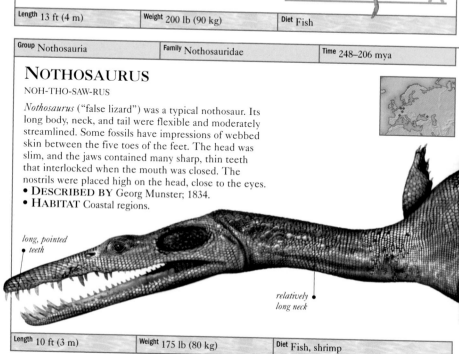

long, pointed teeth

relatively long neck

Length 10 ft (3 m)	Weight 175 lb (80 kg)	Diet Fish, shrimp

Group Nothosauria	Family Nothosauridae	Time 234–227 mya

LARIOSAURUS

LA-REE-OH-SAW-RUS

Lariosaurus was a small member of the nothosaur group of marine reptiles. It had primitive adaptations to an aquatic lifestyle. Its neck and toes were very short, and the webs of skin on its hind feet would have been small, and therefore not very useful for fast swimming. Its front feet formed paddlelike flippers. In common with other members of its group, it had flexible knee and ankle joints. *Lariosaurus* probably spent most of its time on the seashore or paddling in coastal waters.

• **DESCRIBED BY**
Curioni; 1847.
• **HABITAT**
Coastal shallows.

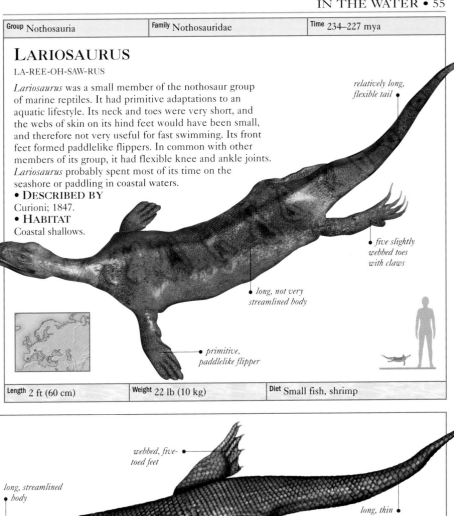

relatively long, flexible tail

five slightly webbed toes with claws

long, not very streamlined body

primitive, paddlelike flipper

Length 2 ft (60 cm)	Weight 22 lb (10 kg)	Diet Small fish, shrimp

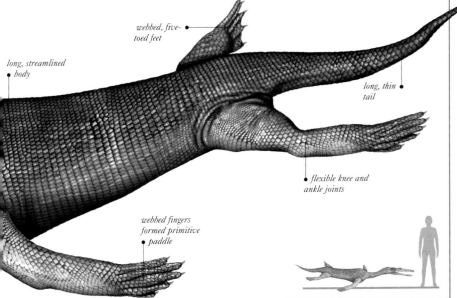

webbed, five-toed feet

long, streamlined body

long, thin tail

flexible knee and ankle joints

webbed fingers formed primitive paddle

Group Ichthyosauria	Family Mixosauridae	Time 225 mya

MIXOSAURUS

MIX-OH-SAW-RUS

This "mixed reptile" is thought to have been an intermediate form between primitive ichthyosaurs and more advanced types. It had a fishlike body, typical of advanced ichthyosaurs, with a dorsal fin on its back. However, it had only a small fin on the top of its tail. Its paddles were short, with the front pair longer than the hind ones.

- **DESCRIBED BY** Baur; 1887.
- **HABITAT** Oceans.

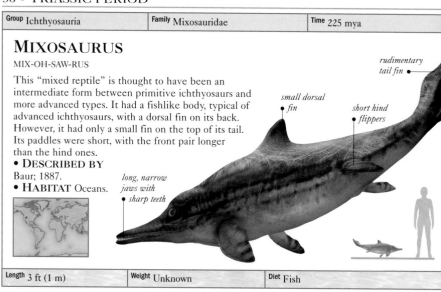

rudimentary tail fin

small dorsal fin

short hind flippers

long, narrow jaws with sharp teeth

Length 3 ft (1 m)	Weight Unknown	Diet Fish

Group Ichthyosauria	Family Shastasauridae	Time 227–206 mya

SHONISAURUS

SHON-EE-SAW-RUS

Shonisaurus ("Shoshone mountain reptile") is the largest ichthyosaur known. It had the typical ichthyosaur shape, with its head and neck, body, and tail making up equal thirds of its length. However, it had several features that indicate that it was an offshoot from the main ichthyosaur line. Its jaws were very long and had teeth only at the front. Its paddles were also unusually long, and of equal length.

- **DESCRIBED BY** Charles L. Camp; 1976.
- **HABITAT** Oceans.

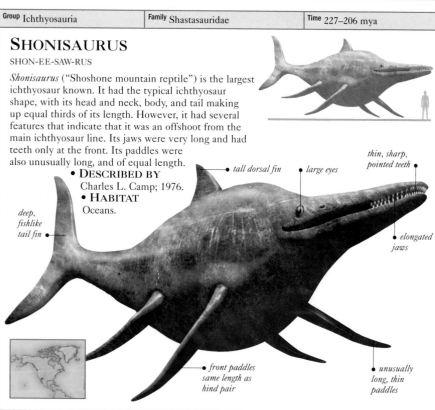

tall dorsal fin

large eyes

thin, sharp, pointed teeth

deep, fishlike tail fin

elongated jaws

front paddles same length as hind pair

unusually long, thin paddles

Length 50 ft (15 m)	Weight 22–38 tons (20–35 metric tons)	Diet Fish, squid, other cephalopods

IN THE AIR

L ate Triassic times saw an amazing evolutionary leap—the first group of vertebrate animals took to the air. These were the pterosaurs (winged reptiles). The earliest and most primitive pterosaurs, the rhamphorhynchoids, were usually small, with a long tail stiffened by bony ligaments. Later, they gave way to a more advanced group, the pterodactyloids.

Pterosaur wings were made of extremely thin membranes of skin stretched from the incredibly long fourth finger to the thigh. Views on flying ability, particularly of the rhamphorynchoids, have changed dramatically over the years. For a long time, it was thought that pterosaurs could not actively fly—they could only glide after climbing to a high takeoff point. Skeletal analysis now shows that pterosaurs were capable of flapping flight, although not as efficiently as birds. They probably had some kind of furry body covering.

Group Rhamphorhynchoidea	Family Dimorphodontidae	Time 228–215 mya

PETEINOSAURUS

PET-INE-OH-SAW-RUS

Peteinosaurus ("winged lizard") is one of the earliest vertebrates to show evidence of active, flapping flight. It had a light-boned skeleton, like that of a modern bird. Its long tail was stiffened with bony ligaments to stabilize it during flight. It had cone-shaped teeth for crunching insects.

- **DESCRIBED BY** Rupert Wild; 1978.
- **HABITAT** Swamps and river valleys.

large, light head

wing membrane stretched from fourth finger

long, bony tail

Length 2 in (60 cm)	Weight Unknown	Diet Flying insects

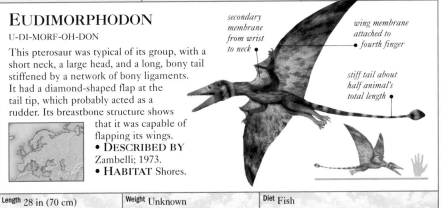

Group Rhamphorhynchoidea	Family Eudimorphodontidae	Time 210 mya

EUDIMORPHODON

U-DI-MORF-OH-DON

This pterosaur was typical of its group, with a short neck, a large head, and a long, bony tail stiffened by a network of bony ligaments. It had a diamond-shaped flap at the tail tip, which probably acted as a rudder. Its breastbone structure shows that it was capable of flapping its wings.

- **DESCRIBED BY** Zambelli; 1973.
- **HABITAT** Shores.

secondary membrane from wrist to neck

wing membrane attached to fourth finger

stiff tail about half animal's total length

Length 28 in (70 cm)	Weight Unknown	Diet Fish

JURASSIC PERIOD

208–144 MILLION YEARS AGO

At the beginning of the Jurassic Period, the world was still hot and arid. Major continental movements caused climate change throughout the period: increased rainfall led to a reduction in desert areas, climates were more humid, and, as the period progressed, habitats in general became more green and luxuriant. However, lake deposits show that there were millions of cycles of dry and wet periods. Most Jurassic plants were still mainly primitive types of gymnosperms. There were also ferns, horsetails, and club mosses, and huge forests of these plants spread worldwide. Continental movements led to the creation of warm, shallow seas, which became filled with coral reefs and new forms of marine life, including large reptiles. Pterosaurs were present in large numbers, and the earliest birds appeared at the end of the period.

JURASSIC LIFE

Prosauropod dinosaurs still dominated Early Jurassic habitats, but as the period progressed, they were usurped by the giant sauropods, such as *Apatosaurus*. The first armored dinosaurs—the stegosaurs—also appeared. Protective armor may have been an evolutionary response to the emergence of ever-larger carnivorous dinosaurs. The first true mammals evolved, and probably survived by remaining small and living a mainly nocturnal existence.

*relatively
short tail*

**LATER
PTEROSAURS**
In the Late Jurassic, new forms of pterosaurs, such as *Anurognathus* (below) appeared. Their main feature was a very short tail that gave them greater agility in the air.

MARINE PREDATORS
Giant pliosaurs such as *Liopleurodon* (above) filled the warm Jurassic seas, hunting large prey including other marine reptiles. They had developed an efficient "flying" action for swimming rapidly through the water.

*wing supported by
greatly elongated
fourth finger*

4,600 mya	4,000 mya	3,000 mya

JURASSIC LANDMASSES

At the start of the Jurassic Period, there was once again a supercontinent called Gondwana south of the Equator. Later in the period (see map), this split to form the landmasses that were to become present-day Australia, Antarctica, India, Africa, and South America. Laurasia (comprising the future North America and Europe) had begun to take shape in the northern hemisphere.

DIVERSITY

In the early Jurassic Period, the maximum size of dinosaurs increased, and this trend continued throughout the period. Because of this, mammals (such as *Sinoconodon*, above) and lizards tended to be rather small in order to maintain their ecological niches. In the seas, the ichthyosaurs, a fishlike group of marine reptiles, were at their zenith, sharing the warm Jurassic oceans with other marine predators, including plesiosaurs, marine crocodiles, and sharks.

TREES

Many forests of evergreen trees spread throughout the world. *Araucaria* were conifers. A fossilized cone is pictured at left.

| 2,000 mya | 1,000 mya | 500 mya | 250 mya | 0 |

ON THE LAND

A minor extinction event at the end of the Triassic Period led to many new groups of dinosaurs appearing during the Early Jurassic. The larger prosauropods were replaced by the giant sauropods—the largest land animals ever to have lived. Herds of these immense herbivores seem to have migrated long distances, probably causing massive damage to the environments they moved through. Once thought to be too heavy to live anywhere but in swamps, modern research shows that their legs were able to carry their weight on land. However, their lifestyle as high browsers has been called into question lately, as some paleontologists have presented evidence suggesting that some could not raise their long necks much above shoulder height.

Jurassic theropod dinosaurs became a little more varied than the Triassic forms. Two main groups existed—the large carnosaurs, and the small, lightly built coelurosaurs.

The Jurassic also saw the first appearances of the armored and plated ornithischian dinosaurs—the ankylosaurs and the stegosaurs.

Despite competition from dinosaurs, early mammals were continuing to diversify into a variety of forms, although remaining small and probably nocturnal animals.

Group Theropoda	Family Coelophysidae	Time 201–189 mya

DILOPHOSAURUS

DI-LOAF-OH-SAW-RUS

Dilophosaurus ("two-ridged lizard") was named for the striking pair of bony crests that adorned its head. These were so thin and fragile that they were almost certainly only used for sexual display. This theory is backed up by the finding that not all specimens have the crest—possibly they only occurred in males. *Dilophosaurus* had a more primitive body structure than that of coelurosaurs and carnosaurs—it had a large head, but was lightly built, with a slender neck, body, and tail. It seems to have been closely related to *Coelophysis*—like that dinosaur, it has a four-fingered hand and a notch in its upper jaw.

• **DESCRIBED BY** Samuel Welles; 1954.
• **HABITAT** Riverbanks.

flexible tail

bony, semicircular crests

long, slim, powerful hind legs

three long, forward-facing, clawed toes

Length 20 ft (6 m)	Weight ½ ton (500 kg)	Diet Small animals, perhaps fish or carrion

Group Theropoda	Family Ceratosauridae	Time 150–144 mya

CERATOSAURUS

KER-AT-OH-SAW-RUS

Ceratosaurus ("horned lizard") was named for the short horn above its nose. Another striking feature was the line of bony plates that ran down its back—so far, it is the only theropod known to have had them. It had strong yet short arms, with four fingers on each hand. Three of the fingers were clawed. It had a deep, broad tail, and feet with three large toes and a reduced back toe. Its teeth were long and bladelike. Although it superficially resembled a carnosaur such as *Allosaurus*, it was more primitive, and its tail was flexible rather than stiffened with bony ligaments, as was the case with the carnosaurs.

• **DESCRIBED BY** Othniel C. Marsh; 1884.
• **HABITAT** Forested plains.

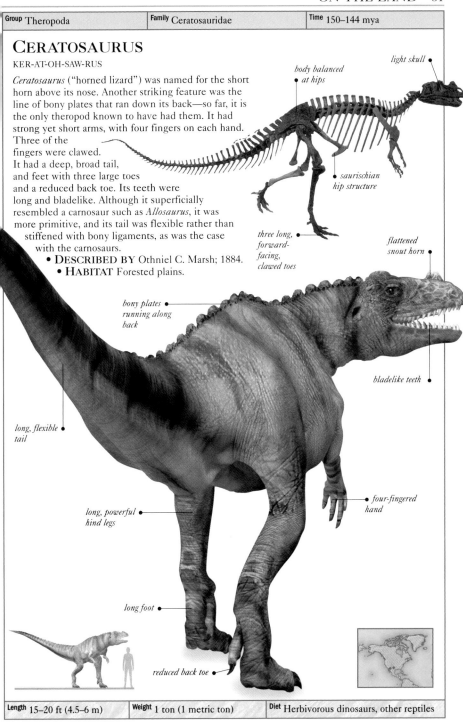

light skull

body balanced at hips

saurischian hip structure

three long, forward-facing, clawed toes

flattened snout horn

bony plates running along back

bladelike teeth

long, flexible tail

four-fingered hand

long, powerful hind legs

long foot

reduced back toe

Length 15–20 ft (4.5–6 m)	Weight 1 ton (1 metric ton)	Diet Herbivorous dinosaurs, other reptiles

Group Theropoda	Family Tetanurae	Time 160–155 mya

GASOSAURUS

GAS-OH-SAW-RUS

This theropod was given its unusual name ("gas lizard") in honor of the Dashanpu gas-mining company, which was working in the quarry where the fossil remains were excavated. The single species *Gasosaurus constructus* is represented by a single specimen. Remains included a humerus, the pelvis, and a femur. Little is known about *Gasosaurus*, and its classification is still uncertain. It may be a primitive carnosaur; however, some features of the leg bones suggest that it may be an early coelurosaur instead. If so, it would be one of the oldest coelurosaurs so far discovered. *Gasosaurus* had the typical theropod body shape of a large head, long, powerful legs ending in three forward-facing clawed toes, and a long, stiff tail. It had very short arms, but they were longer than those of later carnosaurs.

• **DESCRIBED BY** Dong and Tang; 1985.
• **HABITAT** Woodland.

RECONSTRUCTION
This computer-enhanced reconstruction of the skeleton was based on information from other carnosaurs.

bulky body

stiffened tail

large jaws
with sharp teeth

heavily built
hind legs

relatively
long arms

three forward-
facing clawed
toes

Length 13 ft (4 m)	Weight 330 lb (150 kg)	Diet Large herbivorous dinosaurs

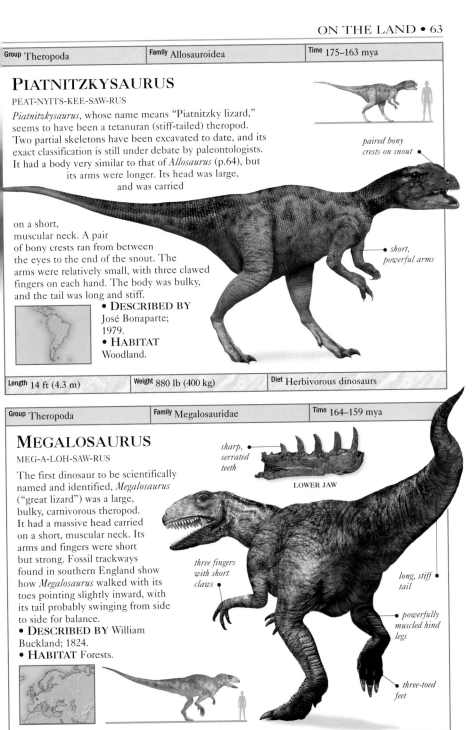

Group Theropoda	Family Allosauroidea	Time 175–163 mya

PIATNITZKYSAURUS

PEAT-NYITS-KEE-SAW-RUS

Piatnitzkysaurus, whose name means "Piatnitzky lizard," seems to have been a tetanuran (stiff-tailed) theropod. Two partial skeletons have been excavated to date, and its exact classification is still under debate by paleontologists. It had a body very similar to that of *Allosaurus* (p.64), but its arms were longer. Its head was large, and was carried

paired bony crests on snout

on a short, muscular neck. A pair of bony crests ran from between the eyes to the end of the snout. The arms were relatively small, with three clawed fingers on each hand. The body was bulky, and the tail was long and stiff.

short, powerful arms

• **DESCRIBED BY** José Bonaparte; 1979.
• **HABITAT** Woodland.

Length 14 ft (4.3 m)	Weight 880 lb (400 kg)	Diet Herbivorous dinosaurs

Group Theropoda	Family Megalosauridae	Time 164–159 mya

MEGALOSAURUS

MEG-A-LOH-SAW-RUS

The first dinosaur to be scientifically named and identified, *Megalosaurus* ("great lizard") was a large, bulky, carnivorous theropod. It had a massive head carried on a short, muscular neck. Its arms and fingers were short but strong. Fossil trackways found in southern England show how *Megalosaurus* walked with its toes pointing slightly inward, with its tail probably swinging from side to side for balance.
• **DESCRIBED BY** William Buckland; 1824.
• **HABITAT** Forests.

sharp, serrated teeth

LOWER JAW

three fingers with short claws

long, stiff tail

powerfully muscled hind legs

three-toed feet

Length 30 ft (9 m)	Weight 1–2¼ tons (1–2 metric tons)	Diet Large herbivorous dinosaurs

Group Theropoda	Family Allosauridae	Time 150–145 mya

ALLOSAURUS

AL-OH-SAW-RUS

Allosaurus ("different lizard") was the most abundant, and probably the largest, predator in the late Jurassic period in the lands that were to become North America. It was typical of its family of meat-eating dinosaurs, with a massive head, short neck, and bulky body. Its tail was long and deep, with a thin, stiff end. Its three-fingered forelimbs were strong, with large claws. *Allosaurus* had distinctive bony bumps over the eyes, and a narrow ridge of bone running between them down to the tip of the snout. These features may have been used for display. Although the head was massive, it was lightened by several large openings (fenestrae) between the bones. Expandable joints between the skull bones allowed the jaws to gape open sideways to swallow large mouthfuls. Despite its large size and lack of speed, some paleontologists believe that *Allosaurus* was agile enough to fell the giant plant-eating dinosaurs of the time.

• **DESCRIBED BY** Othniel C. Marsh, 1877.
• **HABITAT** Plains.

distinctive ridge of bone along snout

teeth with serrated front and back edges

Length 40 ft (12 m)	Weight 2½–3½ tons (2–3 metric tons)	Diet Herbivorous dinosaurs, carrion

massive skull lightened
by large fenestrae
(openings)

2½–5-in-
(5–10-cm-)
long teeth

large attachment
points for
powerful jaw
muscles

bladelike
teeth for slicing

FOSSIL SKULL

powerful upper jaw
had an axlike action

OTHNIEL C. MARSH
The greatest dinosaur
paleontologist of the 19th
century, Othniel C. Marsh,
named *Allosaurus*.

tail held
outstretched
for balance

**FOSSIL
FINDS**
A number of complete
skeletons of *Allosaurus* have
been excavated. Many partial
skeletons have been found in
the Cleveland-Lloyd Dinosaur
Quarry in Utah. This site is
thought to have been a place
where herbivorous dinosaurs
became stuck in mud
and attracted predators,
which also became
trapped as they attacked
their helpless prey.

Group Theropoda	Family Uncertain	Time 157–156 mya

XUANHANOSAURUS

SCHWAN-HAN-OH-SAW-RUS

This poorly
understood
theropod ("Xuan
lizard") was named after Xuanhan County in Sichuan
Province, China, where its fossils were found. At present, it is
known only from vertebrae and bones from the shoulder, arm,
and hand. *Xuanhanosaurus* seems to have been a *Megalosaurus*-like
tetanuran theropod. It is shown here with long, powerful hind legs,
clawed feet with three forward-facing toes, a large head, and a long
stiff tail held outstretched for balance. The hands were short, with
robust claws. The arms were very well developed and strong,
despite their short length: the humerus (upper arm bone)
is slightly longer than the bones of the lower
arm. Its discoverer has suggested that,
although it was probably mainly
bipedal, it walked on all fours
for at least some of the time.
• **DESCRIBED BY** Zhiming Dong; 1984.
• **HABITAT** Forests.

stiff tail held outstretched for balance

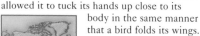

Length 20 ft (6 m)	Weight 550 lb (250 kg)	Diet Meat

Group Theropoda	Family Ornitholestidae	Time 156–145 mya

ORNITHOLESTES

OR-NITH-OH-LESS-TEES

Ornitholestes ("bird robber") was a close relative
of *Coelophysis* (see p.45). It was a slim, lightly built
dinosaur, with a small head, many conical teeth,
and an S-shaped neck. A long, tapering tail
contributed to
greater agility
when running.
Its name arose
because its
grasping hands,
light build, and long hind limbs
indicated that it may have been adapted to
the pursuit of Jurassic birds. Its arms were short
and strong; its hands had three long, clawed
fingers. An additional finger was very small. The
snout bore a small, bony crest. *Ornitholestes* had
many birdlike features, and its wrist structure
allowed it to tuck its hands up close to its
body in the same manner
that a bird folds its wings.
• **DESCRIBED BY**
Henry F. Osborn; 1903.
• **HABITAT** Forests.

long, flexible neck

birdlike, clawed feet

three long and one short finger on each hand

Length 6½ ft (2 m)	Weight 26 lb (12 kg)	Diet Meat, perhaps including birds, carrion

skin may have had distinctive markings

large head

strong, well-developed arms

three clawed fingers on each hand

three long, forward-facing, clawed toes

very long, thin, tapering tail

tail held outstretched

small crest on snout

body balanced at hip

FOSSIL-HUNTING EXPEDITION
Leading US paleontologist Henry F. Osborn (1857–1935) undertook many fossil-hunting expeditions in Mongolia and the United States in the 1900s.

Group Theropoda	Family Compsognathidae	Time 155–145 mya

COMPSOGNATHUS

COMP-SOG-NAY-THUS

This theropod, whose name means "pretty jaw," was about the size of a modern chicken, making it one of the smallest known dinosaurs. Its skeletal structure shows that it must have been a fast runner—its bones were hollow, its shins were much longer than its thighs, and its long tail was held outstretched for balance. Its arms were short, probably with three fingers. Its feet were very birdlike, with three clawed toes facing forward. *Compsognathus* was anatomically very similar to *Archaeopteryx* (p.102), with the exception of wings, and lived in similar areas. The presence of primitive feathers on a closely related genus—*Sinosauropteryx*—suggests that *Compsognathus* could also have had a downy body covering, although there is no direct evidence for this.

• **DESCRIBED BY** Johann A. Wagner; 1859.
• **HABITAT** Warm, moist areas and scrub.

relatively large eyes

slim, pointed head and snout

Length 24 in (70 cm)	Weight 6½ lb (3 kg)	Diet Small lizards, mammals

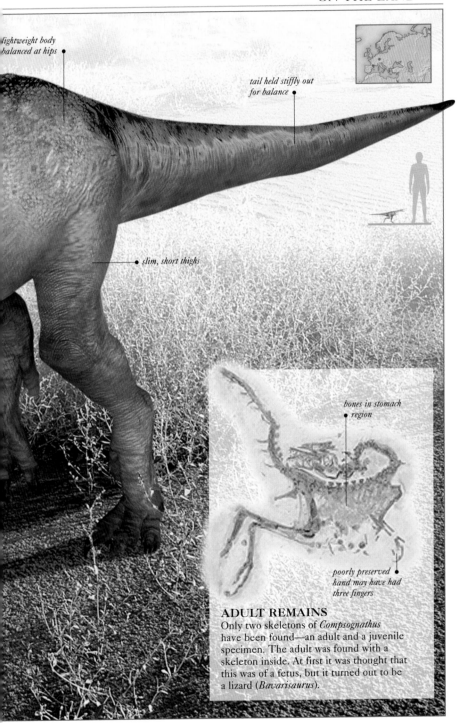

lightweight body balanced at hips

tail held stiffly out for balance

slim, short thighs

bones in stomach region

poorly preserved hand may have had three fingers

ADULT REMAINS

Only two skeletons of *Compsognathus* have been found—an adult and a juvenile specimen. The adult was found with a skeleton inside. At first it was thought that this was of a fetus, but it turned out to be a lizard (*Bavarisaurus*).

Group Prosauropoda	Family Anchisauridae	Time 190 mya

ANCHISAURUS

AN-CHEE-SAW-RUS

Anchisaurus was an early prosauropod. It had a small head with a narrow snout, a long, flexible neck, and a slim body and tail. Although its arms were a third shorter than its legs, it spent most of its time on all fours. The thumbs had a large claw that may have been used for defense.
• **DESCRIBED BY**
Othniel C. Marsh, 1885.
• **HABITAT**
Woodland.

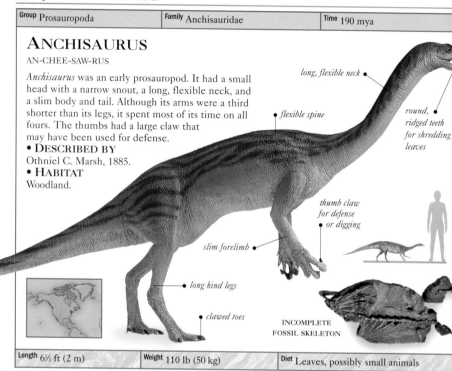

long, flexible neck

flexible spine

round, ridged teeth for shredding leaves

thumb claw for defense or digging

slim forelimb

long hind legs

clawed toes

INCOMPLETE
FOSSIL SKELETON

Length 6½ ft (2 m)	Weight 110 lb (50 kg)	Diet Leaves, possibly small animals

Group Prosauropoda	Family Massospondylidae	Time 208–204 mya

MASSOSPONDYLUS

MASS-OH-SPON-DI-LUSS

Massospondylus ("massive vertebrae") was named for the first remains found—a few large vertebrae. Many fossil finds have now been made, and it appears to have been the most common prosauropod in what is now southern Africa.

Massospondylus had a tiny head on a long, flexible neck. It probably spent most of its time on all fours, but could rear up on its hind legs to feed from trees. It had massive, five-fingered hands that could be used for holding food or for walking on. Each thumb had a large, curved claw. The front teeth were rounded, and the back ones had flat sides, indicating a tough plant diet. There may also have been a horny beak on the lower jaw. Gizzard stones have been found with some skeletons.
• **DESCRIBED BY** Richard Owen; 1854.
• **HABITAT** Scrubland and desert plains.

extremely long, flexible neck

hands with massive span

Length 13 ft (4 m)	Weight 330 lb (150 kg)	Diet Plants, possibly small animals

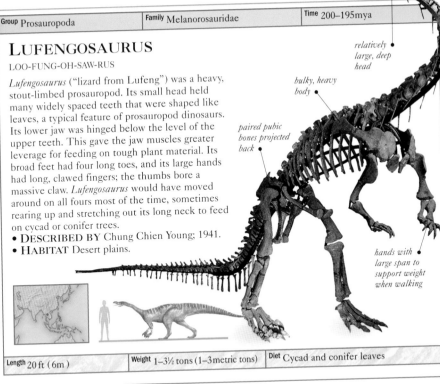

| Group Prosauropoda | Family Melanorosauridae | Time 200–195mya |

LUFENGOSAURUS

LOO-FUNG-OH-SAW-RUS

Lufengosaurus ("lizard from Lufeng") was a heavy, stout-limbed prosauropod. Its small head held many widely spaced teeth that were shaped like leaves, a typical feature of prosauropod dinosaurs. Its lower jaw was hinged below the level of the upper teeth. This gave the jaw muscles greater leverage for feeding on tough plant material. Its broad feet had four long toes, and its large hands had long, clawed fingers; the thumbs bore a massive claw. *Lufengosaurus* would have moved around on all fours most of the time, sometimes rearing up and stretching out its long neck to feed on cycad or conifer trees.

- **DESCRIBED BY** Chung Chien Young; 1941.
- **HABITAT** Desert plains.

relatively large, deep head

bulky, heavy body

paired pubic bones projected back

hands with large span to support weight when walking

| Length 20 ft (6m) | Weight 1–3½ tons (1–3 metric tons) | Diet Cycad and conifer leaves |

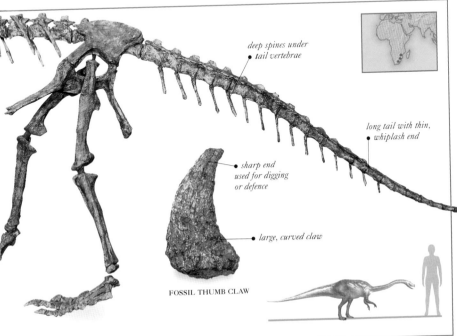

deep spines under tail vertebrae

long tail with thin, whiplash end

sharp end used for digging or defence

large, curved claw

FOSSIL THUMB CLAW

Group Sauropoda	Family Vulcanodontidae	Time 208–201 mya

VULCANODON

VUL-KAN-UH-DON

Vulcanodon was named after the volcanic rock in which the first skeleton was found. With the skeleton were seven teeth, which actually came from a predator that may have eaten it. One of the earliest sauropods known, *Vulcanodon* had blunt claws on its feet and an enlarged claw on each inner toe.
• **DESCRIBED BY** Raath; 1972.
• **HABITAT** Forested plains.

small head •

bulky, sloping • body

nostrils positioned high on nose

• long, slim neck

• long, slim neck

• relatively long front limbs

Length 21 ft (6.5 m)	Weight 4½–5½ tons (4–5 metric tons)	Diet Plants

Group Sauropoda	Family Cetiosauridae	Time 170–160 mya

SHUNOSAURUS

SHOON-OH-SAW-RUS

Nearly complete skeletons of *Shunosaurus* ("Shuno lizard") have been discovered, making it only the second sauropod to be known in its entirety. The skull is long and low with small teeth. A surprising feature is the small bony club at the end of its tail, formed by enlarged vertebrae (not seen in the pictured specimen).
• **DESCRIBED BY** Dong, Zhou, and Zhang; 1983.
• **HABITAT** Plains.

long, flexible neck •

low head with large nostrils

• relatively short forelegs

Length 33 ft (10 m)	Weight 11 tons (10 metric tons)	Diet Plants

Group Sauropoda	Family Vulcanodontidae	Time 189–176 mya

BARAPASAURUS

BA-RAP-A-SAW-RUS

Barapasaurus ("big-legged lizard") is one of the earliest known sauropods. There is fossil evidence for all parts of the skeleton, with the exception of the skull and feet, making it potentially the best-known Early Jurassic sauropod. However, to date it still has not been fully described, and its provisional classification may change in the light of future findings. *Barapasaurus* had slim limbs, spoon-shaped, saw-edged teeth (found in isolation), and unusual hollows in the vertebrae of the back. Paleontologists believe this dinosaur had a short, deep head, but the structure of the skull is unknown at present.
• **DESCRIBED BY** Jain, Cutty, Roy-Chowdhury and Chatterjee; 1975.
• **HABITAT** Plains.

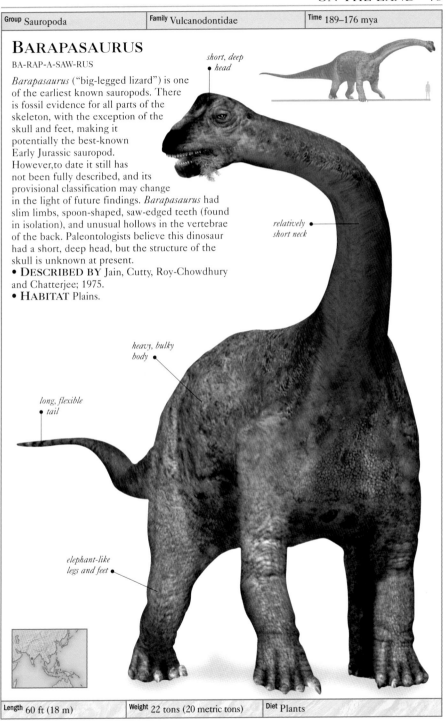

short, deep head

relatively short neck

heavy, bulky body

long, flexible tail

elephant-like legs and feet

Length 60 ft (18 m)	Weight 22 tons (20 metric tons)	Diet Plants

Group Sauropoda	Family Diplodocidae	Time 155–145 mya

BAROSAURUS

BA-ROH-SAW-RUS

Barosaurus ("heavy lizard") had all the typical features of its family—a long neck and tail, a bulky body, a tiny head, and relatively short legs for its size. Its limbs are indistinguishable from those of *Diplodocus* (see p.76), but its neck was much longer. Its 15 cervical vertebrae were greatly elongated—a third longer than in *Diplodocus*.

powerful tail with whiplash end

Barosaurus probably roamed in herds and relied on its huge size for defense against the large predators of the time. However, its tail had a thin whiplash end and would have imparted considerable force if swung against an attacking dinosaur.
• **DESCRIBED BY** Othniel C. Marsh; 1890.
• **HABITAT** Floodplains.

elephant-like limbs

Length 75–90 ft (23–27 m)	Weight 22 tons (20 metric tons)	Diet Plants

Group Sauropoda	Family Cetiosauridae	Time 170–160 mya

CETIOSAURUS

SEE-TEE-OH-SAW-RUS

This dinosaur, whose name means "whale lizard," was discovered early in the 18th century. Its huge bones were thought to belong to some type of immense whale—hence its name. It was a large, heavy sauropod with a shorter neck and tail than other sauropods. It was also different in that its vertebrae were solid, without hollow spaces to lighten them. Its head was blunt, and contained spoon-shaped teeth. *Cetiosaurus* is thought to have roamed in large herds, at an estimated walking speed of 10 mph (15 km/h).
• **DESCRIBED BY** Richard Owen; 1842.
• **HABITAT** Plains.

solid centrum of vertebra

FOSSIL VERTEBRA

tail held outstretched in life

5-ft- (1.5-m-) long shoulder blade (mounted too vertically in this reconstruction)

Length 60 ft (18 m)	Weight 10 tons (9 metric tons)	Diet Plants

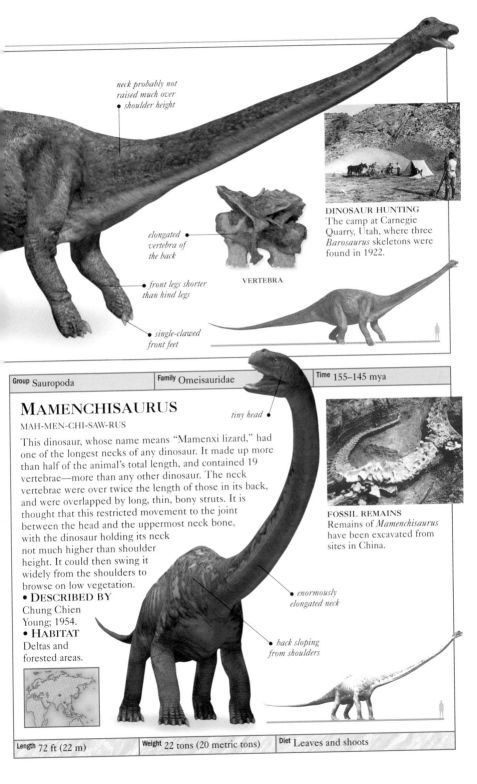

neck probably not raised much over shoulder height

DINOSAUR HUNTING
The camp at Carnegie Quarry, Utah, where three *Barosaurus* skeletons were found in 1922.

elongated vertebra of the back

VERTEBRA

front legs shorter than hind legs

single-clawed front feet

Group Sauropoda	Family Omeisauridae	Time 155–145 mya

MAMENCHISAURUS

MAH-MEN-CHI-SAW-RUS

tiny head

This dinosaur, whose name means "Mamenxi lizard," had one of the longest necks of any dinosaur. It made up more than half of the animal's total length, and contained 19 vertebrae—more than any other dinosaur. The neck vertebrae were over twice the length of those in its back, and were overlapped by long, thin, bony struts. It is thought that this restricted movement to the joint between the head and the uppermost neck bone, with the dinosaur holding its neck not much higher than shoulder height. It could then swing it widely from the shoulders to browse on low vegetation.

FOSSIL REMAINS
Remains of *Mamenchisaurus* have been excavated from sites in China.

- **DESCRIBED BY**
Chung Chien Young; 1954.
- **HABITAT**
Deltas and forested areas.

enormously elongated neck

back sloping from shoulders

Length 72 ft (22 m)	Weight 22 tons (20 metric tons)	Diet Leaves and shoots

| Group Sauropoda | Family Diplodocidae | Time 155–145 mya |

DIPLODOCUS

DIP-LOD-OH-KUS

Diplodocus was one of the longest dinosaurs. Some paleontologists think that *Seismosaurus* was actually an aged *Diplodocus*, in which case, it would be the longest yet discovered. It was lightly built, with slim limbs and a tapered tail with a whiplash end. Its name, meaning "double beam," comes from the chevron bones under its tail vertebrae.

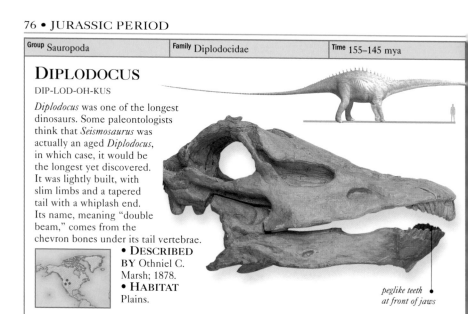

- **DESCRIBED BY** Othniel C. Marsh; 1878.
- **HABITAT** Plains.

peglike teeth at front of jaws

| Length 87 ft (27 m) | Weight 13½ tons (12 metric tons) | Diet Leaves |

| Group Sauropoda | Family Diplodocidae | Time 154–145 mya |

APATOSAURUS

A-PAT-OH-SAW-RUS

One species of *Apatosaurus*, *A. excelsus*, was the dinosaur originally called *Brontosaurus*. This sauropod was shorter, yet heavier and bulkier than its close relatives. It had a tiny head at the end of a long neck made up of 15 vertebrae. Its back vertebrae were hollow, and its long tail had a whiplike end. Its thick hind legs were longer than the front ones, perhaps to allow the dinosaur to rear up when feeding. Whether *Apatosaurus* could actually do this is disputed by some paleontologists.

- **DESCRIBED BY** Othniel C. Marsh; 1877.
- **HABITAT** Wooded plains.

neck with limited mobility

tail comprising over half the total length

relatively short front legs

| Length 70 ft (21 m) | Weight 38½ tons (35 metric tons) | Diet Leaves |

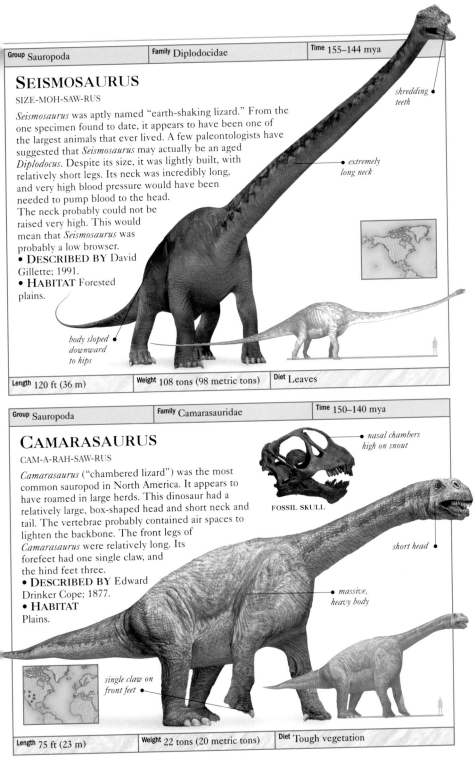

| Group Sauropoda | Family Diplodocidae | Time 155–144 mya |

SEISMOSAURUS

SIZE-MOH-SAW-RUS

Seismosaurus was aptly named "earth-shaking lizard." From the one specimen found to date, it appears to have been one of the largest animals that ever lived. A few paleontologists have suggested that *Seismosaurus* may actually be an aged *Diplodocus*. Despite its size, it was lightly built, with relatively short legs. Its neck was incredibly long, and very high blood pressure would have been needed to pump blood to the head. The neck probably could not be raised very high. This would mean that *Seismosaurus* was probably a low browser.
• **DESCRIBED BY** David Gillette; 1991.
• **HABITAT** Forested plains.

shredding teeth

extremely long neck

body sloped downward to hips

| Length 120 ft (36 m) | Weight 108 tons (98 metric tons) | Diet Leaves |

| Group Sauropoda | Family Camarasauridae | Time 150–140 mya |

CAMARASAURUS

CAM-A-RAH-SAW-RUS

Camarasaurus ("chambered lizard") was the most common sauropod in North America. It appears to have roamed in large herds. This dinosaur had a relatively large, box-shaped head and short neck and tail. The vertebrae probably contained air spaces to lighten the backbone. The front legs of *Camarasaurus* were relatively long. Its forefeet had one single claw, and the hind feet three.
• **DESCRIBED BY** Edward Drinker Cope; 1877.
• **HABITAT** Plains.

nasal chambers high on snout

FOSSIL SKULL

short head

massive, heavy body

single claw on front feet

| Length 75 ft (23 m) | Weight 22 tons (20 metric tons) | Diet Tough vegetation |

Group Sauropoda	Family Brachiosauridae	Time 150–145 mya

BRACHIOSAURUS

BRACK-EE-OH-SAW-RUS

Brachiosaurus ("arm lizard") is known from all parts of the skeleton except for the important neural arches of the vertebrae at the base of the neck. It was one of the tallest and largest sauropods, and the one in which the lengthening of the forelimbs relative to the hind limbs reached its extreme. Together with its long neck, ending in a small head, *Brachiosaurus*' giraffelike stance gave it a great height: up to 50 ft (16 m). The tail was relatively short and thick. Like other members of its family, *Brachiosaurus* had chisel-like teeth—26 on each jaw—toward the front of the mouth. The nostrils were large and were situated on a bulge on the top of the head. The legs were pillarlike, and the feet all had five toes with fleshy pads behind. The first toe of each front foot bore a claw, as did the first three toes of the hind feet. Like other sauropods, it probably traveled in herds. *Brachiosaurus* was adapted for feeding off vegetation from the tops of trees. The length of its neck means that it would have had to have an extremely large, powerful heart, and very high blood pressure to pump blood up to its head. *Brachiosaurus* is thought to have laid its eggs while walking, leaving the young to fend for themselves.

- **DESCRIBED BY** Elmer S. Riggs; 1903.
- **HABITAT** Plains.

chisel-like teeth at front of mouth

long neck made up of 3-ft- (1-m-) long vertebrae

ball-like head of femur

MASSIVE BONES

The femur (thigh bone) of *Brachiosaurus* was over 6 ft (1.8 m) long and massively thick to support the dinosaur's weight. One of the first bones discovered by Elmer S. Riggs, in 1900, was the humerus (upper arm bone). It was over 7 ft (2.1 m) long, which was so much greater than that of any known humerus that Riggs thought it was a crushed femur of an *Apatosaurus* (p.76).

Length 85 ft (26 m)	Weight 55 tons (50 metric tons)	Diet Plants

nostrils on bulge
on top of head •

body sloping
downward from
• shoulder to hip

relatively slim,
pillarlike legs •

Group Ornithiscia	Family Lesothosauridae	Time 208–203 mya

LESOTHOSAURUS

LE-SO-TOE-SAW-RUS

Lesothosaurus ("Lesotho lizard") was an early bipedal herbivorous dinosaur, perhaps the same genus as *Fabrosaurus* (see Glossary). It was small and built for speed, with a lightly built body, long, slim legs, and a thin, flexible tail. It had pointed front teeth, serrated, arrow-shaped cheek teeth,

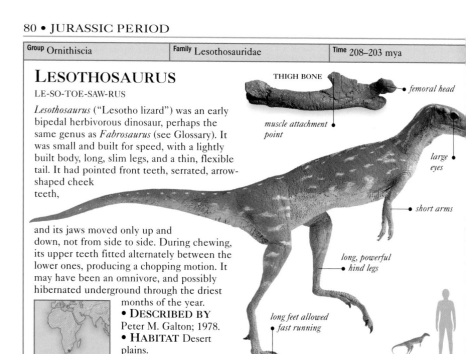

THIGH BONE

femoral head

muscle attachment point

large eyes

short arms

long, powerful hind legs

long feet allowed fast running

and its jaws moved only up and down, not from side to side. During chewing, its upper teeth fitted alternately between the lower ones, producing a chopping motion. It may have been an omnivore, and possibly hibernated underground through the driest months of the year.

• **DESCRIBED BY** Peter M. Galton; 1978.
• **HABITAT** Desert plains.

Length 3¼ ft (1 m)	Weight 9–15 lb (4–7 kg)	Diet Leaves, perhaps carrion and insects

Group Thyreophora	Family Scelidosauridae	Time 208–194 mya

SCELIDOSAURUS

SCEL-EYE-DOH-SAW-RUS

This small, heavy, armored dinosaur, whose name means "lower hind limb lizard," seems to be one of the earliest and most primitive ornithischians. Its classification as either a primitive stegosaur or ankylosaur is is still open to debate. It had impressive defensive armor: its back was covered with bony plates and studded with a double row of bony spikes. Additional rows of studs ran along its sides, and there was a pair of triple-spiked bony plates behind the neck. The head was small and pointed, with a horny beak and small, leaf-shaped teeth. Although the forelimbs were much shorter than the hind limbs, *Scelidosaurus* seems to have walked on all fours.

• **DESCRIBED BY** Richard Owen; 1861.
• **HABITAT** Woodland.

underside of tail covered by bony studs

three long, one short, clawed digits

longer feet than later thyreophorans

FOSSIL FOOT

Length 11 ft (3.5 m)	Weight 550 lb (250 kg)	Diet Plants

Group Thyreophora	Family Scutellosauridae	Time 200–195 mya

SCUTELLOSAURUS

SCOO-TELL-OH-SAW-RUS

This "little shield lizard" had a long body and slim limbs. Its arms were also relatively long and slender. Over 300 low, bony studs covered its back, flanks, and the base of its tail to form a defensive armor. *Scutellosaurus* probably fed and rested on all fours, but ran away from predators on its hind legs, holding its tail stiffly out behind it to counter-balance the weight of the bony armor.

• **DESCRIBED BY** Edwin H. Colbert; 1981.

• **HABITAT** Woodland.

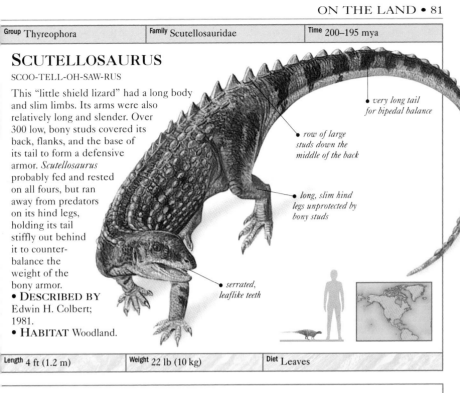

very long tail for bipedal balance

row of large studs down the middle of the back

long, slim hind legs unprotected by bony studs

serrated, leaflike teeth

Length 4 ft (1.2 m)	Weight 22 lb (10 kg)	Diet Leaves

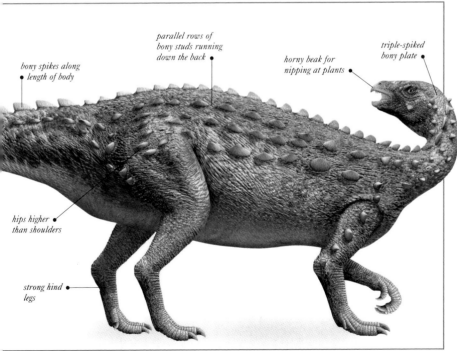

parallel rows of bony studs running down the back

triple-spiked bony plate

bony spikes along length of body

horny beak for nipping at plants

hips higher than shoulders

strong hind legs

Group Stegosauria	Family Stegosauridae	Time 155–144 mya

STEGOSAURUS
STEG-OH-SAW-RUS

Stegosaurus ("roof lizard") was the largest plated dinosaur. It had a tiny head, a toothless beak, and two rows of bony plates running from behind its neck to halfway along its tail. Some of these plates were over 24 in (60 cm) high. The tail also had long spikes, each up to 3 ft (1 m) long, the number of which varied between species. The dinosaur's neck was also armored with many tiny, bony studs. The hind legs were twice as long as the forelegs, meaning that the body's highest point was at the hips. *Stegosaurus* had a toothless beak and small, weak cheek teeth, so it probably used gizzard stones to aid digestion.

- **DESCRIBED BY** Othniel C. Marsh; 1877.
- **HABITAT** Woodland.

pointed tip ●

very sharp, ● bony tail spikes

FOSSIL PLATE

FOSSIL TAIL SPIKE

PLATES AND SPIKES
Some reconstructions of *Stegosaurus* have the plates arranged in pairs or in a zigzag pattern along the back. However, no one is sure exactly how the plates were arranged.

Length 20 ft (6 m)	Weight 2¼ tons (2 metric tons)	Diet Plants

very small
braincase

plates graduated
in size along
the tail

tail spikes varied
in number
between species

massive
body

long spines on
tail vertebrae

SKELETAL RECONSTRUCTION

covering of skin
or tough horn
over plates

Group Stegosauria	Family Stegosauridae	Time 156–150 mya

KENTROSAURUS

KEN-TRO-SAW-RUS

This East African contemporary of *Stegosaurus* was smaller than its more famous relative, but just as well protected. *Kentrosaurus* ("spiked lizard") had paired rectangular plates running down over the neck, shoulders, and half of the back. Over the hips, the plates gave way to sharp spikes, which ran in pairs down to the tip of the tail. Another pair of long spikes jutted out from the hips on each side. The skull, housing a tiny brain, is known only from fragments, but was probably long and slender with a toothless, horny beak.
• **DESCRIBED BY** Edwin Henning; 1915.
• **HABITAT** Forests.

pairs of sharp spikes from mid back to tail tip

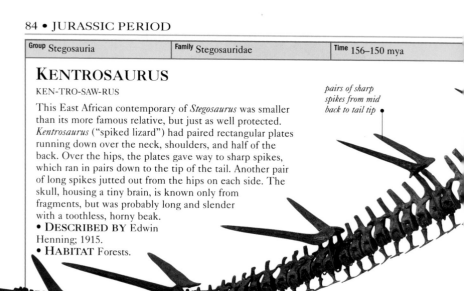

Length 16 ft (5 m)	Weight 1⅔ tons (1.5 metric tons)	Diet Low-lying vegetation

Group Stegosauria	Family Stegosauridae	Time 157–154 mya

TUOJIANGOSAURUS

TOO-YANG-OH-SAW-RUS

Tuojiangosaurus ("Tuojiang lizard") was similar in appearance to *Kentrosaurus*. Fifteen pairs of pointed spines ran down over the neck, shoulders, and back. These became taller and more pointed over the hips and the base of the tail. The end of the tail was armored with two pairs of long spikes. Unlike *Stegosaurus*, another member of the same family, *Tuojiangosaurus* did not have tall vertebral spines over its hips and lower back. It could probably not rear up to feed from trees, and was a low browser instead. The head was long and low, with small cheek teeth and a horny beak at the front of the snout.
• **DESCRIBED BY** Dong, Li, Zhou, and Zhang; 1973.
• **HABITAT** Forests.

paired bony spines running along back

short forelegs for low browsing posture

long, forward-facing, clawed toes

Length 23 ft (7 m)	Weight 4½ tons (4 metric tons)	Diet Low-lying vegetation

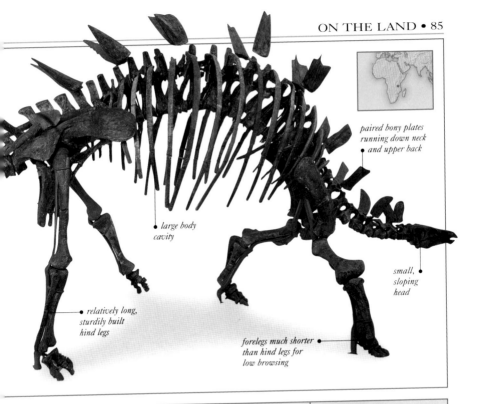

paired bony plates
running down neck
and upper back

large body
cavity

small,
sloping
head

relatively long,
sturdily built
hind legs

forelegs much shorter
than hind legs for
low browsing

Group Ankylosauria	Family Ankylosauridae	Time 156–145 mya

GARGOYLEOSAURUS

GAR-GOYL-EE-OH-SAW-RUS

Gargoyleosaurus ("gargoyle lizard") was a primitive,
early ankylosaur with body armor formed from
irregular, bony oval plates on the
upper surface of its body and tail.
The hind legs were slightly longer
than the front ones. *Gargoyleosaurus*
had many features unusual among
ankylosaurs, including teeth on both the
upper and lower jaw, a straight nasal passage,
and hollow armor plates. The skull shows
features seen in late Cretaceous ankylosaurs,
including fusion of bone armor to the surface
of the skull and jaw.
• **DESCRIBED BY** Kenneth Carpenter
et al.; 1998.
• **HABITAT** Woodland.

large bony plates
along back

long
shoulder
spikes

long, low
skull covered
by bony plates

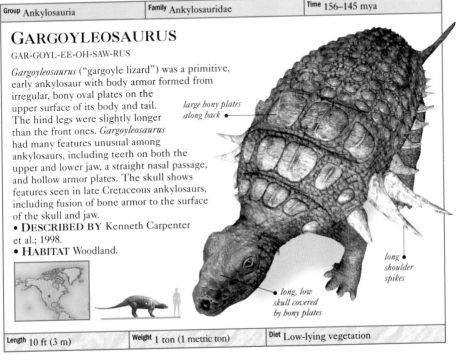

Length 10 ft (3 m)	Weight 1 ton (1 metric ton)	Diet Low-lying vegetation

| Group Ornithopoda | Family Heterodontosauridae | Time 208–200 mya |

HETERODONTOSAURUS
HET-ER-OH-DONT-OH-SAW-RUS

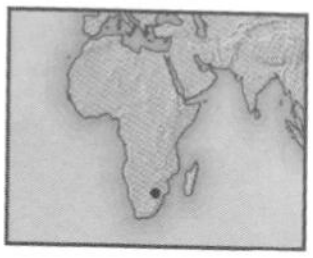

As its name ("different-toothed lizard") suggests, the most remarkable feature of this small bipedal dinosaur was its teeth. *Heterodontosaurus* had three kinds: cutting incisors at the front of the upper jaw, two pairs of large tusklike teeth, and tall, chisel-like teeth used for shredding vegetation. The tusks may have been used for defense, or they may have occurred in males only and been used for sexual display.

• **DESCRIBED BY** Crompton and Charig; 1962.
• **HABITAT** Scrub.

long tail for counterbalance when running •

• *tusks possibly only present in males*

cutting incisors •

hands capable of grasping and supporting weight for four-legged walking •

• *shredding cheek teeth*

FOSSIL SKULL

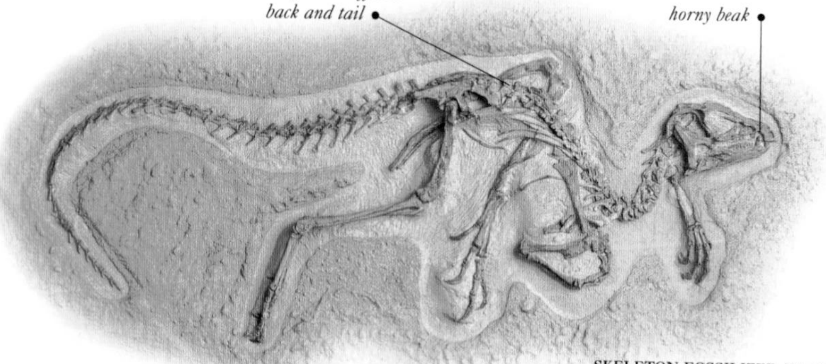

three long, forward-facing, clawed toes •

bony rods stiffened back and tail •

horny beak •

SKELETON FOSSILIZED IN CLAY

| Length 4 ft (1.2 m) | Weight 40 lb (20 kg) | Diet Leaves, tubers, possibly insects |

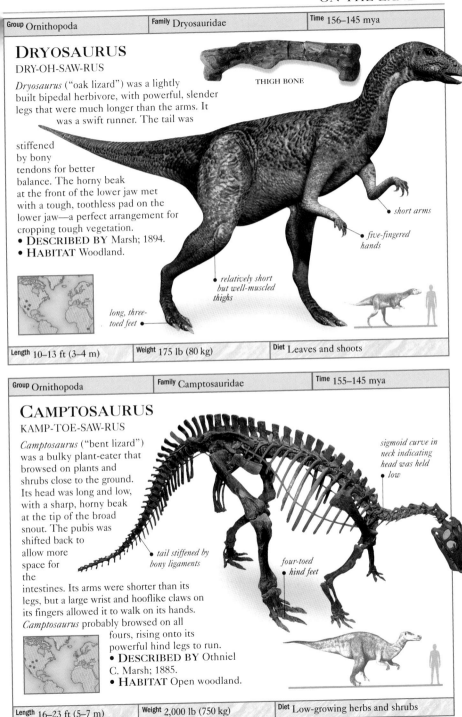

| Group Ornithopoda | Family Dryosauridae | Time 156–145 mya |

DRYOSAURUS
DRY-OH-SAW-RUS

Dryosaurus ("oak lizard") was a lightly built bipedal herbivore, with powerful, slender legs that were much longer than the arms. It was a swift runner. The tail was stiffened by bony tendons for better balance. The horny beak at the front of the lower jaw met with a tough, toothless pad on the lower jaw—a perfect arrangement for cropping tough vegetation.
• **DESCRIBED BY** Marsh; 1894.
• **HABITAT** Woodland.

THIGH BONE

short arms

five-fingered hands

relatively short but well-muscled thighs

long, three-toed feet

| Length 10–13 ft (3–4 m) | Weight 175 lb (80 kg) | Diet Leaves and shoots |

| Group Ornithopoda | Family Camptosauridae | Time 155–145 mya |

CAMPTOSAURUS
KAMP-TOE-SAW-RUS

Camptosaurus ("bent lizard") was a bulky plant-eater that browsed on plants and shrubs close to the ground. Its head was long and low, with a sharp, horny beak at the tip of the broad snout. The pubis was shifted back to allow more space for the intestines. Its arms were shorter than its legs, but a large wrist and hooflike claws on its fingers allowed it to walk on its hands. *Camptosaurus* probably browsed on all fours, rising onto its powerful hind legs to run.
• **DESCRIBED BY** Othniel C. Marsh; 1885.
• **HABITAT** Open woodland.

sigmoid curve in neck indicating head was held low

tail stiffened by bony ligaments

four-toed hind feet

| Length 16–23 ft (5–7 m) | Weight 2,000 lb (750 kg) | Diet Low-growing herbs and shrubs |

Group Mammalia	Family Sinocodontidae	Time 208 mya

SINOCONODON

SINE-OH-CO-DON

Sinoconodon ("Chinese spiky tooth") was a small, primitive mammal resembling a modern shrew. Its skull structure, despite retaining some minor synapsid features, showed that it was truly mammalian. In particular, the structures housing the inner ear are similar to those of true mammals. Although the cheek-teeth were permanent, as in living mammals, its other teeth were still replaced, perhaps several times, during its lifetime. The rear of the braincase had expanded and the eye socket was large. *Sinoconodon* was apparently warm-blooded and was probably covered in fur. It was a quadruped, with five long, clawed toes on each foot, and a long tail. The snout was long and slim.

• **DESCRIBED BY** Patterson and Olsen; 1961.

• **HABITAT** Woodland.

long, flexible tail •

Length 4–6 in (10–15 cm)	Weight 1–2 oz (30–80 g)	Diet Probably mainly insects

Group Mammaliaformes	Family Docodontidae	Time 150–144 mya

DOCODON

DOH-CO-DON

probably fur-covered body •

Docodon ("beam tooth") was a mouse-sized, close mammal relative. So far, this genus is known only from remains of teeth. These had very complex tooth cusp patterns, allowing *Docodon* to chew food effectively. It appears to have been a rodentlike animal, and was probably warm-blooded.

• **DESCRIBED BY** Othniel C. Marsh 1880.

• **HABITAT** Forests.

five-toed feet •

Length 4 in (10 cm)	Weight ¼–1¼ oz (20–50 g)	Diet Possibly omnivorous

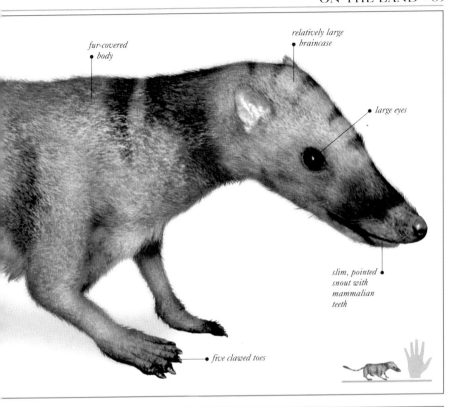

fur-covered body

relatively large braincase

large eyes

slim, pointed snout with mammalian teeth

five clawed toes

Group Mammalia	Family Triconodontidae	Time 150–144 mya

TRICONODON

TRY-CON-OH-DON

Triconodon ("three-spiked tooth") was a small raccoon- or opossum-like primitive mammal. Originally classed in the same group as *Eozostrodon* (p. 51), recent analysis shows that it was a true mammal, perhaps a marsupial. Its teeth were rather unspecialized and versatile, suggesting an omnivorous lifestyle, including insects and small reptiles. The development of a mammalian middle ear seems to have coincided with an increase in brain size.
• **DISCOVERED** Richard Owen; 1859.
• **HABITAT** Woodland.

molars with three sharp points

FOSSIL JAWBONE

large teeth at the front of the jaw

Length 20 in (50 cm)	Weight 1¾ lb (750 g)	Diet Omnivorous

IN THE WATER

J urassic oceans teemed with fish, giant ammonites, squid, sharks, and the first rays. There were also extensive ranges of coral reefs. The nothosaurs and the placodonts died out at the end of the Triassic Period, and were replaced by the plesiosaurs. These were more adapted for marine life, and lived in both sea- and fresh water. There were two main groups: the long-necked plesiosaurs, which had a short body and tail and a long neck with a small head; and the pliosaurs. These were generally larger than the plesiosaurs and had a relatively short neck and large head. The two groups appear to have occupied different hunting niches, with the plesiosaurs feeding in shallow or surface waters, and the pliosaurs hunting at greater depths.

Ichthyosaurs survived into the Jurassic, and many new forms appeared. Some of these reached immense sizes. They all had half-moon-shaped tail fins, and swam using their tails, rather than their paddles, for propulsion. Fossil remains of some ichthyosaurs are quite remarkable—fossil droppings and stomach contents have often been found. This evidence shows that their diet consisted of small fish and cephalopods. Numerous fossils have also been found of young ichthyosaurs inside the body of an adult, or emerging tail-first from an adult's body. This is the same way that modern dolphins give birth.

In the late Jurassic, ichthyosaurs seem to have become rarer, possibly because of competition from the more modern forms of fish that had evolved.

Group Ichthyosauria	Family Leptopterygidae	Time 209–194 mya

TEMNODONTOSAURUS

TEM-NOH-DON-TOH-SAW-RUS

This large ichthyosaur looked a bit like a modern dolphin. Its body was long, smooth, and streamlined, and it had a long, narrow snout, with many large teeth set into a dental groove. Its tail was large, and it had four long, narrow paddles. Unusually, the rear paddles were almost the same length as the front ones. *Temnodontosaurus* also had a large triangular dorsal fin, as did all advanced ichthyosaurs. Fossil finds of ichthyosaur young preserved inside the body of adults show that these creatures were viviparous—they gave birth to live young in the sea without having to come ashore to lay eggs.

• **DESCRIBED BY** William D. Conybeare; 1922.
• **HABITAT** Shallow seas.

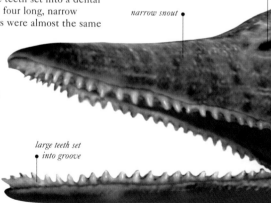

nostrils set far back on snout

narrow snout

large teeth set into groove

Length 30 ft (9 m)	Weight 16½ tons (15 metric tons)	Diet Large squid and ammonites

Group Ichthyosauria	Family Ichthyosauridae	Time 206–140 mya

ICHTHYOSAURUS

IK-THEE-OH-SAW-RUS

Many hundred complete skeletons of *Ichthyosaurus* have been discovered, making it one of the best-known of all prehistoric animals. It had a high dorsal fin and broad front paddles. The end section of the tail was angled downward to support the vertical tail fin. *Ichthyosaurus* had massive ear bones, perhaps to pick up underwater vibrations created by potential prey.

• **DESCRIBED BY** Charles Koenig; 1818.

• **HABITAT** Oceans.

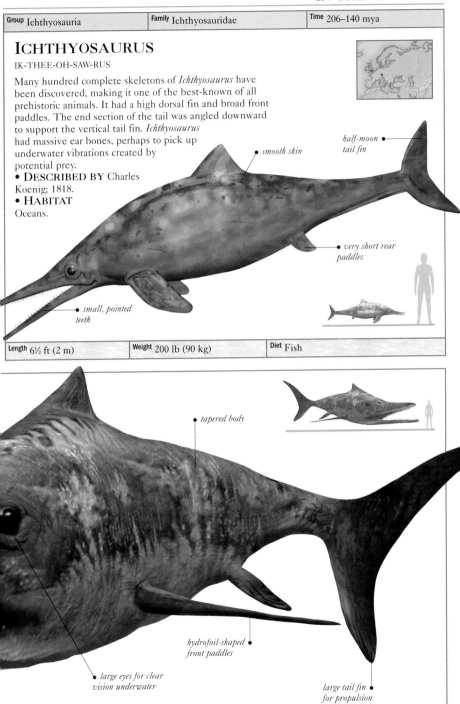

half-moon tail fin

smooth skin

very short rear paddles

small, pointed teeth

Length 6½ ft (2 m)	Weight 200 lb (90 kg)	Diet Fish

tapered body

hydrofoil-shaped front paddles

large eyes for clear vision underwater

large tail fin for propulsion

Group Ichthyosauria	Family Ichthyosauridae	Time 161–145 mya

OPHTHALMOSAURUS

OFF-THAL-MO-SAW-RUS

It is not difficult to see why *Ophthalmosaurus* ("eye lizard") was so named. Its eyes were the largest of any creature, relative to body size. As in other ichthyosaurs, the eyes were surrounded by the sclerotic ring—a circular arrangement of bony plates that prevented the soft tissues from collapsing at high pressures. Some paleontologists think that *Ophthalmosaurus* had such large eyes because it was a night hunter, others that it swam at very deep depths. *Ophthalmosaurus* had a teardrop-shaped body. The tail had a crescent-shaped fin. The paddles were short and broad.

nostrils set high on snout, close to eyes

huge eye sockets

long, thin snout

• **DESCRIBED BY** C.W. Andrews; 1907.
• **HABITAT** Oceans.

Length 16 ft (5 m)	Weight 3⅓ tons (3 metric tons)	Diet Fish, squid, other mollusks

Group Plesiosauroidea	Family Plesiosauridae	Time 135–120 mya

PLESIOSAURUS

PLEEZ-EE-OH-SAW-RUS

Plesiosaurus was built for maneuverability rather than speed. It had the typical plesiosaur shape of a short and wide body that tapered toward the tail. Its neck was much longer than the body, and was very flexible. Although its head was relatively small, its jaws were long, and held many sharp, conical teeth. *Plesiosaurus* had four wide, paddle-shaped flippers, which it is thought to have used in a combination of rowing (back and forth) and flying (up and down) motions.

small head

flexible neck longer than body

• **DESCRIBED BY** H.T. De La Beche, William D. Conybeare; 1821.
• **HABITAT** Oceans.

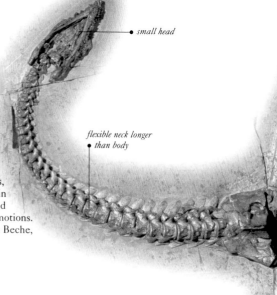

Length 7½ ft (2.5 m)	Weight 200 lb (90 kg)	Diet Fish, squidlike mollusks

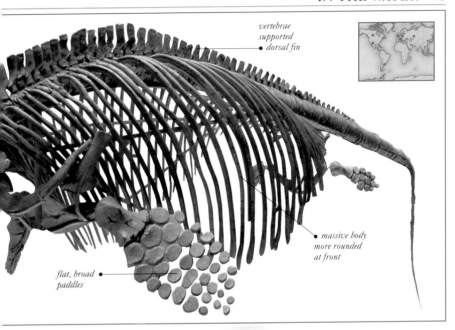

vertebrae
supported
• dorsal fin

• massive body
more rounded
at front

flat, broad •
paddles

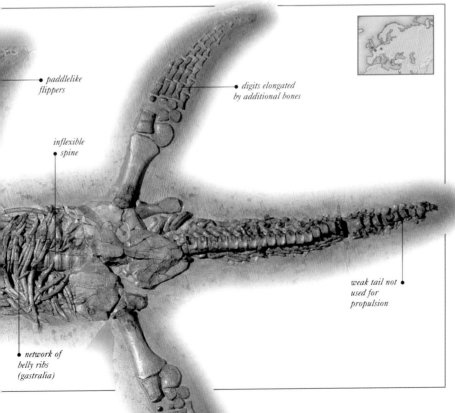

• paddlelike
flippers

• digits elongated
by additional bones

inflexible
• spine

weak tail not •
used for
propulsion

• network of
belly ribs
(gastralia)

Group Plesiosauroidea	Family Cryptoclididae	Time 165–150 mya

CRYPTOCLIDUS

CRIP-TOH-CLID-US

Cryptoclidus was a plesiosaur with a moderately long neck
made up of 30 vertebrae. Its small skull had a long snout,
with the nostrils set far back. Its jaw contained many
sharp, pointed teeth. These interlocked when
the jaw was closed to make a fine trap for
small fish or shrimplike prey.
Cryptoclidus had a relatively
short tail, and four hydrofoil-
shaped flippers. These are
thought to have been
moved in steady, vertical
strokes to propel the
animal along. The
belly ribs were molded
into plates that provided
protection when *Cryptoclidus*
came ashore to lay its eggs.
• **DESCRIBED BY** Harry G. Seeley; 1892.
• **HABITAT** Shallow oceans.

*long, relatively
inflexible neck*

*collar bones
formed plates
under the body*

Length 13 ft (4 m)	Weight 9 tons (8 metric tons)	Diet Fish, small marine animals

Group Pliosauroidea	Family Pliosauridae	Time 165–150 mya

LIOPLEURODON

LIE-OH-PLOOR-OH-DON

*streamlined
body*

Liopleurodon was a massive marine carnivore. It had a
whalelike appearance, with a large, heavy head, a short,
thick neck, and a streamlined body. It is thought to have
used its front and rear flippers in different swimming
motions, with the front pair moving up and down, and
the rear ones used in a kicking and turning motion.
Its teeth were arranged in a rosette at the front
of its mouth. It may have swum with its
mouth open, allowing water to pass
into its nostrils so that it could
smell its prey.
• **DESCRIBED BY**
H.E. Sauvage;
1873.
• **HABITAT**
Oceans.

*rosette of teeth
at front of jaw*

large eyes

Length 33–50 ft (10–15 m)	Weight 22–33 tons (20–30 metric tons)	Diet Large squid, ichthyosaurs

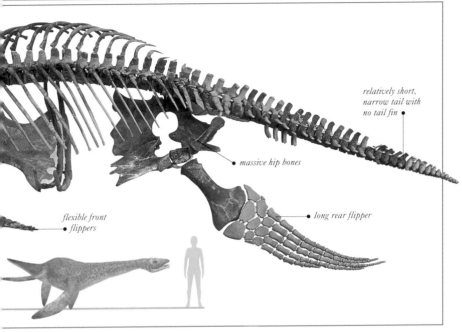

relatively short, narrow tail with no tail fin

massive hip bones

flexible front flippers

long rear flipper

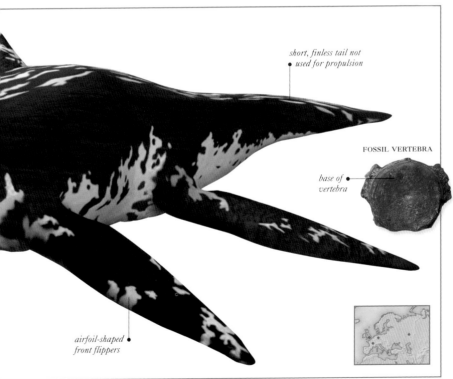

short, finless tail not used for propulsion

FOSSIL VERTEBRA

base of vertebra

airfoil-shaped front flippers

Group Thalattosuchia	Family Metriorhynchidae	Time 178–157 mya

GEOSAURUS

GEE-OH-SAW-RUS

This "earth lizard" was a highly specialized aquatic crocodilian. It had a streamlined shape and had lost the heavy back armor that crocodiles normally have. Its smoother skin meant that *Geosaurus* was more maneuverable when swimming, and could move its body, as well as its tail, from side to side to propel itself along. It had two pairs of flippers and a large, fishlike tail fin, which was supported by a steep downward bend of the spine. One fossil specimen of *Geosaurus* was found outlined by a thin film of carbon. This showed the shape of the limbs in life. The hind flippers were longer than the front pair, which were shaped like hydrofoils. The long, slim snout was filled with sharp, pointed teeth.

• **DESCRIBED BY** Baron Georges Cuvier; 1842.

• **HABITAT** Seas.

• *vertical tail fin*

• *long, thin tail*

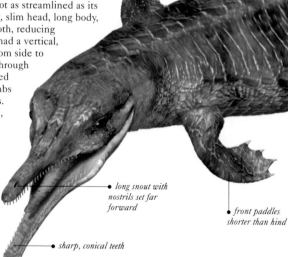

Length 10 ft (3 m)	Weight 265 lb (120 kg)	Diet Fish

Group Thalattosuchia	Family Metriorhynchidae	Time 157–154 mya

METRIORHYNCHUS

MET-REE-OR-RINE-CUS

An aquatic crocodilian, *Metriorhynchus* is thought to have come ashore only when laying eggs. It had a streamlined shape (although not as streamlined as its relative *Geosaurus*), with a long, slim head, long body, and thin tail. Its skin was smooth, reducing resistance in the water, and it had a vertical, fishlike tail fin. Moving this from side to side propelled *Metriorhynchus* through the water. Its limbs were formed into paddles, with the hind limbs being larger than the forelimbs. Its snout was long and pointed, and the jaws had long muscles to allow the animal to open its mouth very wide. The teeth were conical.

• **DESCRIBED BY** Hermann von Meyer; 1832.

• **HABITAT** Tropical seas.

• *long snout with nostrils set far forward*

• *front paddles shorter than hind*

• *sharp, conical teeth*

Length 10 ft (3 m)	Weight 265 lb (120 kg)	Diet Fish

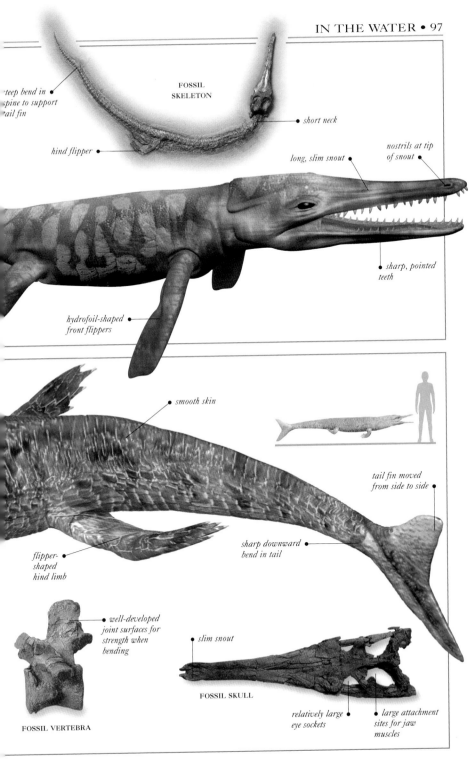

FOSSIL
SKELETON

teep bend in
pine to support
ail fin

short neck

hind flipper

long, slim snout

nostrils at tip
of snout

sharp, pointed
teeth

hydrofoil-shaped
front flippers

smooth skin

tail fin moved
from side to side

flipper-
shaped
hind limb

sharp downward
bend in tail

well-developed
joint surfaces for
strength when
bending

slim snout

FOSSIL SKULL

FOSSIL VERTEBRA

relatively large
eye sockets

large attachment
sites for jaw
muscles

IN THE AIR

The pterosaurs, which had first appeared in the Triassic Period, continued to evolve during the Jurassic, and many new forms appeared. The more advanced pterodactyls, which had a longer neck and skull and a shorter tail than the rhamphorhynchoids, became well-established by the end of the period. The rhamphorhynchoids did not survive into the Cretaceous.

The discovery in 1971 of a fossil of the rhamphorhynchoid *Sordes* provided strong evidence that pterosaurs had a fast metabolism and were warm-blooded. Impressions in the deposits around the skeleton showed that the body was covered in a fine, dense fur, while the tail and wings were not.

Remains of feathered dinosaurs have been found in Jurassic deposits, and in this period, the first true bird, *Archaeopteryx*, appeared. Since its discovery in 1860, there has been great debate about its classification and its ability to fly. Despite early accusations of fraud, the presence of feathers is indisputable. They probably evolved first for insulation, and only later to improve flying efficiency. The action of wing flapping may have originated as an extension of the grabbing forearm motions that small theropods used to capture their prey. Current opinion is that *Archaeopteryx* could sustain powered flight for short distances, but was not a strong flier.

Group Rhamphorhynchoidea	Family Dimorphodontidae	Time 175–159 mya

DIMORPHODON

DIE-MOR-FOH-DON

The most striking feature of *Dimorphodon* ("two-form tooth") was its enormous puffinlike head. It had a short neck and a long tail. The tail could only be moved near the base, helping to steer the animal. It was probably a clumsy walker. It has been suggested that it spent most of its time hanging from cliffs or branches, from which it launched itself into flight. *Dimorphodon* had two types of teeth—long front ones and small cheek teeth.
• **DESCRIBED BY** Richard Owen; 1859.
• **HABITAT** Shores.

• *diamond-shaped flap of skin at tail end used as a rudder*

Length 4 ft (1.2 m)	Weight Unknown	Diet Fish

Group Rhamphorhynchoidea	Family Rhamphorhynchidae	Time 165–150 mya

RHAMPHORHYNCHUS

RAM-FOR-RINK-US

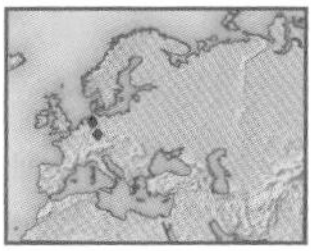

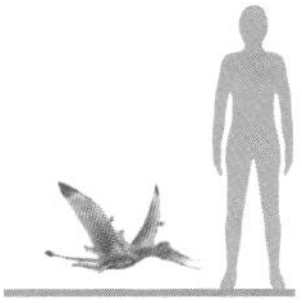

This pterosaur is well-known from beautifully preserved specimens found along with *Archaeopteryx*. Details of the wing structure and the tail can be seen, and a throat pouch has even been preserved in a few fossils. *Rhamphorhynchus* had long narrow jaws to act as a fish spear. Its sharp teeth pointed outward. It had a long tail with a diamond-shaped flap of skin at the end, and small legs. The wing membrane stretched down to the ankle.

• **DESCRIBED BY** Hermann von Meyer; 1847.
• **HABITAT** Shores.

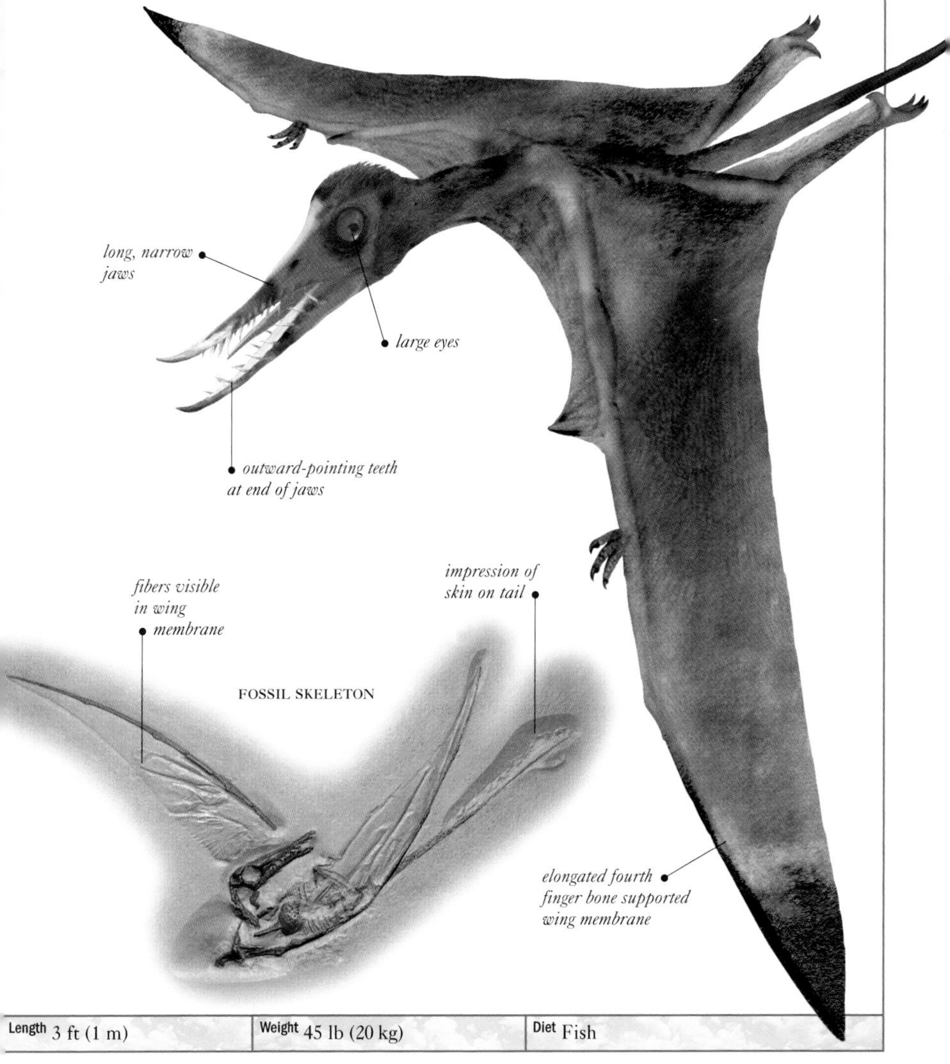

long, narrow jaws

large eyes

outward-pointing teeth at end of jaws

fibers visible in wing membrane

impression of skin on tail

FOSSIL SKELETON

elongated fourth finger bone supported wing membrane

Length 3 ft (1 m)	Weight 45 lb (20 kg)	Diet Fish

Group Rhamphorhynchoidea	Family Anurognathidae	Time 150–145 mya

ANUROGNATHUS

AN-YOOR-OG-NATH-US

This tiny pterosaur was unlike other rhamphorhynchoids in that it only had a very short tail. In fact, its name means "without tail and jaw." Along with the short tail, its small body size would have made maneuvering on the wing very easy. Its narrow head had short yet strong jaws with many peglike teeth designed for crushing or grinding. Its wings, which reached a maximum span of about 20 in (50 cm), were composed of a thin flap of skin that stretched from the elongated fourth finger to the ankle. A secondary wing, supported by the pteroid bone, stretched from each wrist to the neck. Some paleontologists have surmised that *Anurognathus* spent most of their time on the backs of the huge sauropods of the period, hunting for insects from this elevated vantage point.

• **DESCRIBED BY** Doerderline; 1923.
• **HABITAT** Wooded plains.

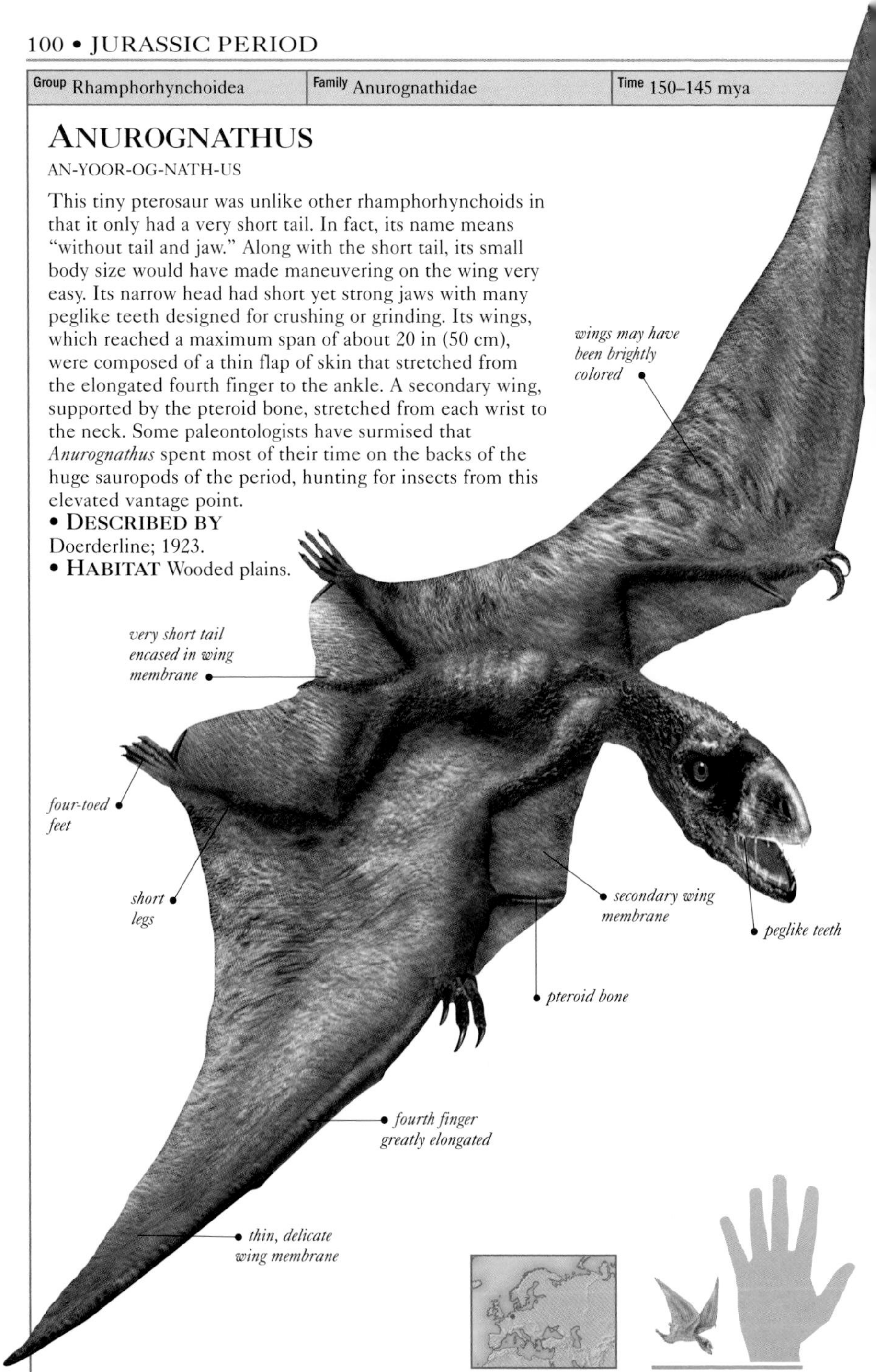

wings may have been brightly colored

very short tail encased in wing membrane

four-toed feet

short legs

secondary wing membrane

peglike teeth

pteroid bone

fourth finger greatly elongated

thin, delicate wing membrane

Length 3½ in (9 cm)	Weight ¼ oz (7 g)	Diet Insects

Group Pterodactyloidea	Family Pterodactylidae	Time 144–150 mya

PTERODACTYLUS

TER-OH-DAK-TIL-US

Many species of *Pterodactylus* ("wing finger") have been discovered—the main differences between them are their size, and the shape and length of the head. All species had the typical pterodactyl features of a short tail, large head, and hollow bones. *Pterodactylus* had a long, curved, pelican-like neck, and a long skull with many small, pointed teeth. Skeletal analysis shows that it was a powerful, active flyer.

• **DESCRIBED BY** Georges Cuvier as Ptero-Dactyle; 1809: name amended by Rafinesque; 1815.

• **HABITAT** Shores.

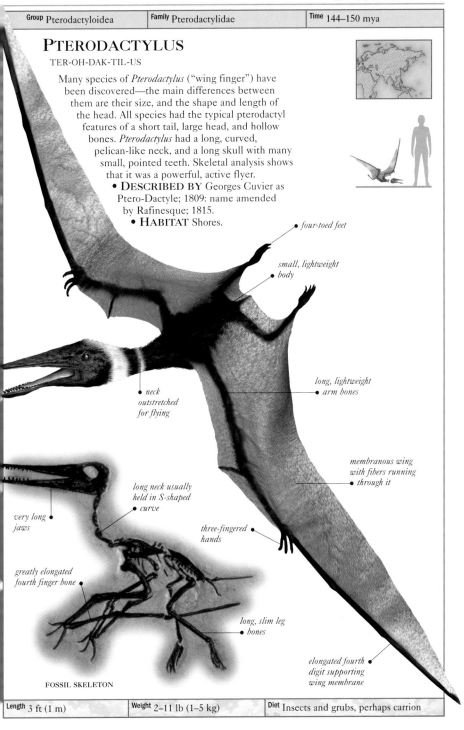

four-toed feet

small, lightweight body

long, lightweight arm bones

neck outstretched for flying

membranous wing with fibers running through it

long neck usually held in S-shaped curve

very long jaws

three-fingered hands

greatly elongated fourth finger bone

long, slim leg bones

elongated fourth digit supporting wing membrane

FOSSIL SKELETON

Length 3 ft (1 m)	Weight 2–11 lb (1–5 kg)	Diet Insects and grubs, perhaps carrion

Group Theropoda	Family Archaeopteridae	Time 150 mya

ARCHAEOPTERYX

AR-KAY-OP-TER-IKS

Archaeopteryx ("ancient wing") was about the size of a modern pigeon, with a small head, large eyes, and pointed teeth in its jaws. Its lower leg bones were long and slim, indicating that it could move well on land. Unlike modern birds, *Archaeopteryx* had a flat breastbone, a long, bony tail, and three grasping claws on each wing. However, its feathers, wings, and furcula (wishbone) are characteristics shared by modern birds. Recent analysis shows that *Archaeopteryx* could probably fly, although it was probably not a strong flier. It was almost certainly warm-blooded.

• **DESCRIBED BY** Hermann von Meyer; 1861.
• **HABITAT** Lakeshores or open forests.

feathered wings for effective flight

three clawed digits on elongated hand

Length 12 in (30 cm)	Weight 11–18 oz (300–500 g)	Diet Insects

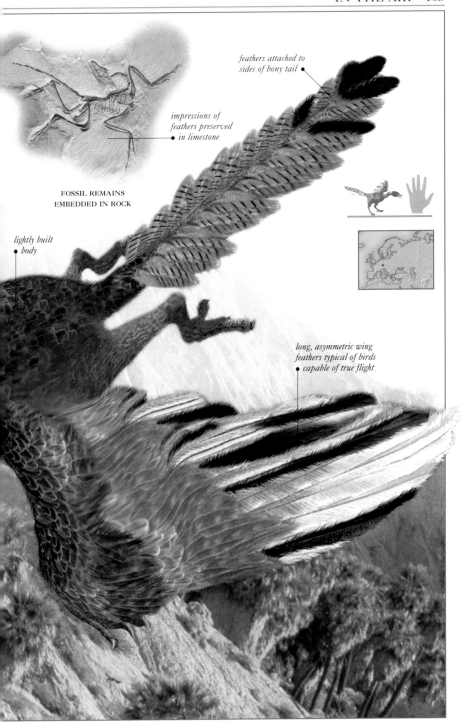

feathers attached to
sides of bony tail •

impressions of
feathers preserved
• in limestone

FOSSIL REMAINS
EMBEDDED IN ROCK

lightly built
• body

long, asymmetric wing
feathers typical of birds
• capable of true flight

CRETACEOUS PERIOD

144–65 MILLION YEARS AGO

The climate in the Cretaceous was similar to that in the Jurassic—warm and humid. Sea levels were very high, resulting in large areas of flooding and consequent isolation of landmasses. A major evolutionary development— the appearance of the angiosperms (flowering plants) led to important changes in the landscape and animal life on Earth. Many new insect groups appeared. Dinosaurs continued to flourish, but populations of certain groups, such as sauropods and stegosaurs, were greatly reduced as their staple food supply was taken over by new dinosaur groups, including the advanced ornithopods and ceratopsians. These flourished until the mass extinction event at the end of the period.

FLOWERING PLANTS
Late in the Cretaceous, forests were composed of flowering trees, such as birc and magnolia. *Betulites* (abo is an extinct birch species.

| 4,600 mya | 4,000 mya | 3,000 mya |

CRETACEOUS LANDMASSES

During the Cretaceous, continental drift led to the breakup of the supercontinents of Laurasia and Gondwana. This process was augmented by the very high sea levels of 640 ft (200 m). The Atlantic Ocean started to open up between the future South America and Africa, and Antarctica was almost in its modern position. India started to move northward. There was still a land link between Eurasia and North America.

CRETACEOUS LIFE

Dinosaurs were still the dominant land animals. They increased in diversity throughout the period, with new groups including the hadrosaurs, horned dinosaurs, and giant tyrannosaurs appearing. Birds continued to evolve, and snakes appeared. Mammals were still small, but continued to diversify.

MAMMAL EVOLUTION
Mammals remained only minor elements of the fauna. Like the early marsupial *Alphadon* (right) they were shrew- or rabbit-sized animals.

• *toes adapted for climbing*

neck frill with • large openings

CERATOPSIANS
The Cretaceous saw the appearance of the frilled ceratopsian dinosaurs, such as *Chasmosaurus* (left). These had brow and nose horns, and a large, bony frill covering the neck and shoulders.

• *wide feet*

2,000 mya   1,000 mya   500 mya   250 mya   0

ON THE LAND

The Cretaceous Period was the heyday of the dinosaurs. Many new forms of dinosaurs evolved, most probably in response to the rapid spread of flowering plants.

Sauropodomorphs were once thought not to have survived the Jurassic–Cretaceous boundary. However, they continued to be present, and remained abundant in the lands that were to become South America, but declined in other areas. Stegosaurs seem to have died out early in the Cretaceous.

Other groups of ornithischian dinosaurs flourished. Ankylosaurs became more numerous and developed extensive armor plating and defensive tail clubs. Ornithopods and hadrosaurs

(duckbills) seem to have formed large herds. The Mid- and Late Cretaceous also saw the appearance of the pachycephalosaurs and the ceratopians, such as *Triceratops*. These became more varied as the period progressed.

Theropods also diversified greatly in the Cretaceous. New dinosaur groups that evolved included the immense tyrannosaurs, the highly intelligent dromaeosaurs, such as *Deinonychus*, the bird mimics (ornithomimosaurs), and the oviraptorids. The two latter groups were birdlike in appearance. They had lost their teeth, having a beak instead, and had a varied diet that probably included fruit, small animals, insects, and eggs.

Group Theropoda	Family Abelisauridae	Time 74–70 mya

ABELISAURUS

AH-BEL-EE-SAW-RUS

This large theropod, named after its discoverer, Roberto Abel, is known only from a single skull. It seems to have been rather a primitive form related to *Carnotaurus*. Its head was large, with a rounded snout, and its teeth were relatively small for a carnivorous dinosaur of its size. Its skull is peculiar, in that it has a huge opening at the side just above the jaws that is much larger than in other dinosaurs. Reconstructions of the rest of its body are necessarily hypothetical. The illustration here is based on the body structure of *Carnotaurus* and similar theropod dinosaurs.
• **DESCRIBED BY** José Bonaparte and F. Novas; 1985.
• **HABITAT** River plains.

probably three clawed toes

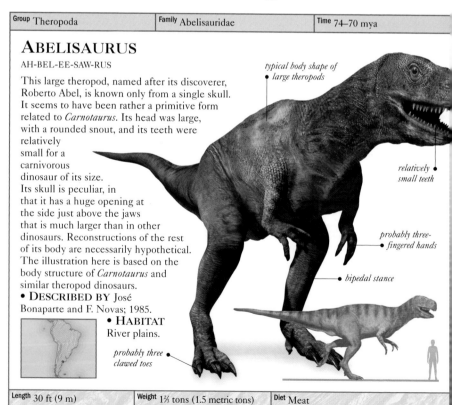

typical body shape of large theropods

relatively small teeth

probably three-fingered hands

bipedal stance

Length 30 ft (9 m)	Weight 1¾ tons (1.5 metric tons)	Diet Meat

| Group Theropoda | Family Abelisauridae | Time 70 mya |

CARNOTAURUS

KAR-NOH-TAW-RUS

The most distinctive feature of *Carnotaurus*
("meat-eating bull") were the broad, triangular
horns over its eyes. Otherwise, it looked
much
like other
large theropods.
It had long legs and a
lightly built body covered
in scales and studs. Its forearms were
incredibly small. Its three fingers were short
and stubby, and the thumbs bore a small spike.
Its tail was long, thick, and flexible.
• **DESCRIBED BY** José Bonaparte; 1985.
• **HABITAT** Dry plains, perhaps desert.

very short forearms

slim, powerful legs

three-toed feet

| Length 25 ft (7.5 m) | Weight 1 ton (1 metric ton) | Diet Meat |

| Group Theropoda | Family Carcharodontosauridae | Time 112–90 mya |

GIGANOTOSAURUS

GIG-AN-OH-TOE-SAW-RUS

large eyes

Giganotosaurus ("giant southern lizard")
is the largest carnivorous dinosaur
yet discovered. Its skull was
longer than an average man,
and held long, serrated teeth.
Its hands had three fingers, and it
had a slim, pointed tail. Although larger
than *Tyrannosaurus*, it was less heavily built
than that dinosaur, and seems to have hunted
in a different fashion—by slashing at its prey
rather than charging and biting head on.
Despite its huge size, some paleontologists
maintain that, like other large theropods, it
may have been able to run relatively fast.
• **DESCRIBED BY** Coria and
Salgado; 1995.
• **HABITAT** Warm swamps.

serrated teeth 8 in (20 cm) long

three clawed fingers

| Length 40 ft (12.5 m) | Weight 9 tons (8 metric tons) | Diet Meat |

Group Theropoda	Family Spinosauridae	Time 98–95 mya

SPINOSAURUS

SPINE-OH-SAW-RUS

Spinosaurus ("spine lizard") was an immense theropod with an impressive sail-like structure running all the way down its back. This was held up by bladelike spines sticking out from the vertebrae. The function of the sail is not known. Some paleontologists believe that it served as a primitive heat-exchanging device, others that it was brightly colored and was used for sexual display. The herbivorous dinosaur *Ouranosaurus*, which lived in the same region during this period, had a similar structure, so it seems most likely that the sail was an adaptation to the hot climate. *Spinosaurus* had relatively long arms.

• **DESCRIBED BY** Ernst Stromer; 1915.
• **HABITAT** Tropical swamps.

vertical "sail" supported by spines

stiff tail

powerful hind legs

large, straight teeth

longer than usual arms for a large theropod

tooth socket

three long, forward-facing, clawed toes

FOSSIL TOOTH BATTERY

Length 50 ft (15 m)	Weight 7¾ tons (7 metric tons)	Diet Meat, perhaps fish

Group Theropoda	Family Spinosauridae	Time 110–100 mya

SUCHOMIMUS

SOOK-OH-MIME-US

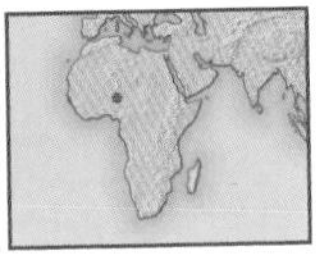

This dinosaur, whose name means "crocodile-mimic," had several features that indicate that it ate fish. It had a very long snout, and huge, curved thumb claws that could be used for hooking fish from the water. The jaws had over 100 teeth that pointed slightly backward, and the end of the snout had a rosette of longer teeth. A low ridge ran along the length of its back. Its arms were relatively long, which would have enabled *Suchomimus* to reach into the water to grasp prey.

- **DESCRIBED BY** Paul C. Sereno; 1998.
- **HABITAT** Lush forests.

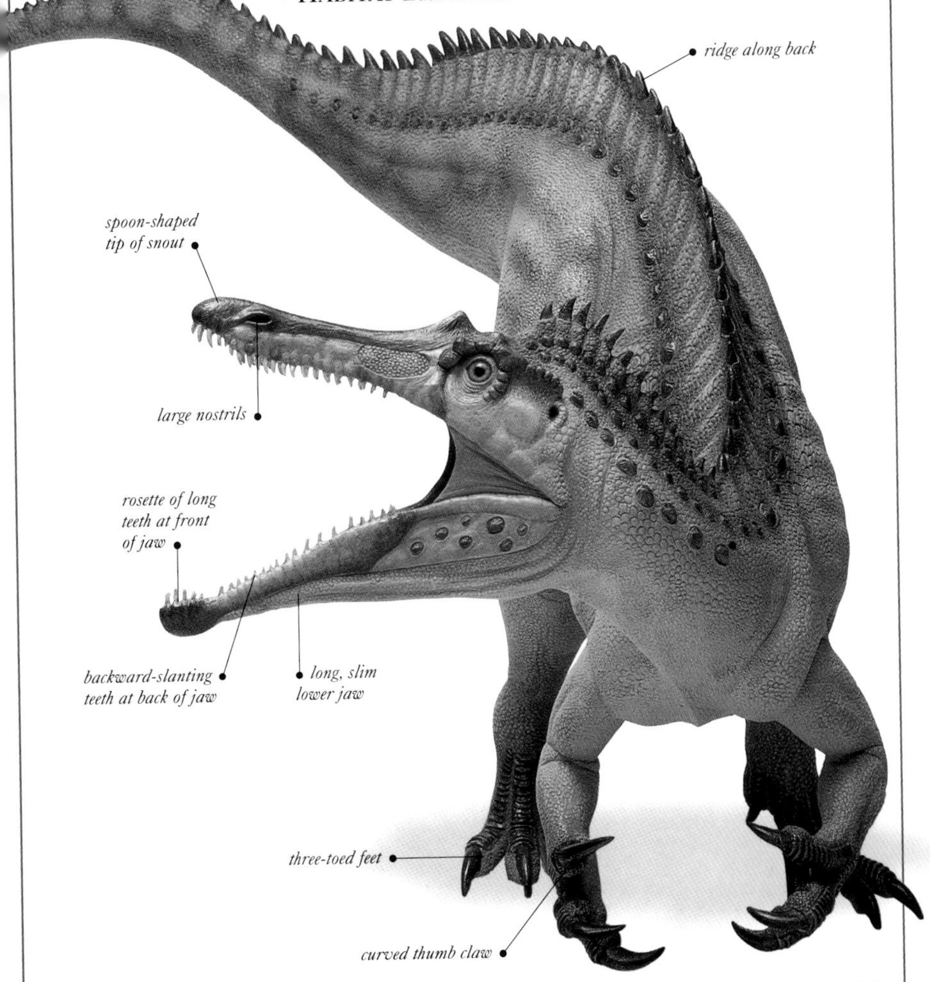

ridge along back

spoon-shaped tip of snout

large nostrils

rosette of long teeth at front of jaw

backward-slanting teeth at back of jaw

long, slim lower jaw

three-toed feet

curved thumb claw

Length 36 ft (11 m)	Weight 5½ tons (5 metric tons)	Diet Fish, possibly meat

Group Theropoda	Family Spinosauridae	Time 125 mya

BARYONYX

BAR-EE-ON-ICKS

Baryonyx ("heavy claw") was named for one of its unusual features—its huge, curved thumb claws. Its skull was also an unusual shape for a theropod, being long and narrow—somewhat like that of a crocodile. There was a bony crest on the top of the head, and the jaws were filled with 96 pointed and serrated teeth. This is twice as many as theropods usually possessed. The neck was not as flexible as in other theropods and could not have been carried in the characteristic S-bend. Its arms were thick and unusually powerful. These features, along with the remains of fish found with the skeleton, have led paleontologists to surmise that *Baryonyx* fished using its claws as hooks, in the same way as a modern bear does.

- **DESCRIBED BY** Charig and Milner; 1986.
- **HABITAT** Riverbanks.

BARYONYX CLAW

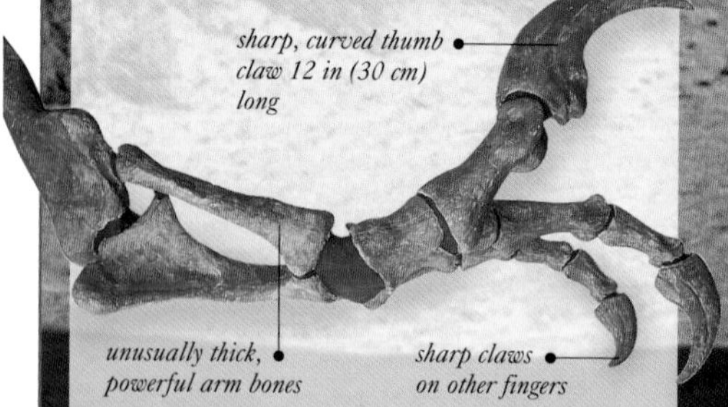

sharp, curved thumb claw 12 in (30 cm) long

unusually thick, powerful arm bones

sharp claws on other fingers

Although the claws were not found attached to the skeleton, and it is therefore not certain that they formed part of the hand, paleontologists have reconstructed Baryonyx with the claw in this position because the length and thickness of the arms seemed to match its proportions.

Length 33 ft (10 m)	Weight 2 tons (2 metric tons)	Diet Fish, possibly meat

fenestrae lightened weight of skull

long, narrow jaws

BARYONYX SKULL

many small, serrated teeth

bony ridge along spine

relatively inflexible neck

bony head crest

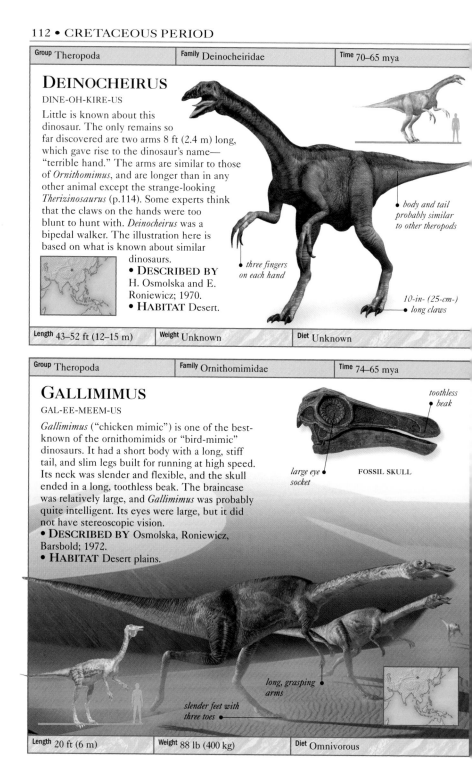

| Group Theropoda | Family Deinocheiridae | Time 70–65 mya |

DEINOCHEIRUS

DINE-OH-KIRE-US

Little is known about this dinosaur. The only remains so far discovered are two arms 8 ft (2.4 m) long, which gave rise to the dinosaur's name— "terrible hand." The arms are similar to those of *Ornithomimus*, and are longer than in any other animal except the strange-looking *Therizinosaurus* (p.114). Some experts think that the claws on the hands were too blunt to hunt with. *Deinocheirus* was a bipedal walker. The illustration here is based on what is known about similar dinosaurs.

• **DESCRIBED BY** H. Osmolska and E. Roniewicz; 1970.
• **HABITAT** Desert.

• *body and tail probably similar to other theropods*

• *three fingers on each hand*

10-in- (25-cm-) long claws

| Length 43–52 ft (12–15 m) | Weight Unknown | Diet Unknown |

| Group Theropoda | Family Ornithomimidae | Time 74–65 mya |

GALLIMIMUS

GAL-EE-MEEM-US

Gallimimus ("chicken mimic") is one of the best-known of the ornithomimids or "bird-mimic" dinosaurs. It had a short body with a long, stiff tail, and slim legs built for running at high speed. Its neck was slender and flexible, and the skull ended in a long, toothless beak. The braincase was relatively large, and *Gallimimus* was probably quite intelligent. Its eyes were large, but it did not have stereoscopic vision.
• **DESCRIBED BY** Osmolska, Roniewicz, Barsbold; 1972.
• **HABITAT** Desert plains.

toothless beak

large eye socket   FOSSIL SKULL

long, grasping arms

slender feet with three toes

| Length 20 ft (6 m) | Weight 88 lb (400 kg) | Diet Omnivorous |

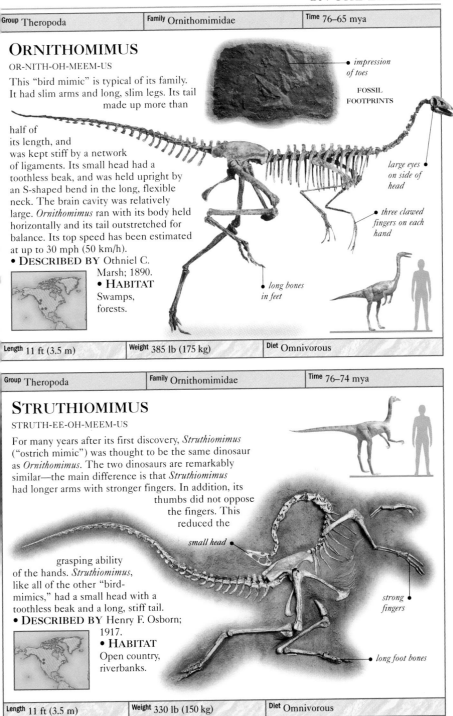

| Group Theropoda | Family Ornithomimidae | Time 76–65 mya |

ORNITHOMIMUS

OR-NITH-OH-MEEM-US

This "bird mimic" is typical of its family. It had slim arms and long, slim legs. Its tail made up more than half of its length, and was kept stiff by a network of ligaments. Its small head had a toothless beak, and was held upright by an S-shaped bend in the long, flexible neck. The brain cavity was relatively large. *Ornithomimus* ran with its body held horizontally and its tail outstretched for balance. Its top speed has been estimated at up to 30 mph (50 km/h).
• **DESCRIBED BY** Othniel C. Marsh; 1890.
• **HABITAT** Swamps, forests.

impression of toes

FOSSIL FOOTPRINTS

large eyes on side of head

three clawed fingers on each hand

long bones in feet

| Length 11 ft (3.5 m) | Weight 385 lb (175 kg) | Diet Omnivorous |

| Group Theropoda | Family Ornithomimidae | Time 76–74 mya |

STRUTHIOMIMUS

STRUTH-EE-OH-MEEM-US

For many years after its first discovery, *Struthiomimus* ("ostrich mimic") was thought to be the same dinosaur as *Ornithomimus*. The two dinosaurs are remarkably similar—the main difference is that *Struthiomimus* had longer arms with stronger fingers. In addition, its thumbs did not oppose the fingers. This reduced the grasping ability of the hands. *Struthiomimus*, like all of the other "bird-mimics," had a small head with a toothless beak and a long, stiff tail.
• **DESCRIBED BY** Henry F. Osborn; 1917.
• **HABITAT** Open country, riverbanks.

small head

strong fingers

long foot bones

| Length 11 ft (3.5 m) | Weight 330 lb (150 kg) | Diet Omnivorous |

Group Theropoda	Family Therizinosauridae	Time 85–70 mya

THERIZINOSAURUS

THER-IZ-IN-OH-SAW-RUS

One of the strangest dinosaurs, the reconstruction of *Therizinosaurus* ("scythe lizard") is based on finds of other members of the family. Little is known of it, apart from its incredibly long arms. These had three fingers that ended in curved, flat-sided claws, the first of which was longer than a man's arm. The claws seem too blunt for use in attack. Suggestions for their function have included that they were used in courtship, for raking plants, or for ripping open termite nests. This bipedal dinosaur may have occasionally rested on all fours. *Therizinosaurus* seems to have been related to *Oviraptor*.

- **DESCRIBED BY** E. A. Maleev; 1954.
- **HABITAT** Woodland.

fine, hairy feathers may have covered the skin

toothless beak

FOSSIL SCYTHE CLAW

claws up to 24 in (60 cm) long

three clawed fingers

Length 36 ft (11 m)	Weight Unknown	Diet Meat, or possibly plants or insects

Group Theropoda	Family Oviraptoridae	Time 85–75 mya

OVIRAPTOR

OV-EE-RAP-TOR

This dinosaur, whose name means "egg thief," seems to have been very closely related to birds, and was probably feathered. Its most distinctive feature was its head, which was short and deep, with a stumpy beak. It had no teeth, but there were two bony projections on the upper palate of the mouth. The jaws were so powerful that they could have crushed objects as hard as bones. The first specimen (see below left) of *Oviraptor* was discovered preserved with eggs, thought to be those of *Protoceratops*, and this led to its name. Later research proved that this *Oviraptor* was actually sitting on its own nest. This dinosaur may have had feathers, but some reconstructions, such as that of the head below right, show it without them.

• **DESCRIBED BY** Henry F. Osborn; 1924.
• **HABITAT** Semi-desert.

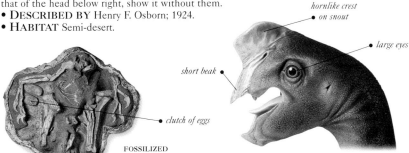

hornlike crest on snout

large eyes

short beak

clutch of eggs

FOSSILIZED
NEST SITE

DETAIL OF
HEAD

birdlike feet

Length 8 ft (2.5 m)	Weight 75 lb (34 kg)	Diet Uncertain

Group Theropoda	Family Tyrannosauridae	Time 67–65 mya

TYRANNOSAURUS

TIE-RAN-OH-SAW-RUS

Tyrannosaurus ("tyrant lizard") was one of the largest terrestrial carnivores ever. It was a heavily built theropod, with thick, long, powerful legs and a large, deep head. Paleontologists are still hotly debating whether it was an active predator or simply a scavenger, and how fast it actually was. Arguments against predation include its small eyes and arms, and presumed slow speed. Evidence supporting scavenging includes the fact that *Tyrannosaurus* had very large olfactory lobes (the area in the brain used for processing odors), and that its legs were built for walking long distances. Recent analysis indicates its top speed may have been as slow as 10 mph.
- **DESCRIBED BY** Henry F. Osborn; 1905.
- **HABITAT** Open forests, coastal forested swamps.

6-in- (15-cm-) long, serrated teeth

large fenestrae to lighten skull

12 back vertebrae with holes to reduce weight

tail made up of about 40 vertebrae

58 teeth

TYRANNOSAURUS SKELETON
The first skeletal reconstruction of *Tyrannosaurus* was prepared in 1915, showing the dinosaur standing upright with its tail along the ground. Recent analysis has shown that the backbone was held horizontally, with the body perfectly balanced at the hips.

relatively slim, birdlike foot

saurischian hip

Length 40 ft (12 m)	Weight 7½ tons (6.5 metric tons)	Diet Hadrosaurs, ceratopsians

NEW DISCOVERY
In 1990 a new
specimen of
Tyrannosaurus was
discovered in South
Dakota. The new
skeleton was at least
70 percent complete,
and is the largest
specimen yet found.

pebbled skin
texture

tail held stiffly
for balance

tail heavily
muscled at base

long, heavily
muscled legs

Group Theropoda	Family Dromaeosauridae	Time 110–100 mya

DEINONYCHUS

DIE-NON-EE-KUS

One of the most fearsome predators of the Cretaceous, *Deinonychus* ("terrible claw") was named for the sickle-shaped claws on the second toe of each foot. These were used alternately to slash at prey as the dinosaur stood on one leg. A group found preserved with the skeleton of a large *Tenontosaurus* (see p.208) suggests that *Deinonychus* was a pack hunter.

lightweight body

- **DESCRIBED BY** John H. Ostrom; 1969.
- **HABITAT** Forests.

tail held rigid

long hind legs

sickle-shaped claw of second toe held off ground while running

Length 9¾–13 ft (3–4 m)	Weight 155 lb (70 kg)	Diet Herbivorous dinosaurs

Group Theropoda	Family Dromaeosauridae	Time 76–74 mya

DROMAEOSAURUS

DROM-AY-OH-SAW-RUS

Dromaeosaurus ("running lizard") was the first sickle-clawed dinosaur to be discovered. However, the difficulty in reconstructing it from the few bones found meant that its true classification was only realized after *Deinonychus* was described. This dinosaur was smaller than *Deinonychus*, but otherwise very similar. Its body was slender, with long limbs and a large head. Its sharp claws would have been effective slashing weapons.

large braincase indicating relatively high intelligence

- **DESCRIBED BY** Matthew, Brown; 1922.
- **HABITAT** Forests, plains.

large eye sockets

sharp, backward-facing teeth

Length 5½ ft (1.8 m)	Weight 33 lb (15 kg)	Diet Herbivorous dinosaurs

Group Theropoda	Family Dromaeosauridae	Time 85–80 mya

SAURORNITHOIDES

SAWR-OR-NITH-OID-EEZ

relatively large braincase •

Only the skull, a few arm bones, and teeth of *Saurornithoides* ("lizard bird form") have been found to date, and its classification as a dromaeosaur is therefore uncertain. Its long, narrow skull had a relatively large braincase. Its long, powerful arms ended in three-fingered hands capable of grasping prey.
• **DESCRIBED BY** Osborn; 1924.
• **HABITAT** Plains.

long, narrow snout •

jaw containing many sharp teeth •

Length 6½–11 ft (2–3.5 m)	Weight 30–60 lb (13–27 kg)	Diet Meat

Group Theropoda	Family Troodontidae	Time 74–65 mya

TROODON

TROH-OH-DON

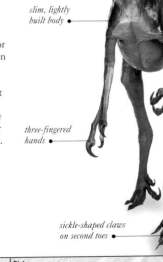

Troodon ("wounding tooth") was named for its sharp, serrated teeth. Its remains are very rare, and no complete skeleton has been found to date. Its reconstruction is based on the fossils found and details known from similar, closely related dinosaurs. It was probably an efficient hunter. It had long, slim hind legs, a large sickle-shaped claw on both second toes, and three long, clawed fingers that were capable of grasping prey. The sickle claws were smaller than in *Deinonychus* (opposite) and *Velociraptor* (see p.120). This has led some paleontologists to suggest that they were mainly used for defense. The shape of the teeth has prompted debate on whether it was omnivorous. *Troodon* could undoubtedly run quickly on its long legs, with its stiff tail held out behind for balance. Analysis of the slim skull shows that it had sharp eyesight and may have had good hearing. Its braincase was also very large in proportion to its body size, indicating an unusually high level of intelligence for a dinosaur. *Troodon* eggs have been found in fossil nests.
• **DESCRIBED BY** Joseph Leidy; 1856.
• **HABITAT** Plains.

large eyes •

slim, lightly built body •

three-fingered hands •

sickle-shaped claws on second toes •

Length 6½ ft (2 m)	Weight 110 lb (50 kg)	Diet Meat, carrion

Group Theropoda	Family Dromaeosauridae	Time 85–80 mya

VELOCIRAPTOR

VEL-O-SEE-RAP-TOR

Many well-preserved skeletons of *Velociraptor* ("fast thief") have been found, making it the best-known member of its family. The main feature that sets it apart from other members of the family is its low, long, flat-snouted head. *Velociraptor* must have been a formidable predator: its jaws held about 80 very sharp teeth, and the second toe of each foot ended in a slashing, sickle-shaped claw. The neck was S-shaped, and the hands bore three clawed fingers. It is probable that *Velociraptor* hunted in packs. Traditionally reconstructed with scaly skin, recent analysis has shown that this dinosaur was probably at least partly covered in a downy coat or primitive feathers.

• **DESCRIBED BY** Henry F. Osborn; 1924.
• **HABITAT** Woodland.

PRESERVED IN DEATH
One of the most famous fossil finds is a *Velociraptor* and *Protoceratops* locked together in battle at the time of their deaths.

stiff tail held
outstretched for
balance

slim legs with long
shins for speed

Length 6 ft (1.8 m)	Weight 33 lb (15 kg)	Diet Lizards, mammals, smaller dinosaurs

large eye socket

FOSSIL SKULL

long, slim jaws
with pointed,
recurved teeth

probable downy
covering over
much of body

three-fingered
grasping hands
with claws

large, sickle-shaped
second claw

Group Theropoda	Family Not yet assigned	Time 120–136 mya

CAUDIPTERYX

CAWD-IP-TER-IKS

The discovery of this small, feathered dinosaur provided firm evidence of a theropod ancestry for birds. *Caudipteryx* ("tail feather") was a theropod with feathers covering its arms, most of its body, and its short tail. The feathers varied in structure—some were downy, and others were structured quills with shafts and veins. The feathers were symmetrical, showing that this animal did not fly. Some paleontologists regard *Caudipteryx's* feathers as an example of convergent evolution, since this dinosaur lived after the time of *Archaeopteryx*. Others contend that *Caudipteryx* was a true bird that had lost the power of flight.
• **DESCRIBED BY** Ji Q., Currie, Norell, Ji S.; 1998.
• **HABITAT** Lakesides.

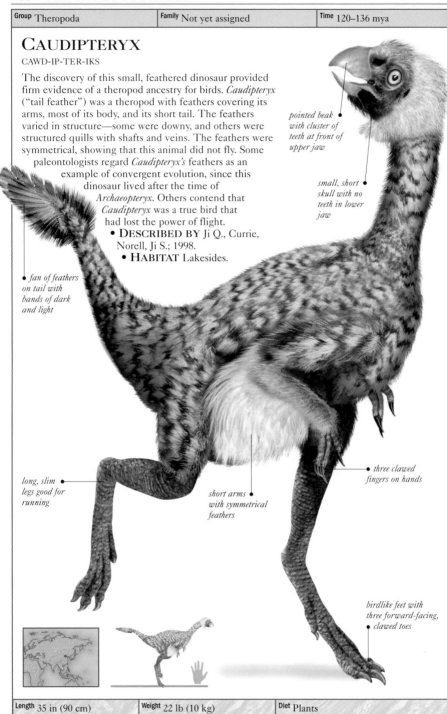

pointed beak with cluster of teeth at front of upper jaw

small, short skull with no teeth in lower jaw

fan of feathers on tail with bands of dark and light

three clawed fingers on hands

long, slim legs good for running

short arms with symmetrical feathers

birdlike feet with three forward-facing, clawed toes

Length 35 in (90 cm)	Weight 22 lb (10 kg)	Diet Plants

Group Sauropoda	Family Titanosauridae	Time 90 mya

ARGENTINOSAURUS

AR-GEN-TEEN-OH-SAW-RUS

Only a few bones of *Argentinosaurus* (Argentina lizard) have been found to date, including some enormous vertebrae from the back, which were over 5 ft (1.5 m) wide in cross-section. Other bones found were the sacrum, a tibia (shin bone), and a few ribs. Because of the sparsity of fossil evidence, very little is known about *Argentinosaurus*. However, it appears to have been the longest dinosaur ever found. It is thought to have been a titanosaur, which had some body structures similar to those of *Diplodocus* (p.76).

As in other titanosaurs, the neck and tail would have been very long and thin, and the skull is likely to have been small and triangular.

• **DESCRIBED BY** José Bonaparte and R. Coria; 1993.
• **HABITAT** Forested areas.

DISCOVERY IN ARGENTINA
The first bone of *Argentinosaurus* was found on an Argentinian sheep ranch in 1988.

long, slim neck

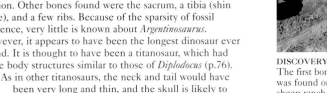

body thought to resemble that of other titanosaurs

long, whiplash tail

elephant-like, thick limbs with clawed toes

Length 130 ft (40 m)	Weight 110 tons (100 metric tons)	Diet Conifers

Group Sauropoda	Family Titanosauridae	Time 83–65 mya

TITANOSAURUS

TI-TAN-OH-SAW-RUS

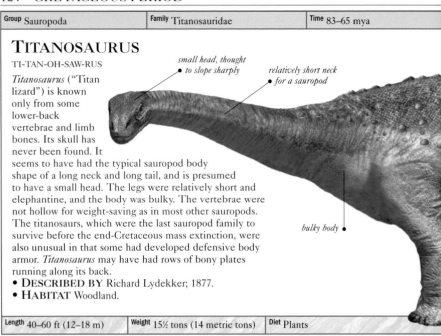

small head, thought to slope sharply

relatively short neck for a sauropod

bulky body

Titanosaurus ("Titan lizard") is known only from some lower-back vertebrae and limb bones. Its skull has never been found. It seems to have had the typical sauropod body shape of a long neck and long tail, and is presumed to have a small head. The legs were relatively short and elephantine, and the body was bulky. The vertebrae were not hollow for weight-saving as in most other sauropods. The titanosaurs, which were the last sauropod family to survive before the end-Cretaceous mass extinction, were also unusual in that some had developed defensive body armor. *Titanosaurus* may have had rows of bony plates running along its back.
- **DESCRIBED BY** Richard Lydekker; 1877.
- **HABITAT** Woodland.

Length 40–60 ft (12–18 m)	Weight 15½ tons (14 metric tons)	Diet Plants

Group Sauropoda	Family Titanosauridae	Time 83–65 mya

SALTASAURUS

SALT-AH-SAW-RUS

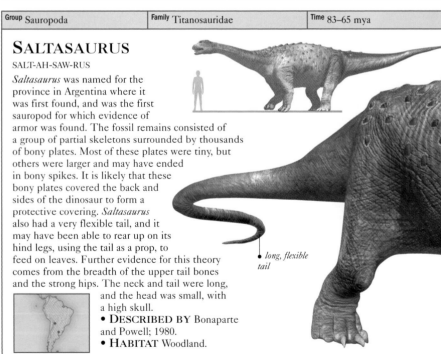

long, flexible tail

Saltasaurus was named for the province in Argentina where it was first found, and was the first sauropod for which evidence of armor was found. The fossil remains consisted of a group of partial skeletons surrounded by thousands of bony plates. Most of these plates were tiny, but others were larger and may have ended in bony spikes. It is likely that these bony plates covered the back and sides of the dinosaur to form a protective covering. *Saltasaurus* also had a very flexible tail, and it may have been able to rear up on its hind legs, using the tail as a prop, to feed on leaves. Further evidence for this theory comes from the breadth of the upper tail bones and the strong hips. The neck and tail were long, and the head was small, with a high skull.
- **DESCRIBED BY** Bonaparte and Powell; 1980.
- **HABITAT** Woodland.

Length 40 ft (12 m)	Weight 22 tons (20 metric tons)	Diet Plants

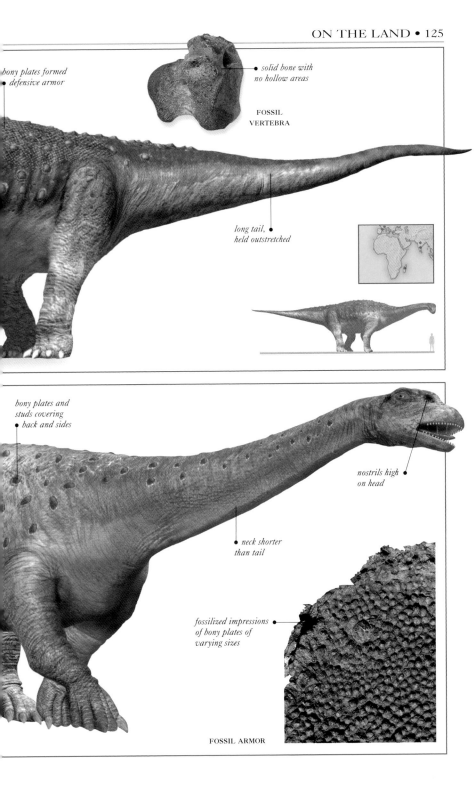

bony plates formed
defensive armor

solid bone with
no hollow areas

FOSSIL
VERTEBRA

long tail,
held outstretched

bony plates and
studs covering
back and sides

nostrils high
on head

neck shorter
than tail

fossilized impressions
of bony plates of
varying sizes

FOSSIL ARMOR

Group Ceratopsia	Family Psittacosauridae	Time 120–100 mya

PSITTACOSAURUS

SIT-AH-KOH-SAW-RUS

teeth behind toothless beak

horn

Its characteristic square skull and curved beak were the features that led to this dinosaur being given its name, which means "parrot lizard." Its cheek bones formed a pair of horns, believed to have been used for fighting or sexual display. Its hind legs were long and thin, suggesting that it was a fast bipedal runner. The long toes with blunt claws were perhaps used for digging. Its long tail was stiffened by bony tendons along its length.
- **DESCRIBED BY** Henry F. Osborn; 1923.
- **HABITAT** Desert and scrubland.

FOSSIL SKULL

four clawed toes on hind feet

tail to maintain balance

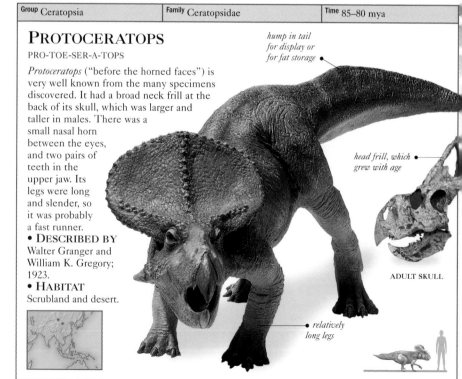

Length 6½ ft (2 m)	Weight 175 lb (80 kg)	Diet Plants

Group Ceratopsia	Family Ceratopsidae	Time 85–80 mya

PROTOCERATOPS

PRO-TOE-SER-A-TOPS

hump in tail for display or for fat storage

Protoceratops ("before the horned faces") is very well known from the many specimens discovered. It had a broad neck frill at the back of its skull, which was larger and taller in males. There was a small nasal horn between the eyes, and two pairs of teeth in the upper jaw. Its legs were long and slender, so it was probably a fast runner.
- **DESCRIBED BY** Walter Granger and William K. Gregory; 1923.
- **HABITAT** Scrubland and desert.

head frill, which grew with age

ADULT SKULL

relatively long legs

Length 6 ft (1.8 m)	Weight 400 lb (180 kg)	Diet Plants

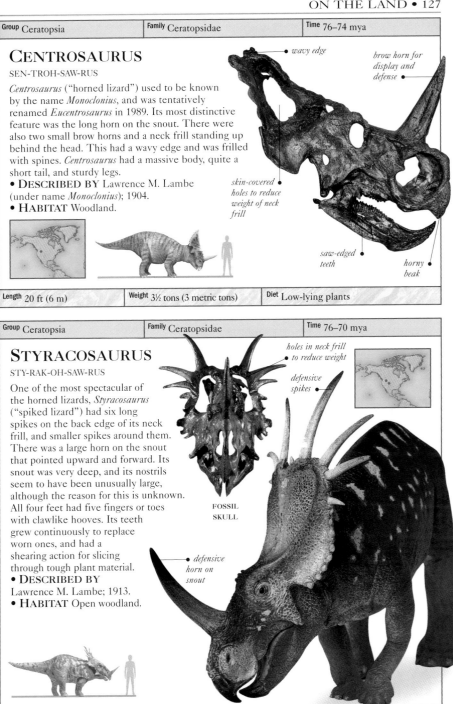

| Group Ceratopsia | Family Ceratopsidae | Time 76–74 mya |

CENTROSAURUS

SEN-TROH-SAW-RUS

Centrosaurus ("horned lizard") used to be known by the name *Monoclonius*, and was tentatively renamed *Eucentrosaurus* in 1989. Its most distinctive feature was the long horn on the snout. There were also two small brow horns and a neck frill standing up behind the head. This had a wavy edge and was frilled with spines. *Centrosaurus* had a massive body, quite a short tail, and sturdy legs.
• **DESCRIBED BY** Lawrence M. Lambe (under name *Monoclonius*); 1904.
• **HABITAT** Woodland.

wavy edge

brow horn for display and defense

skin-covered holes to reduce weight of neck frill

saw-edged teeth

horny beak

| Length 20 ft (6 m) | Weight 3½ tons (3 metric tons) | Diet Low-lying plants |

| Group Ceratopsia | Family Ceratopsidae | Time 76–70 mya |

STYRACOSAURUS

STY-RAK-OH-SAW-RUS

One of the most spectacular of the horned lizards, *Styracosaurus* ("spiked lizard") had six long spikes on the back edge of its neck frill, and smaller spikes around them. There was a large horn on the snout that pointed upward and forward. Its snout was very deep, and its nostrils seem to have been unusually large, although the reason for this is unknown. All four feet had five fingers or toes with clawlike hooves. Its teeth grew continuously to replace worn ones, and had a shearing action for slicing through tough plant material.
• **DESCRIBED BY** Lawrence M. Lambe; 1913.
• **HABITAT** Open woodland.

holes in neck frill to reduce weight

defensive spikes

FOSSIL SKULL

defensive horn on snout

| Length 17 ft (5.2 m) | Weight 3 tons (2.8 metric tons) | Diet Ferns and cycads |

Group Ceratopsia	Family Ceratopsidae	Time 76–74 mya

CHASMOSAURUS

KAZ-MOH-SAW-RUS

Chasmosaurus ("cleft lizard") was a typical frilled, horned dinosaur. It had a large body with four stocky legs. Its most distinctive feature—its enormous neck frill—was likely to have been brightly colored in life for sexual display. The frill was so long that it reached over the shoulders. Its bony structure was lightened by two large holes that were covered with skin. Triangular, bony protrusions ran along the edge of the frill. *Chasmosaurus* had a small nose horn, and two blunt brow horns, which were of different lengths in different species or sexes. There was also a parrotlike beak at the front of the snout. The skin was covered in knobby bumps with five or six sides.

• **DESCRIBED BY** Lawrence Lambe; 1914.
• **HABITAT** Woodland.

bony protrusions along frill edge

large nasal cavity

FRONT VIEW OF SKULL

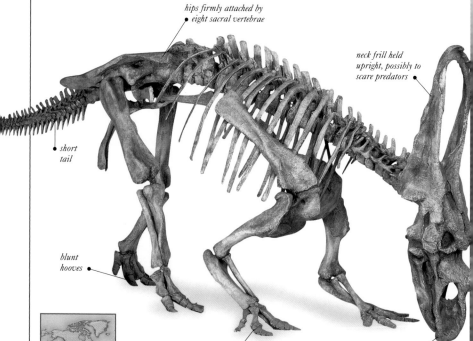

hips firmly attached by eight sacral vertebrae

neck frill held upright, possibly to scare predators

short tail

blunt hooves

five short toes on all four feet

horny, parrot-like beak

Length 16 ft (5 m)	Weight 2¾ tons (2.5 metric tons)	Diet Cycads, palms, other plants

Group Ceratopsia	Family Ceratopsidae	Time 75–65 mya

PENTACERATOPS

PEN-TAH-SER-A-TOPS

Pentaceratops ("five-horn face") was so named because it was originally thought to have had five horns on its face. In fact, it had the usual three horns—a straight horn on the snout and two curved brow horns. The two smaller "horns" were simply outgrowths of the cheekbones. *Pentaceratops'* most unusual feature is the size of its head—a skull reconstructed in 1998 was over 10 ft (3 m) long. Its neck frill was also enormous, and edged with triangular, bony projections. The body was stockily built, with a short, pointed tail.

• **DESCRIBED BY** Henry F. Osborn; 1923.
• **HABITAT** Wooded plains.

SKULL FRAGMENT

scalloped edges on neck frill

large neck frill, possibly elaborately colored for sexual display

heavily built body with thick hide

curved brow horns longer in males

straight nose horn

cheek horn

short legs

curved beak made of horn

hooflike claws

Length 16–26 ft (5–8 m)	Weight 2¼–9 tons (2.5–8 metric tons)	Diet Plants

Group Ceratopsia	Family Ceratopsidae	Time 70–65 mya

TRICERATOPS

TRY-SER-A-TOPS

Probably the best-known of the horned dinosaurs, *Triceratops* ("three-horned face") lived at the end of the Cretaceous Period, throughout the lands that now form North America. The nose horn was short and thick, and the two long brow horns, each over 3 ft (1 m) long, curved forward and slightly outward over the snout. There were pointed studs set around the edge of the neck frill for further protection and ornamentation. Many of the fossil skulls found have evidence of scarring. This suggests that *Triceratops* may have fought in territorial or mating battles by locking horns with rivals.

- **DESCRIBED BY** Othniel C. Marsh; 1889.
- **HABITAT** Woodland.

bony studs •
around margin
of frill

Length 30 ft (9 m)	Weight 5–11 tons (4.5–10 metric tons)	Diet Plants

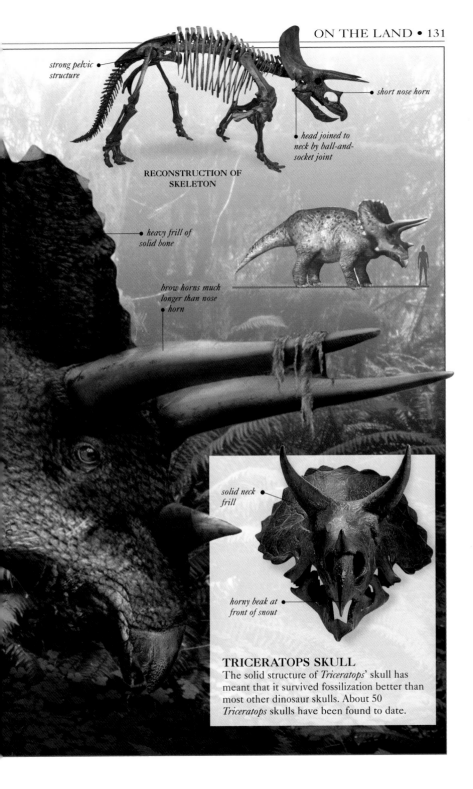

strong pelvic structure

short nose horn

head joined to neck by ball-and-socket joint

RECONSTRUCTION OF SKELETON

heavy frill of solid bone

brow horns much longer than nose horn

solid neck frill

horny beak at front of snout

TRICERATOPS SKULL

The solid structure of *Triceratops'* skull has meant that it survived fossilization better than most other dinosaur skulls. About 50 *Triceratops* skulls have been found to date.

| Group Ankylosauria | Family Nodosauridae | Time 115–91 mya |

ACANTHOPHOLIS

A-CAN-THUH-FOE-LIS

Acanthopholis ("spiny scales") is a poorly known nodosaur with a low-slung, bulky body. Its formidable armor was formed from rows of oval plates (scutes) set into the skin. It also had long, bony spikes jutting out of its neck and shoulder area along the spine.

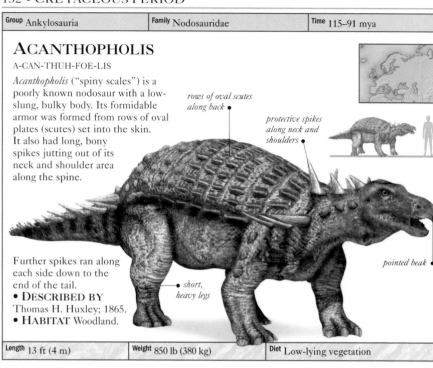

rows of oval scutes along back

protective spikes along neck and shoulders

pointed beak

short, heavy legs

Further spikes ran along each side down to the end of the tail.
• **DESCRIBED BY** Thomas H. Huxley; 1865.
• **HABITAT** Woodland.

| Length 13 ft (4 m) | Weight 850 lb (380 kg) | Diet Low-lying vegetation |

| Group Ankylosauria | Family Anklyosauridae | Time 76–74 mya |

EDMONTONIA

ED-MON-TONE-EE-AH

This ankylosaur (whose name means "from Edmonton") had a bulky body, four short, thick legs, wide feet, and a short neck. The back and tail were covered with rows of bony plates (scutes) and spikes. The shoulders of this dinosaur were particularly well-armored with long spikes and large scutes. Fossil scutes that have been found are not symmetrical, meaning that they would have projected not straight out from the hide, but at an angle. *Edmontonia*'s skull was long and flat, with large nasal cavities and weak jaws. The front of the snout was formed into a horny, toothless beak, with small, weak cheek teeth inside the mouth. Some paleontologists have suggested that *Edmontonia* may have used its shoulder spines for fighting with others of its own kind, as modern deer species do. It is also possible that the large spines were used for sexual display or for dominance signaling.
• **DESCRIBED BY** C.M. Sternberg; 1928.
• **HABITAT** Woodland.

sloping back

short neck protected by bony scutes

long skull

double shoulder spike

horny beak

| Length 20 ft (6 m) | Weight 4 tons (3.5 metric tons) | Diet Low-lying vegetation |

Group Ankylosauria	Family Nodosauridae	Time 119 –113 mya

MINMI

MIN-ME

This small, heavily built, and thickly armored ankylosaur, named after Minmi Crossing in Australia, had rows of small, bony plates running down its back and triangular spikes over the hips. There were also large, bony plates over the neck and shoulders. Unlike other ankylosaurs, there were horizontal plates of bone running along each side of the vertebrae. The head was box-shaped, with a very narrow snout ending in a horny beak. Four small horns jutted out from the back of the face.

• **DESCRIBED BY** Ralph E. Molnar; 1980.
• **HABITAT** Scrubby and wooded plains.

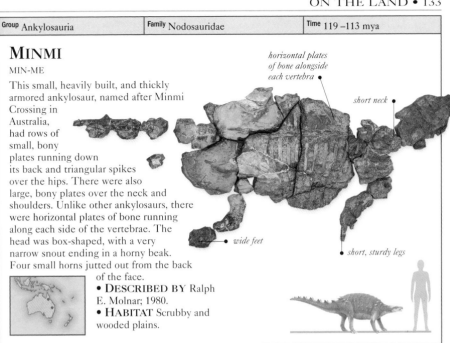

horizontal plates of bone alongside each vertebra

short neck

wide feet

short, sturdy legs

Length 10 ft (3 m)	Weight Unknown	Diet Low-lying vegetation

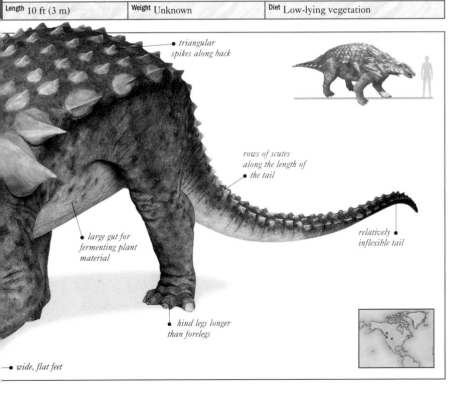

triangular spikes along back

rows of scutes along the length of the tail

large gut for fermenting plant material

relatively inflexible tail

hind legs longer than forelegs

wide, flat feet

Group Ankylosauria	Family Nodosauridae	Time 131–124 mya

GASTONIA

GAS-TONE-EE-A

Gastonia (named after Robert Gaston) had a mixture of ankylosaur and nodosaur features. This herbivore's defensive armor was impressive: there were four horns on the head, and bony rings covering the neck; rows of spikes covered the back and the flanks, and fused, bony armoured plates protected the hips. The tail, which could lash from side to side, had rows of triangular blades along each side. The long spikes running along each side of the spine curved up and outward, forming a formidable defensive shield against attack by predators.
• **DESCRIBED BY** J. I. Kirkland; 1998.
• **HABITAT** Woodland.

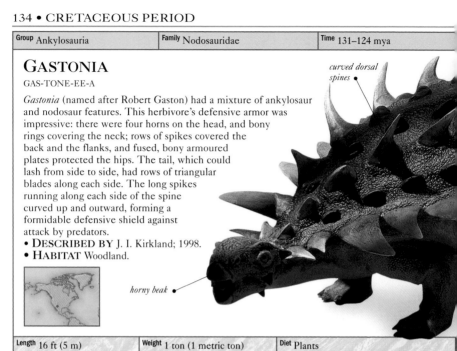

curved dorsal spines

horny beak

Length 16 ft (5 m)	Weight 1 ton (1 metric ton)	Diet Plants

Group Ankylosauria	Family Ankylosauridae	Time 76–70 mya

EUOPLOCEPHALUS

YOU-OH-PLO-SEF-AH-LUSS

Built like a military tank, the back of *Euoplocephalus* ("well-armored head") was embedded with bands of armor and bony studs. Fused plates covered the neck, and triangular horns protected the shoulders, the base of the tail, and the face. A large ball of fused bone at the end of the tail acted as a club that could be swung at attacking predators.
• **DESCRIBED BY** Lawrence Lambe as *Stereocephalus*; 1910.
• **HABITAT** Woodland.

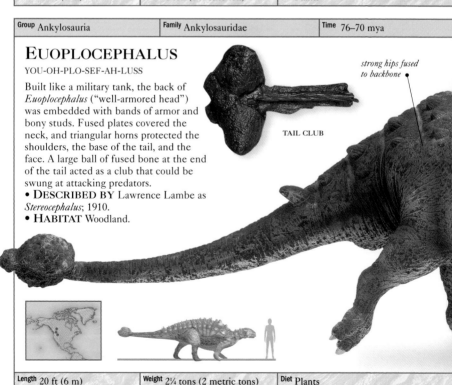

strong hips fused to backbone

TAIL CLUB

Length 20 ft (6 m)	Weight 2¼ tons (2 metric tons)	Diet Plants

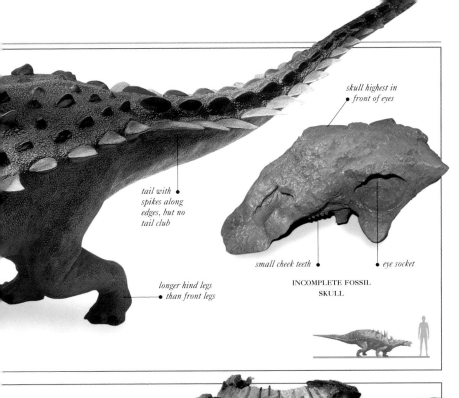

skull highest in
front of eyes

tail with
spikes along
edges, but no
tail club

small cheek teeth

eye socket

INCOMPLETE FOSSIL
SKULL

longer hind legs
than front legs

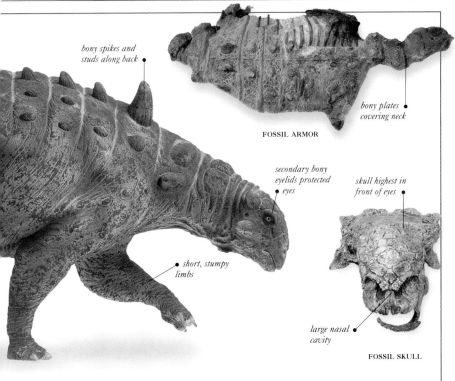

bony spikes and
studs along back

bony plates
covering neck

FOSSIL ARMOR

secondary bony
eyelids protected
eyes

skull highest in
front of eyes

short, stumpy
limbs

large nasal
cavity

FOSSIL SKULL

Group Ankylosauria	Family Ankylosauridae	Time 74–67 mya

ANKYLOSAURUS

AN-KIE-LOH-SAW-RUS

Ankylosaurus ("fused lizard") has aptly been described as a
living tank. Its stocky body, neck, and head were protected
by thick bands of armor-plating. The skin was thick and
leathery, and was studded with hundreds of oval bony
plates and rows of spikes. A pair of long spikes stuck out
from the back of the head, and the cheekbones were drawn
out into another pair of spikes on the face. The tail was
armed with a bony club, which could be swung with great
force. The legs were strong, although short, and the body
was wide and squat. The face was also broad, with a
blunt snout that ended in a toothless beak.

• **DESCRIBED BY** Barnum Brown; 1908.
• **HABITAT** Woodland.

terminal plate

lateral plate

bony tendons to support end of tail

FOSSIL TAIL CLUB

nostril

head spike

FOSSIL SKULL

bony spikes

teeth

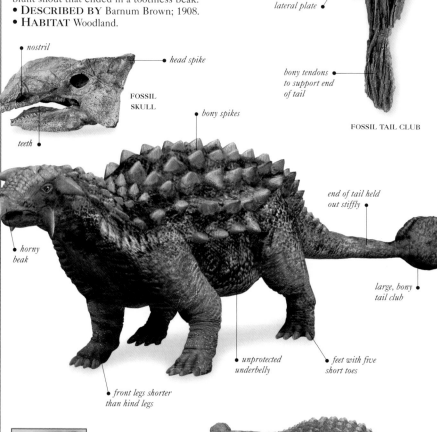

horny beak

end of tail held out stiffly

large, bony tail club

unprotected underbelly

feet with five short toes

front legs shorter than hind legs

Length 25–35 ft (7.5–10.5 m)	Weight 5–7¾ tons (4.5–7 metric tons)	Diet Large herbivorous dinosaurs

Group Ornithopoda	Family Hypsilophodontidae	Time 125–120 mya

HYPSILOPHODON

HIP-SILL-OH-FO-DON

This primitive ornithischian, whose name means "high-ridge tooth," is generally believed to have been a fully terrestrial dinosaur that was capable of running at high speeds. It walked on its hind legs; its short thigh bones and long shins meant that it was capable of taking long strides. The tail, stiffened by a network of bony ligaments, helped to balance the animal as it ran. Its small head had a horny beak and large eyes. The jaws held 28 or 30 cheek teeth that were self-sharpening, and the mouth had cheek pouches that could be used for storing food. Groups of fossils found together in bone beds suggest that this was a herding dinosaur.

• **DESCRIBED BY** Thomas H. Huxley; 1869.
• **HABITAT** Forests.

small beak

slim tail held out straight behind body

short, relatively weak forelimbs

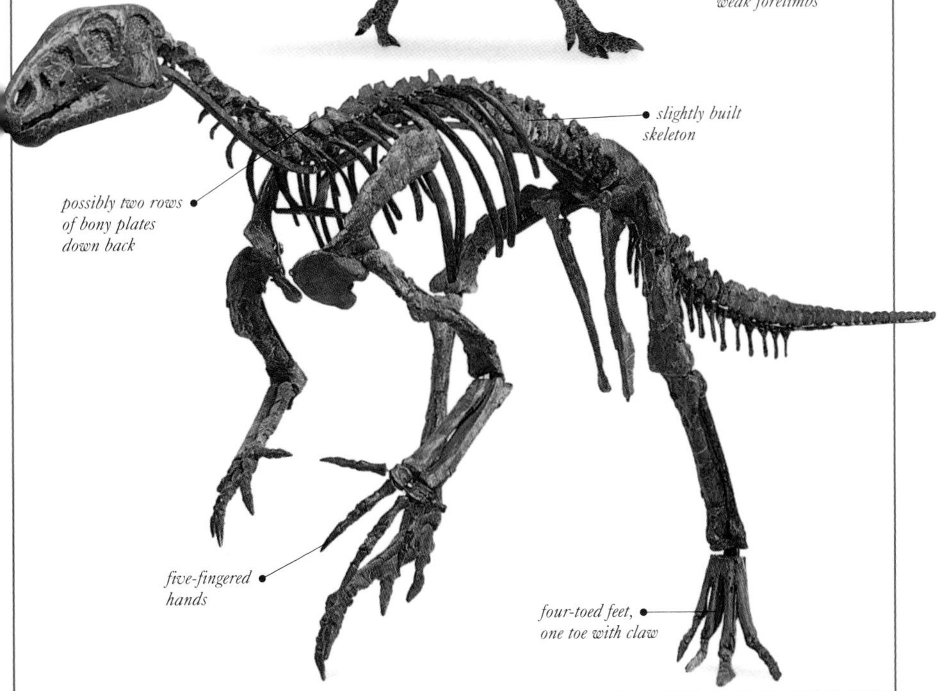

slightly built skeleton

possibly two rows of bony plates down back

five-fingered hands

four-toed feet, one toe with claw

Length 6½ ft (2 m)	Weight 150 lb (68 kg)	Diet Plants

Group Ornithopoda	Family Iguanodontidae	Time 135–125 mya

IGUANODON

IG-WAH-NOH-DON

Originally thought to have been entirely quadrupedal, *Iguanodon* ("iguana tooth") is now thought to have been primarily quadrupedal, but also capable of bipedal walking. Its hind legs were thick and columnlike, while the front legs were considerably shorter and thinner. The middle three fingers on each hand were joined together by a pad of skin, and the fifth finger could curl to grasp food. The thumb was armed with a vicious, long spike. *Iguanodon* could chew food; it had a hinged upper jaw that allowed the teeth in the upper jaw to grind over those in the lower jaw.

• **DESCRIBED BY** Gideon A. Mantell; 1825.

• **HABITAT** Woodland.

body held horizontally and balanced at hips

deep tail held stiffly out for balance

Length 30 ft (9 m)	Weight 4½–5½ tons (4–5 metric tons)	Diet Plants

batteries of grinding
cheek teeth

horny beak at
front of jaw

FOSSIL SKULL

**FOSSIL THUMB
SPIKE**

6-in- (15-cm-) long
thumb spike

Group Ornithopoda	Family Iguanodontidae	Time 115–100 mya

OURANOSAURUS

OO-RAH-NOH-SAW-RUS

The most remarkable feature of *Ouranosaurus*, whose name means "brave lizard," was the row of spines growing out from the spinal and caudal vertebrae. They ran from the shoulders to halfway along the tail. Some paleontologists think they supported a sail that acted as a heat controller in the hot conditions in which it lived. Others suggest that *Ouranosaurus* may have had a fatty hump as modern bison do (and as illustrated here). *Ouranosaurus* had a pair of bony bumps between the eyes, and a horny beak.

• **DESCRIBED BY** Philippe Taquet; 1976.

• **HABITAT** Tropical plains and forest.

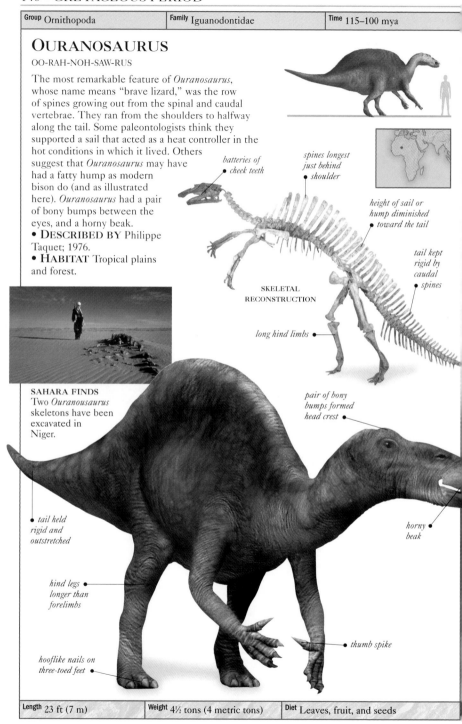

batteries of cheek teeth

spines longest just behind shoulder

height of sail or hump diminished toward the tail

tail kept rigid by caudal spines

SKELETAL RECONSTRUCTION

long hind limbs

SAHARA FINDS
Two *Ouranousaurus* skeletons have been excavated in Niger.

pair of bony bumps formed head crest

tail held rigid and outstretched

horny beak

hind legs longer than forelimbs

hooflike nails on three-toed feet

thumb spike

Length 23 ft (7 m)	Weight 4½ tons (4 metric tons)	Diet Leaves, fruit, and seeds

Group Ornithopoda	Family Hadrosauridae	Time 80–74 mya

HADROSAURUS

HAD-ROW-SAW-RUS

Hadrosaurus ("sturdy lizard") was one of the first dinosaurs discovered in North America. Its skull had a toothless, horny beak used for nipping off vegetation, and hundreds of blunt cheek teeth. These were continually replaced as they wore down from chewing tough plant material. Although its forelimbs were much shorter than its hind legs, *Hadrosaurus* spent most of its time browsing on all fours. It walked with its tail held outstretched for balance.

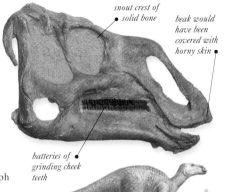

snout crest of solid bone

beak would have been covered with horny skin

batteries of grinding cheek teeth

• **DESCRIBED BY** Joseph Leidy; 1859.
• **HABITAT** Swamps and forests.

Length 30 ft (9 m)	Weight 7¾ tons (7 metric tons)	Diet Leaves and twigs

Group Ornithopoda	Family Hadrosauridae	Time 80–74 mya

MAIASAURA

MAY-A-SAW-RA

This dinosaur's name means "good earth-mother lizard." It was so named because remains were found close to fossilized nests scooped out of mud. The nests were each about 6½ ft (2 m) across and contained eggs arranged in circular layers. Remains of juvenile dinosaurs at various stages of development showed that the parents brought food to their young at the nest site for a considerable time. It appears that *Maisaura* migrated and nested each year in large herds. It had numerous cheek teeth adapted to grinding tough plant material.
• **DESCRIBED BY** John R. Horner, R. Makela; 1979.
• **HABITAT** Coastal plains.

NEST-SITE RECONSTRUCTION

large eye sockets characterize juvenile

stiff, narrow tail

long hind legs

hundreds of grinding cheek teeth

SKELETON OF JUVENILE

Length 30 ft (9 m)	Weight 5½ tons (5 metric tons)	Diet Leaves

| Group Ornithopoda | Family Hadrosauridae | Time 76–74 mya |

CORYTHOSAURUS

KOH-RITH-OH-SAW-RUS

Corythosaurus ("Corinthian helmet lizard") was named for the distinctive hollow crest on top of its head. This seems to have been larger in males. The crest was made up of greatly altered nasal bones, and the hollows were expanded nasal passages. Models of the crest have been made; they produce a booming foghornlike sound when blown through, adding to the current theory that the crest served as a resonating device for signaling among herds. *Corythosaurus* was a low browser that spent most of its time on all fours. It had a broad, toothless beak.

- **DESCRIBED BY** Barnum Brown; 1914.
- **HABITAT** Forests.

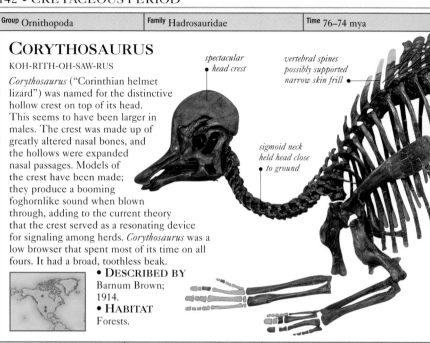

spectacular head crest

vertebral spines possibly supported narrow skin frill

sigmoid neck held head close to ground

| Length 33 ft (10 m) | Weight 5 tons (4.5 metric tons) | Diet Leaves, seeds, pine needles |

| Group Ornithopoda | Family Hadrosauridae | Time 76–74 mya |

PARASAUROLOPHUS

PA-RA-SAW-ROL-OFF-US

This dinosaur, whose name means "beside *Saurolophus*," is instantly recognizable from its trombonelike head crest. This was up to 6 ft (1.8 m) long, and was probably used for display and as a resonating device for sound signaling. The crest was longer in males than in females. A frill of skin may have joined the crest to the neck.

- **DESCRIBED BY** William A. Parks; 1922
- **HABITAT** Woodland.

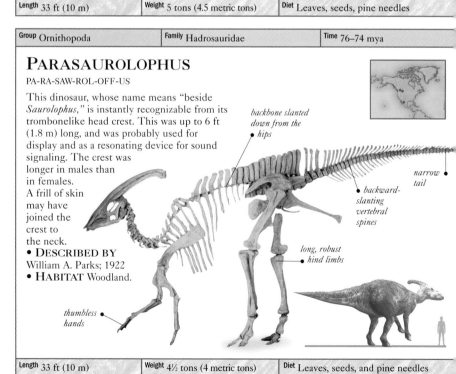

backbone slanted down from the hips

narrow tail

backward-slanting vertebral spines

long, robust hind limbs

thumbless hands

| Length 33 ft (10 m) | Weight 4½ tons (4 metric tons) | Diet Leaves, seeds, and pine needles |

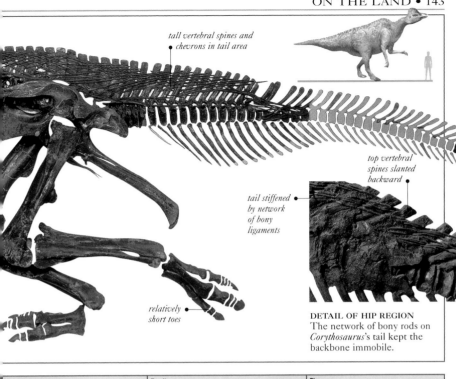

tall vertebral spines and chevrons in tail area

top vertebral spines slanted backward

tail stiffened by network of bony ligaments

relatively short toes

DETAIL OF HIP REGION
The network of bony rods on *Corythosaurus*'s tail kept the backbone immobile.

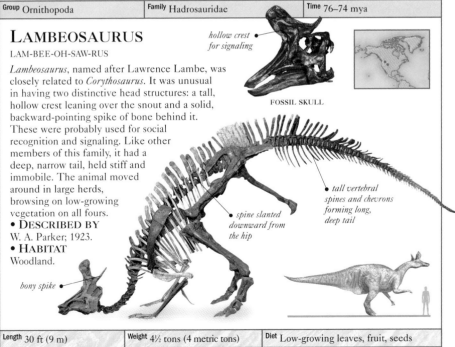

Group Ornithopoda	Family Hadrosauridae	Time 76–74 mya

LAMBEOSAURUS

LAM-BEE-OH-SAW-RUS

Lambeosaurus, named after Lawrence Lambe, was closely related to *Corythosaurus*. It was unusual in having two distinctive head structures: a tall, hollow crest leaning over the snout and a solid, backward-pointing spike of bone behind it. These were probably used for social recognition and signaling. Like other members of this family, it had a deep, narrow tail, held stiff and immobile. The animal moved around in large herds, browsing on low-growing vegetation on all fours.
• **DESCRIBED BY**
W. A. Parker; 1923.
• **HABITAT**
Woodland.

hollow crest for signaling

FOSSIL SKULL

tall vertebral spines and chevrons forming long, deep tail

spine slanted downward from the hip

bony spike

Length 30 ft (9 m)	Weight 4½ tons (4 metric tons)	Diet Low-growing leaves, fruit, seeds

Group Pachycephalosauria	Family Pachycephalosauridae	Time 74–65 mya

PACHYCEPHALOSAURUS

PACK-EE-CEF-AL-OH-SAW-RUS

It is easy to see why *Pachycephalosaurus* ("thick-headed lizard") was so named. The top of the dinosaur's skull was thickened into a dome of solid bone 10 in (25 cm) thick. It is thought that *Pachycephalosaurus* used its head as a battering ram for defense or in territorial fighting. It had a beak, and clusters of bony knobs surrounded the snout. Further groups of round knobs encircled the back of the head. Its relatively slim leg and foot bones indicate that this dinosaur may have been able to run more quickly than its heavy build might suggest. *Pachycephalosaurus* is the largest member of the Pachycephalosauridae family of dinosaurs discovered so far, and was the last to exist before the extinction of the dinosaurs at the end of the Cretaceous Period.

- **DESCRIBED BY** Barnum Brown and Erich Schlaiker; 1943.
- **HABITAT** Forests.

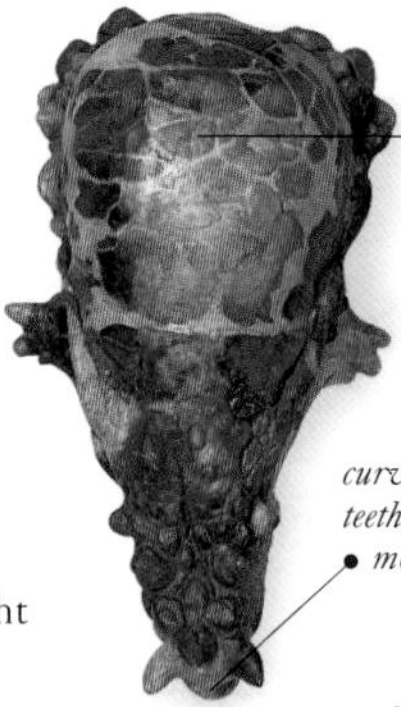

greatly thickened bone on top of skull forming a dome

curved, fanglike teeth at front of mouth

SKULL

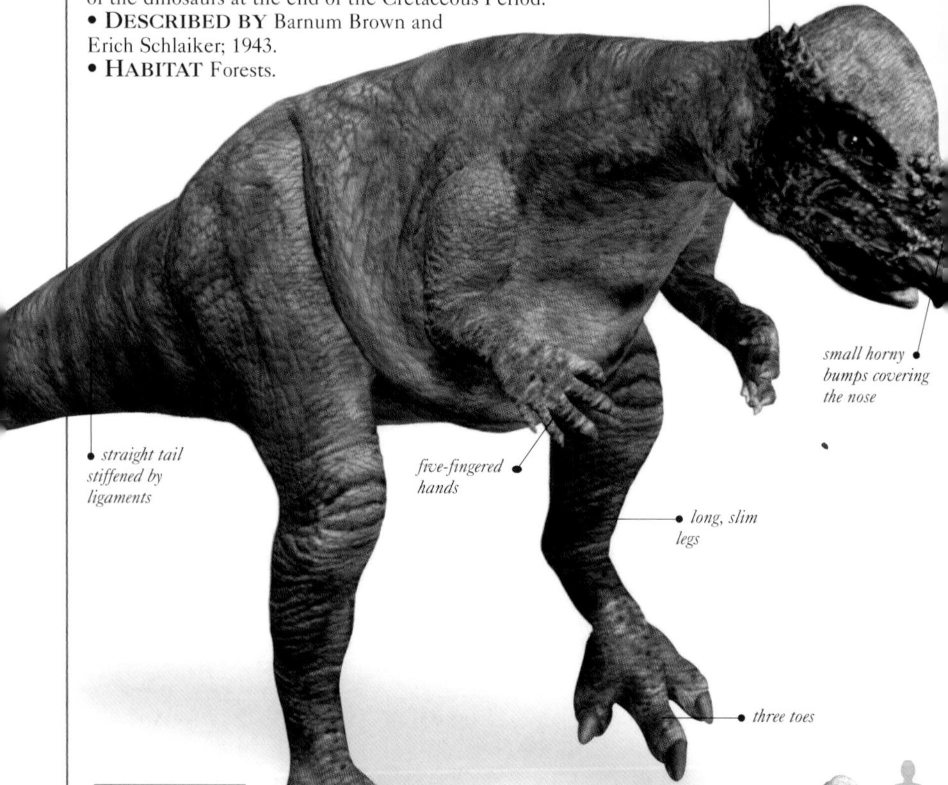

bony protuberances around back of head

small horny bumps covering the nose

straight tail stiffened by ligaments

five-fingered hands

long, slim legs

three toes

long claws

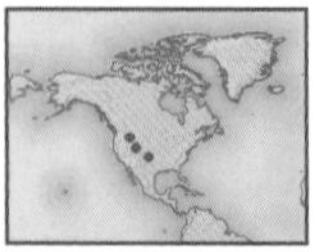

Length 16 ft (5 m)	Weight 2¼ tons (2 metric tons)	Diet Leaves, fruit, perhaps small animals

Group Pachycephalosauria	Family Pachycephalosauridae	Time 76–74 mya

STEGOCERAS

STEG-OH-SER-AS

A fast runner, *Stegoceras* (meaning "roof horn") had a body designed to withstand vigorous head-butting activity. When charging, its head was lowered at right angles, balanced by its neck, body, and tail held in a straight line. The skullcap was thickened into a dome of solid bone, and the grain of bone was angled to the surface, enabling it to withstand impact more effectively. Two types of skull have been found—some with low, flat domes, and others with tall, rounded ones. These variations may indicate sexual differences. Stegoceras had small, serrated teeth that were ideal for shredding plant material.

• **DESCRIBED BY** Lawrence M. Lambe; 1902.

• **HABITAT** Upland forests.

ridge of bone over eye and round back of head

skullcap thickened into dome of bone

slightly curved, serrated teeth   FOSSIL SKULL

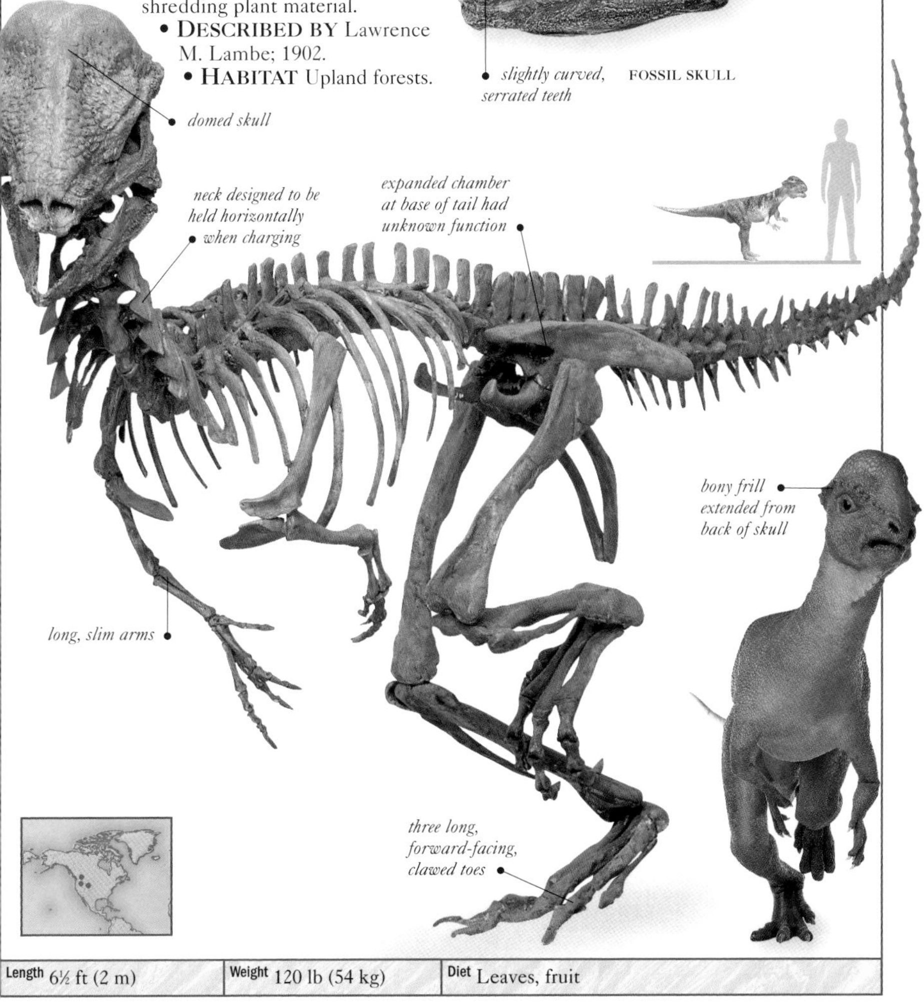

domed skull

neck designed to be held horizontally when charging

expanded chamber at base of tail had unknown function

bony frill extended from back of skull

long, slim arms

three long, forward-facing, clawed toes

Length 6½ ft (2 m)	Weight 120 lb (54 kg)	Diet Leaves, fruit

Group Crocodylia	Family Eusuchia	Time 85–66 mya

DEINOSUCHUS

DEI-NOH-SOOK-US

Only the skull of this "terrible crocodile" has been found, but the size of that suggests that *Deinosuchus* was one of the largest crocodilians ever to have existed. Paleontologists are still debating its size, body proportions, and way of life. Like other members of its group, *Deinosuchus* had a secondary bony palate, allowing it to open its mouth underwater without swallowing water. It probably fed on fish and land-dwelling animals as they came close to river banks.

large eye sockets

mouth with two bony palates

long sharp teeth

6½-ft- (2-m-) long skull

- **DESCRIBED BY** John H. Ostrom; 1969.
- **HABITAT** Swamps.

Length 50 ft (15 m)	Weight Unknown	Diet Fish, medium to large dinosaurs

Group Theria	Family Placentalia	Time 83.5–71 mya

ZALAMBDALESTES

ZAH-LAM-DAL-ES-TEES

Zalambdalestes was a shrewlike mammal, with a long tail and powerful hind legs that were longer than the front ones. The legs had elongated foot bones, and the hands were small, with nonopposable fingers. This suggests that *Zalambdalestes* was probably not a tree-dweller. The eyes were very large, and the snout turned up sharply at the end. The incisors were long and sharp. The recent discovery of an epipubic bone (present only in nonplacental mammals) in a skeleton of *Zalambdalestes* means its classification as a placental mammal is in dispute.

small brain cavity

sensitive, long, upturned snout

- **DESCRIBED BY** W.K. Gregory, G.G. Simpson; 1926.
- **HABITAT** Prairie.

Length 8 in (20 cm)	Weight 1 oz (25 g)	Diet Insects

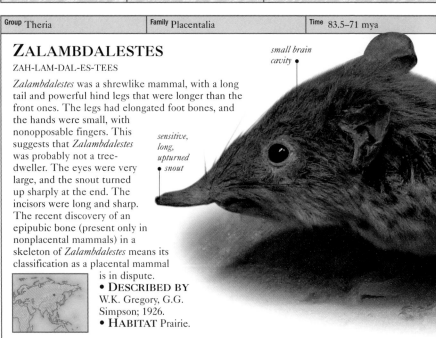

Group Theria	Family Marsupialia	Time 70 mya

ALPHADON

AL-FA-DON

Alphadon, whose name means "first tooth," was
a primitive marsupial that resembled
a modern opossum. It was
probably a tree-dweller that
used its feet, which had
opposable toes, and its
prehensile tail to
grasp branches and
climb. Its hind
legs were longer
than the front ones, and its
body was lightly built. *Alphadon's* head
was small, with a slim, pointed snout,
and large ears. Its forward-facing eyes
provided effective binocular vision, needed
for judging distances accurately.

• **DESCRIBED BY**
G. G. Simpson;
1929.
• **HABITAT**
Forests.

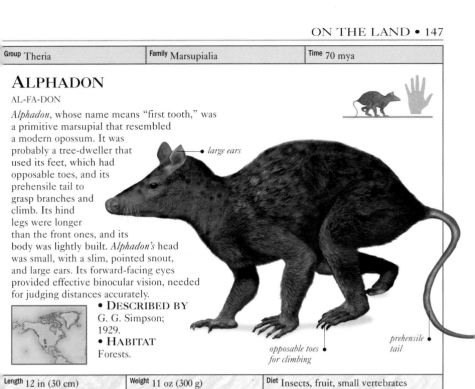

large ears

*opposable toes
for climbing*

*prehensile
tail*

Length 12 in (30 cm)	Weight 11 oz (300 g)	Diet Insects, fruit, small vertebrates

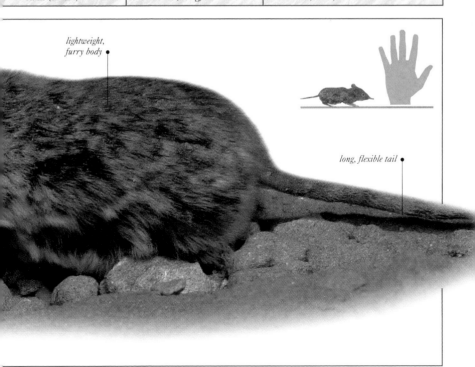

*lightweight,
furry body*

long, flexible tail

IN THE WATER

During the Cretaceous Period, oceans were generally warm, and there was a consequent increase in plankton growth, leading to greater diversity and larger sizes in marine species. Teleost fish, a group of advanced bony fish, which had first appeared during the Jurassic Period, now outnumbered the more primitive forms. Some species in this group, such as *Xiphactinus*, grew to 16 ft (5 m) or more in length. The ammonoids, which were the largest group of marine predators, were also abundant and grew to great sizes.

However, reptiles remained the largest marine carnivores. Plesiosaurs were still present in moderately large numbers, but ichthyosaurs had become rare by the end of the Jurassic, possibly due to competition from sharks.

The ecological niche vacated by the ichthyosaurs at the beginning of the Cretaceous was filled by the mosasaurs (a group of large marine reptiles distantly related to monitor lizards). During this period, they became the dominant carnivores in many marine environments around the world. They hunted squid, ammonoids, fish, and other mosasaurs. Like ichthyosaurs, mosasaurs gave birth to live young. Other large marine carnivores of the Cretaceous Period included giant turtles, such as *Archelon*, and sharks, such as *Cretoxyrhina*.

Group Cryptodira	Family Protostegidae	Time 75 mya

ARCHELON

AR-KAY-LON

This marine animal, whose name means "ruling turtle," was twice the length of modern species. It had a wide, flattened shell. This was was formed from belly ribs (gastralia) that grew out from the body wall. The shell was composed of a leathery covering or horny plates over a framework of bony struts that may have been visible underneath.
• **DESCRIBED BY** Wieland; 1895.
• **HABITAT** Oceans.

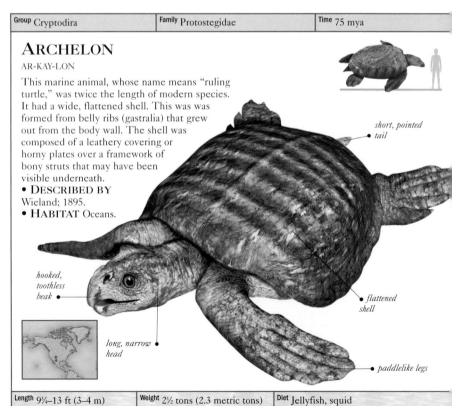

short, pointed tail

hooked, toothless beak

flattened shell

long, narrow head

paddlelike legs

Length 9¾–13 ft (3–4 m)	Weight 2½ tons (2.3 metric tons)	Diet Jellyfish, squid

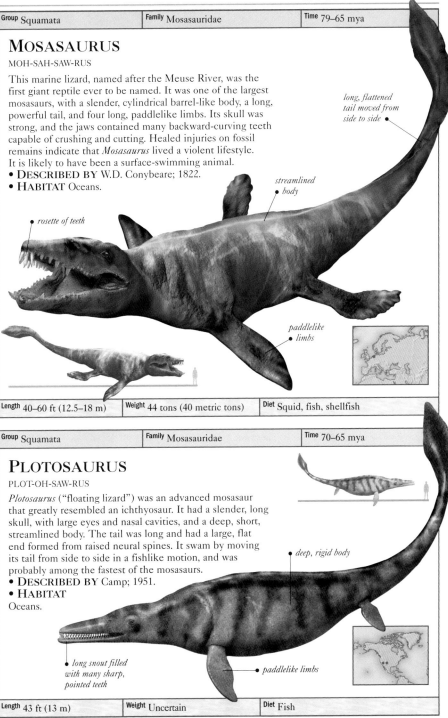

Group Squamata	Family Mosasauridae	Time 79–65 mya

MOSASAURUS

MOH-SAH-SAW-RUS

This marine lizard, named after the Meuse River, was the first giant reptile ever to be named. It was one of the largest mosasaurs, with a slender, cylindrical barrel-like body, a long, powerful tail, and four long, paddlelike limbs. Its skull was strong, and the jaws contained many backward-curving teeth capable of crushing and cutting. Healed injuries on fossil remains indicate that *Mosasaurus* lived a violent lifestyle. It is likely to have been a surface-swimming animal.

• **DESCRIBED BY** W.D. Conybeare; 1822.

• **HABITAT** Oceans.

long, flattened tail moved from side to side •

streamlined • body

• rosette of teeth

paddlelike • limbs

Length 40–60 ft (12.5–18 m)	Weight 44 tons (40 metric tons)	Diet Squid, fish, shellfish

Group Squamata	Family Mosasauridae	Time 70–65 mya

PLOTOSAURUS

PLOT-OH-SAW-RUS

Plotosaurus ("floating lizard") was an advanced mosasaur that greatly resembled an ichthyosaur. It had a slender, long skull, with large eyes and nasal cavities, and a deep, short, streamlined body. The tail was long and had a large, flat end formed from raised neural spines. It swam by moving its tail from side to side in a fishlike motion, and was probably among the fastest of the mosasaurs.

• **DESCRIBED BY** Camp; 1951.

• **HABITAT** Oceans.

• deep, rigid body

• long snout filled with many sharp, pointed teeth

• paddlelike limbs

Length 43 ft (13 m)	Weight Uncertain	Diet Fish

Group Squamata	Family Mosasauridae	Time 85–78 mya

TYLOSAURUS

TIE-LOW-SAW-RUS

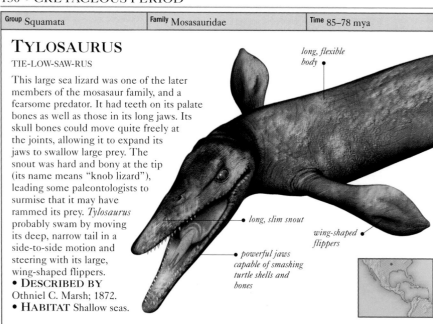

This large sea lizard was one of the later members of the mosasaur family, and a fearsome predator. It had teeth on its palate bones as well as those in its long jaws. Its skull bones could move quite freely at the joints, allowing it to expand its jaws to swallow large prey. The snout was hard and bony at the tip (its name means "knob lizard"), leading some paleontologists to surmise that it may have rammed its prey. *Tylosaurus* probably swam by moving its deep, narrow tail in a side-to-side motion and steering with its large, wing-shaped flippers.
• **DESCRIBED BY** Othniel C. Marsh; 1872.
• **HABITAT** Shallow seas.

long, flexible body

long, slim snout

wing-shaped flippers

powerful jaws capable of smashing turtle shells and bones

Length 36 ft (11 m)	Weight 7¾ tons (7 metric tons)	Diet Turtles, fish, other mosasaurs

Group Plesiosauroidea	Family Pliosauridae	Time 110 mya

KRONOSAURUS

CRO-NO-SAW-RUS

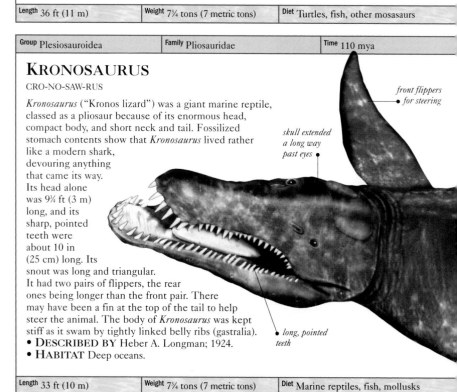

Kronosaurus ("Kronos lizard") was a giant marine reptile, classed as a pliosaur because of its enormous head, compact body, and short neck and tail. Fossilized stomach contents show that *Kronosaurus* lived rather like a modern shark, devouring anything that came its way. Its head alone was 9¾ ft (3 m) long, and its sharp, pointed teeth were about 10 in (25 cm) long. Its snout was long and triangular. It had two pairs of flippers, the rear ones being longer than the front pair. There may have been a fin at the top of the tail to help steer the animal. The body of *Kronosaurus* was kept stiff as it swam by tightly linked belly ribs (gastralia).
• **DESCRIBED BY** Heber A. Longman; 1924.
• **HABITAT** Deep oceans.

front flippers for steering

skull extended a long way past eyes

long, pointed teeth

Length 33 ft (10 m)	Weight 7¾ tons (7 metric tons)	Diet Marine reptiles, fish, mollusks

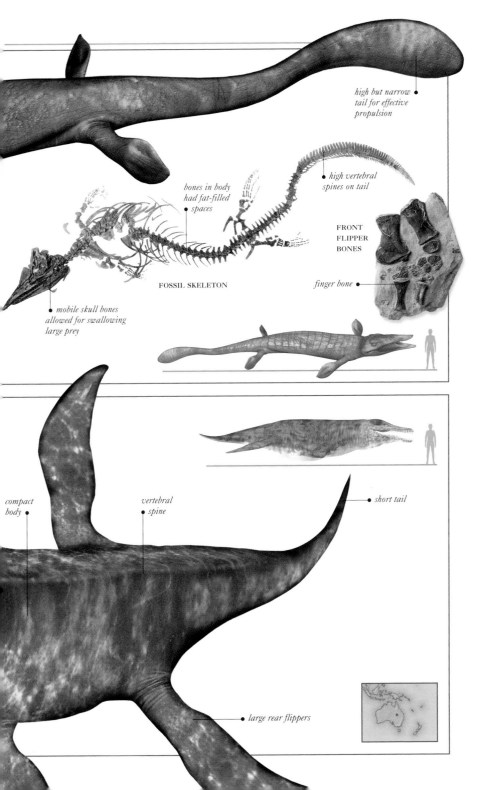

high but narrow
tail for effective
propulsion

bones in body
had fat-filled
spaces

high vertebral
spines on tail

FRONT
FLIPPER
BONES

finger bone

FOSSIL SKELETON

mobile skull bones
allowed for swallowing
large prey

compact
body

vertebral
spine

short tail

large rear flippers

Group Plesiosauria	Family Elasmosauridae	Time 69–66 mya

ELASMOSAURUS

EH-LAZ-MOH-SAW-RUS

Elasmosaurus ("ribbon lizard") was the longest known plesiosaur.
More than half of its body length consisted of the greatly elongated
neck. This had 71 vertebrae, whereas earlier plesiosaurs had only
28. The length and structure of its neck meant that *Elasmosaurus*
would have been able to bend it around its body sideways to feed.
However, calculations of the water resistance it would have met
have led some paleontologists to suggest an alternative method
of feeding. It is possible that *Elasmosaurus* paddled along on the
surface, holding its neck high to spot prey in the
water. The long neck would then have been
plunged into the water to catch it.
Elasmosaurus' body was similar to that
of other plesiosaurs: it had four long,
paddlelike flippers, a tiny head, sharp teeth
in strong jaws, and a short, pointed tail.
• **DESCRIBED BY** E.D. Cope; 1868.
• **HABITAT** Oceans.

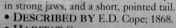

*greatly elongated
• neck*

*tiny head and mouth
• with small, sharp teeth*

Length 45 ft (14 m)	Weight 3⅓ tons (3 metric tons)	Diet Fish, squid, shellfish

front flippers slightly longer than hind ones •

• short, stiff body

short, pointed tail •

LEPIDOTES

Elasmosaurus feasted   large fish such as *Lepidotes* (right) and many other forms of marine life that abounded in the Cretaceous oceans. *Lepidotes* was almost the length of a human and was itself a voracious predator of smaller marine creatures, such as shellfish, which it crunched with its strong teeth.

bony rays supported each fin •

rigid, overlapping • scales

IN THE AIR

By the early Cretaceous Period, bird species had greatly radiated and diversified. Most of these early birds still had very primitive features, such as teeth. However, by the Late Cretaceous they were looking far more like modern birds. Some species of wading and diving birds had even lost the ability to fly.

Cretaceous skies still seem to have been dominated by the pterosaurs, at least until later on in the period. In the Cretaceous, these reached immense sizes. It was at this time that the largest-ever flying animal existed. This was the pterosaur *Quetzalcoatlus*, which has a wingspan as large as a modern small glider.

The fossil record suggests that the diversity of pterosaurs declined in the Late Cretaceous, and by the end of the period, only a few species were left. To date, no fossil remains have been found of these creatures from sediments younger than the Cretaceous, so it seems likely that they died out along with the dinosaurs in the end-Cretaceous extinction. However, the reasons why birds survived while the pterosaurs did not are unclear.

It is possible that the increasing numbers and diversity of birds had some impact on pterosaur populations and evolution. Birds may have filled ecological niches that the pterosaurs vacated through normal extinction processes, and thus slowly displaced pterosaurs. However, for most of the Cretaceous Period, it seems that pterosaurs and birds overlapped only to a small extent, with the two groups apparently coexisting quite easily.

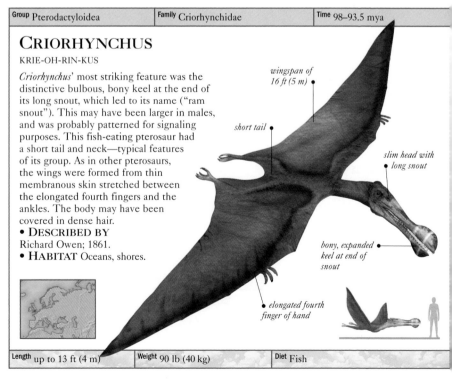

Group Pterodactyloidea	Family Criorhynchidae	Time 98–93.5 mya

CRIORHYNCHUS

KRIE-OH-RIN-KUS

Criorhynchus' most striking feature was the distinctive bulbous, bony keel at the end of its long snout, which led to its name ("ram snout"). This may have been larger in males, and was probably patterned for signaling purposes. This fish-eating pterosaur had a short tail and neck—typical features of its group. As in other pterosaurs, the wings were formed from thin membranous skin stretched between the elongated fourth fingers and the ankles. The body may have been covered in dense hair.
• **DESCRIBED BY** Richard Owen; 1861.
• **HABITAT** Oceans, shores.

wingspan of 16 ft (5 m)

short tail

slim head with long snout

bony, expanded keel at end of snout

elongated fourth finger of hand

Length up to 13 ft (4 m)	Weight 90 lb (40 kg)	Diet Fish

Group Pterodactyloidea	Family Pterodaustridae	Time 125 mya

PTERODAUSTRO

TER-OH-DAW-STROH

The most remarkable feature of this large pterodactyl was its long, curved jaws. The lower jaw contained thousands of very thin teeth, which were probably used to sieve plankton. The upper teeth were used to comb out the lower teeth.
• **DESCRIBED BY** José Bonaparte; 1969.
• **HABITAT** Seashores, lakes.

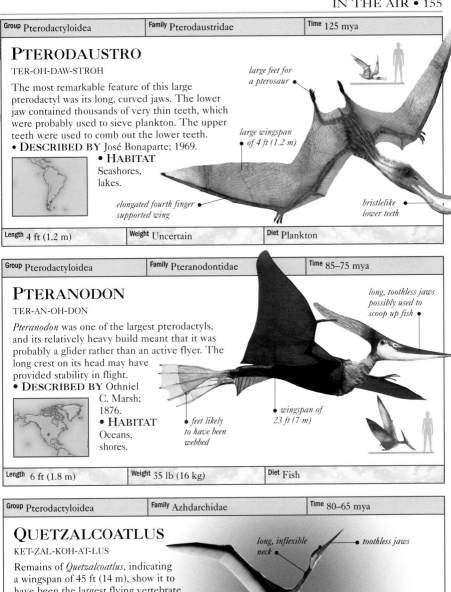

large feet for a pterosaur

large wingspan of 4 ft (1.2 m)

elongated fourth finger supported wing

bristlelike lower teeth

Length 4 ft (1.2 m)	Weight Uncertain	Diet Plankton

Group Pterodactyloidea	Family Pteranodontidae	Time 85–75 mya

PTERANODON

TER-AN-OH-DON

Pteranodon was one of the largest pterodactyls, and its relatively heavy build meant that it was probably a glider rather than an active flyer. The long crest on its head may have provided stability in flight.
• **DESCRIBED BY** Othniel C. Marsh; 1876.
• **HABITAT** Oceans, shores.

long, toothless jaws possibly used to scoop up fish

feet likely to have been webbed

wingspan of 23 ft (7 m)

Length 6 ft (1.8 m)	Weight 35 lb (16 kg)	Diet Fish

Group Pterodactyloidea	Family Azhdarchidae	Time 80–65 mya

QUETZALCOATLUS

KET-ZAL-KOH-AT-LUS

Remains of *Quetzalcoatlus*, indicating a wingspan of 45 ft (14 m), show it to have been the largest flying vertebrate known to date. Its wings were narrow and relatively inflexible. It was probably a glider. There was a small bony crest on the head.
• **DESCRIBED BY** Lawson; 1975.
• **HABITAT** All.

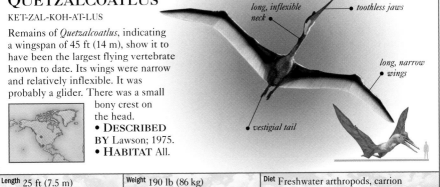

long, inflexible neck

toothless jaws

long, narrow wings

vestigial tail

Length 25 ft (7.5 m)	Weight 190 lb (86 kg)	Diet Freshwater arthropods, carrion

Group Aves	Family Confuciusornithidae	Time 150–120mya

CONFUCIUSORNIS

CON-FUSH-EE-US-OAR-NIS

Confuciusornis ("Confucius bird") was the first bird known to have a true, horny beak. It had a mixture of primitive features (clawed wing fingers and a flat breastbone) and modern adaptations, such as a deeper chest and shortened tail core. The foot claws were highly curved, and the large toe was reversed, indicating that it was a tree-dweller. Males had long tail feathers.

three wing fingers with curved claws

toothless, horny beak with slight upward curve

Its beak turned up slightly at the end, leading to debate about its diet. *Confuciusornis* was most probably a side-shoot from the modern bird lineage.
• **DESCRIBED BY** Lianhai Hou; 1997.
• **HABITAT** Woodland.

e gth 31cm (1ft)	Weight Unknown	Diet Seeds, possibly fish

Group Aves	Family Hesperornithidae	Time 75mya

HESPERORNIS

HESS-PER-OAR-NISS

This large, toothed seabird lived a lifestyle very similar to that of modern penguins. It had lost the power of flight, and its vestigial wings were tiny and stubby.

long neck that could be held in S-shape over shoulders

The head was long and low, with a long beak armed with sharp, pointed teeth for catching fish and other small marine creatures. *Hesperornis* ("western bird") was probably a powerful swimmer, using its large, webbed feet for propulsion, but may have moved clumsily on land. It probably nested on seashores.
• **DESCRIBED BY** Othniel C. Marsh; 1872.
• **HABITAT** Seashores.

legs set far back

splint-like bones supported tiny wings

long, pointed, toothed beak

e gth 2m (6½ft)	Weight Unknown	Diet Fish, squid

Group Aves	Family Ichthyornithidae	Time 135–70mya

ICHTHYORNIS

IK-THEE-OAR-NISS

When the jaw of this toothed, primitive bird was re-examined in 1952, it was thought for a time, incorrectly, to belong to a juvenile mosasaur. The jaws and teeth of *Ichthyornis* ("fish bird") are indeed similar to those of a marine reptile. *Ichthyornis* was a seabird, similar in size and build to a modern seagull, but its head and beak were much larger. It had a well-developed, keeled breastbone, and a deep chest, suggesting it may have been a strong flyer. Its webbed feet had claws.
• **DESCRIBED BY** Othniel C. Marsh; 1872.
• **HABITAT** Seashores.

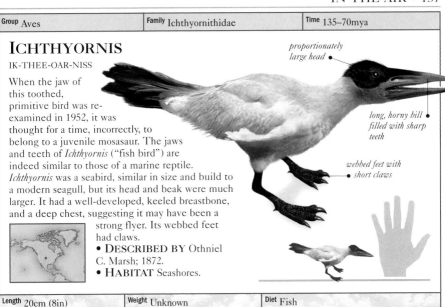

proportionately large head

long, horny bill filled with sharp teeth

webbed feet with short claws

Length 20cm (8in)	Weight Unknown	Diet Fish

Group Theropoda	Family Alvezsauria	Time 85–75mya

SHUVUUIA

SHU-VOO-EE-A

Since its discovery, *Shuvuuia* (its name is derived from "shuvuu", the Mongolian word for bird) has provoked great debate as to whether it was a dinosaur-like bird, or a bird-like dinosaur. It did look superficially like a dinosaur, but examination of its skull shows it to have been more closely related to modern birds than, for example, *Archaeopteryx*. Although *Shuvuuia* did not have a true beak, its slender jaws bore tiny teeth, and it may have been able to raise its upper jaw in relation to the braincase, a facility only modern birds have. Chemical analysis also shows that it was feathered. The legs were long and slim, suggesting that it may have been a fast runner. The forelimbs were short and stubby, and ended in a single, clawed digit.
• **DESCRIBED BY** Chiappe, Norell, and Clark; 1998.
• **HABITAT** Plains.

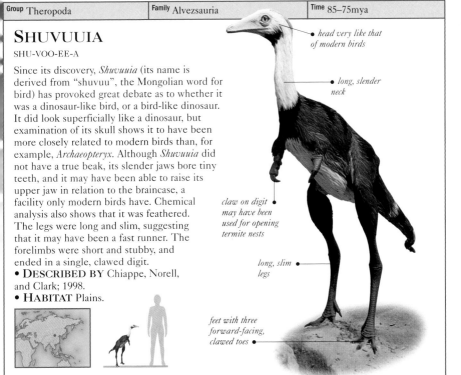

head very like that of modern birds

long, slender neck

claw on digit may have been used for opening termite nests

long, slim legs

feet with three forward-facing, clawed toes

Length 1m (3½ft)	Weight 2.5kg (5½lb)	Diet Insects, small reptiles

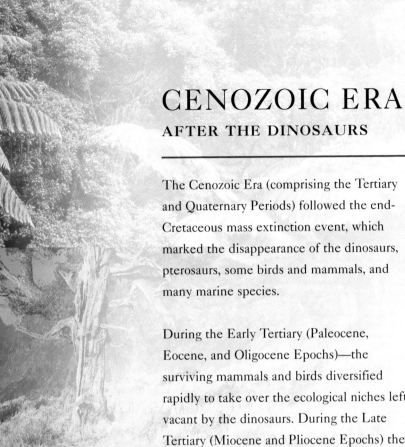

CENOZOIC ERA
AFTER THE DINOSAURS

The Cenozoic Era (comprising the Tertiary and Quaternary Periods) followed the end-Cretaceous mass extinction event, which marked the disappearance of the dinosaurs, pterosaurs, some birds and mammals, and many marine species.

During the Early Tertiary (Paleocene, Eocene, and Oligocene Epochs)—the surviving mammals and birds diversified rapidly to take over the ecological niches left vacant by the dinosaurs. During the Late Tertiary (Miocene and Pliocene Epochs) the spread of grasslands led to the evolution of modern forms of grazing mammals.

By the Quaternary Period (Pleistocene and Holocene Epochs), animal and plant life generally resembled modern forms, although some species that were adapted to recurring ice ages did not survive into modern times.

EARLY TERTIARY PERIOD

65–23.5 MILLION YEARS AGO

The Early Tertiary, including the Paleocene, Eocene, and Oligocene epochs, was the beginning of the "Age of Mammals." Many ecological niches had been left vacant by the end-Cretaceous mass extinction of dinosaurs, and mammal and bird populations evolved and expanded rapidly to fill the gaps. Climates worldwide were warm or hot, with high rainfall. Vast areas of swampy forest and tropical rainforest developed. Toward the mid-Tertiary, a large ice cap formed over the South Pole. This resulted in a fall in sea levels, and the climate became much cooler. Tropical forests disappeared in temperate regions and were replaced by woodlands dominated by deciduous and coniferous trees.

EARLY TERTIARY LIFE

Despite the rapid evolution of mammals into many ecological niches, large herbivores only appeared at the end of the Paleocene (about 53 mya). There were no large mammalian carnivores at all—their niche was filled by very large, flightless birds, such as *Gastornis* (p.167). The reptile groups, including crocodiles and lizards, that had survived the end-Cretaceous extinction flourished in the warm, swampy conditions, as did smaller amphibians.

ICARONYCTERIS

The first bats, such as *Icaronycteris* (right), first appeared in the Paleocene. They filled the niche left by insectivorous pterosaurs, and like them, had wings formed from membranous skin.

• *wings supported on all fingers*

• *feet thought to have been webbed for swimming*

AMBULOCETUS

As well as diversifying on the land, mammals took to the oceans. The ancestors of whales, such as *Ambulocetus* (left), evolved from piglike mammals. These primitive animals showed few adaptations to marine life.

4,600 mya	4,000 mya	3,000 mya

EARLY TERTIARY LANDMASSES

At the start of the Tertiary Period, the supercontinent of Gondwana was continuing to split up. South America was still an isolated island, and the Atlantic Ocean was becoming wider. By the mid-Tertiary (see map) most of the continents were in positions similar to those they occupy today. India had begun to collide with Asia. Australia was moving north, away from Antarctica, but had not yet reached its present-day position.

UINTATHERIUM
Large herbivores, such as the uintatheres, only appeared in the late Paleocene. They included the bizarre rhino-sized *Uintatherium*, which had three distinctive pairs of knobs on its head, and tusklike canine teeth.

| 2,000 mya | 1,000 mya | 500 mya | 250 mya | 0 |

ON THE LAND

T he first epoch of the Tertiary Period, the Paleocene, started with no large land animals. This left many ecological niches available for the animal groups that had survived the end-Cretaceous mass extinction. Non-dinosaurian reptiles, such as crocodiles, lizards, and snakes, flourished in the warm climate and tropical forests. Amphibians also did well in these conditions. However, these groups did not dominate the land as the dinosaurs had done. Instead, mammals and birds evolved to fill the roles of land herbivores and predators.

Mammals entered the Tertiary as mostly nocturnal, rodent-sized animals, and rapidly diversified into many new forms. Marsupials, which had been as common as placental mammals in the Cretaceous Period, were still plentiful during the Early Tertiary Period. Australia's separation from Antarctica left the marsupials there to evolve in isolation, while in other areas of the world, they gradually lost ground to placentals. Large mammalian herbivores appeared only at the very end of the Paleocene Epoch. Carnivorous mammals also appeared at this time, including the hoofed mesonychids. However, these were only small predators. The niche of large carnivores was taken instead by giant, flightless birds, such as *Gastornis*.

Through the Eocene and Oligocene, mammals became established as the major life form in all the main habitats. Large mammalian carnivores appeared during late Eocene times, and mammals similar to modern forms began to appear in the Oligocene.

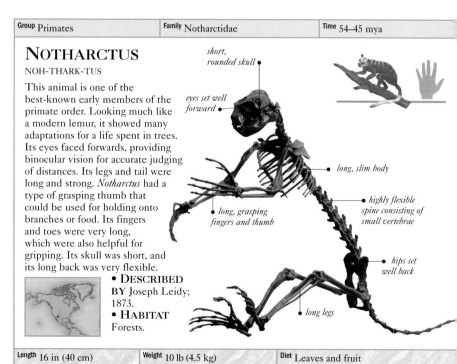

Group Primates	Family Notharctidae	Time 54–45 mya

NOTHARCTUS

NOH-THARK-TUS

This animal is one of the best-known early members of the primate order. Looking much like a modern lemur, it showed many adaptations for a life spent in trees. Its eyes faced forwards, providing binocular vision for accurate judging of distances. Its legs and tail were long and strong. *Notharctus* had a type of grasping thumb that could be used for holding onto branches or food. Its fingers and toes were very long, which were also helpful for gripping. Its skull was short, and its long back was very flexible.

short, rounded skull

eyes set well forward

long, slim body

highly flexible spine consisting of small vertebrae

long, grasping fingers and thumb

hips set well back

long legs

• **DESCRIBED BY** Joseph Leidy; 1873.
• **HABITAT** Forests.

Length 16 in (40 cm)	Weight 10 lb (4.5 kg)	Diet Leaves and fruit

Group Dinocerata	Family Uintatheriidae	Time 45–35 mya

UINTATHERIUM

YOU-IN-TAH-THEER-EE-UM

At the time when *Uintatherium* ("Uinta beast") existed, it was one of the largest land mammals. The size of a modern rhinoceros, it was heavy-limbed, with massive bones. On its face it had three pairs of horns, which varied in size. The largest horns were at the back of the head. All of them seem to have been covered in skin and possibly hair. Males appear to have had larger horns than females. It is possible that the males fought using their horns and tusklike canine teeth. The barrel-shaped body was carried on columnlike legs. *Uintatherium* walked only on its toes, which were very short, as were the other "hand" and "foot" bones. Its elephant-like feet were designed for weight-bearing and walking on dry ground. *Uintatherium* had a very small brain for its skull size, compared with modern hoofed mammals.

• **DESCRIBED BY** Joseph Leidy; 1873.

• **HABITAT** Forests.

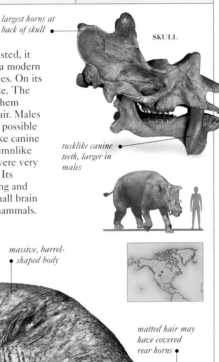

largest horns at back of skull •

SKULL

tusklike canine teeth, larger in males

massive, barrel-shaped body

coarse, thick hide •

matted hair may have covered rear horns •

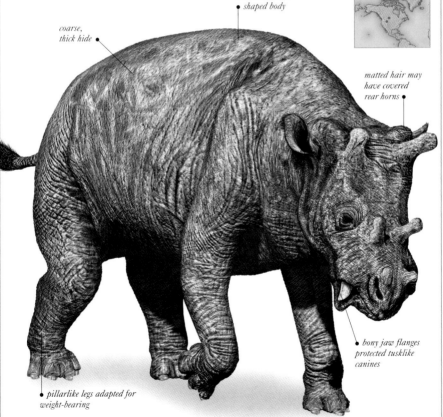

bony jaw flanges protected tusklike canines

pillarlike legs adapted for weight-bearing

Length 11 ft (3.5 m)	Weight 2¼ tons (2 metric tons)	Diet Leaves, fruit, water plants

Group Litopterna	Family Didolodontidae	Time 60–50 mya

DIDOLODUS

DIE-DOH-LOH-DUS

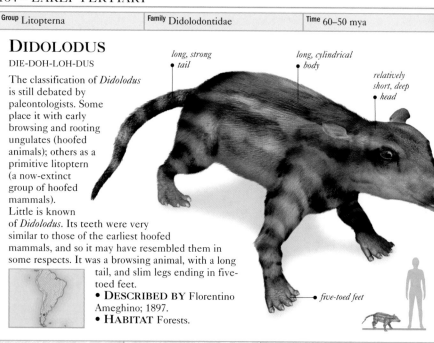

long, strong tail

long, cylindrical body

relatively short, deep head

five-toed feet

The classification of *Didolodus* is still debated by paleontologists. Some place it with early browsing and rooting ungulates (hoofed animals); others as a primitive litoptern (a now-extinct group of hoofed mammals). Little is known of *Didolodus*. Its teeth were very similar to those of the earliest hoofed mammals, and so it may have resembled them in some respects. It was a browsing animal, with a long tail, and slim legs ending in five-toed feet.

- **DESCRIBED BY** Florentino Ameghino; 1897.
- **HABITAT** Forests.

Length 24 in (60 cm)	Weight 33–44 lb (15–20 kg)	Diet Leaves

Group Condylarthra	Family Phenacodontidae	Time 57.8–52 mya

PHENACODUS

FEN-A-CO-DUS

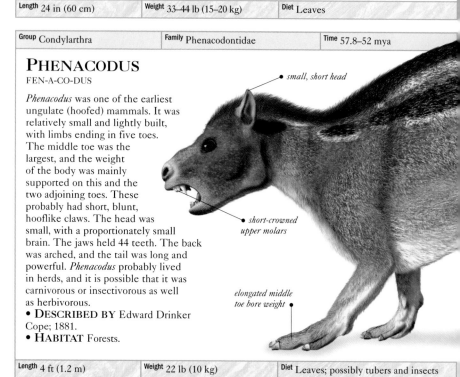

small, short head

short-crowned upper molars

elongated middle toe bore weight

Phenacodus was one of the earliest ungulate (hoofed) mammals. It was relatively small and lightly built, with limbs ending in five toes. The middle toe was the largest, and the weight of the body was mainly supported on this and the two adjoining toes. These probably had short, blunt, hooflike claws. The head was small, with a proportionately small brain. The jaws held 44 teeth. The back was arched, and the tail was long and powerful. *Phenacodus* probably lived in herds, and it is possible that it was carnivorous or insectivorous as well as herbivorous.

- **DESCRIBED BY** Edward Drinker Cope; 1881.
- **HABITAT** Forests.

Length 4 ft (1.2 m)	Weight 22 lb (10 kg)	Diet Leaves; possibly tubers and insects

Group Condylarthra	Family Mesonychidae	Time 45 mya

MESONYX

MEE-ZON-ICKS

This mesonychid carnivore, whose name means "middle claw," had a wolflike body and agile limbs that ended in five toes with small, blunt claws. The long skull had a bony crest to which the large jaw muscles were anchored. This gave a powerful bite. The canine teeth were long and sharp, and the lower molars were thin and bladelike. Paleontologists have suggested that the mesonychids were the ancestors of modern whales. However, it is now thought that whales are descended from piglike ancestors.

- **DESCRIBED BY** Joseph Leidy; 1894.
- **HABITAT** Scrubland, open woodland.

wide mouth with powerful bite

Length 6 ft (1.8 m)	Weight Unknown	Diet Meat, carrion, possibly plants

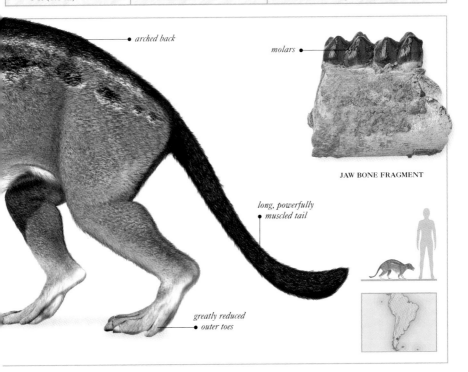

arched back

molars

JAW BONE FRAGMENT

long, powerfully muscled tail

greatly reduced outer toes

Group Embrithopoda	Family Arsinoitheriidae	Time 38–23 mya

ARSINOTHERIUM

AR-SIN-OH-THEER-EE-UM

Arsinotherium is the best-known member of the embrithopods—large, rhinolike animals that were closely related to elephants. Its most notable feature were the two huge, conical horns that jutted out from its snout. These were composed of hollow bone and may have been covered in skin. Adult animals had pointed horns, while juveniles had rounded ones.

• **DESCRIBED BY** Hugh Beadnell; 1906.
• **HABITAT** Forests near rivers.

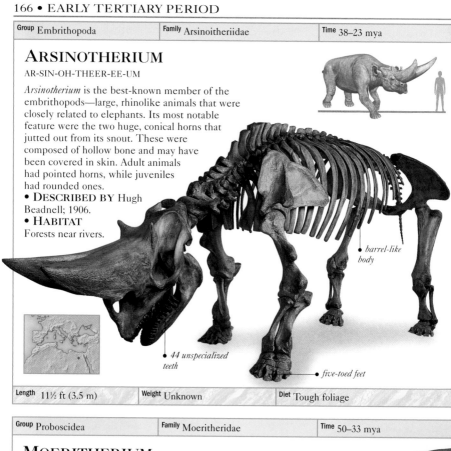

barrel-like body

44 unspecialized teeth

five-toed feet

Length 11½ ft (3.5 m)	Weight Unknown	Diet Tough foliage

Group Proboscidea	Family Moeritheridae	Time 50–33 mya

MOERITHERIUM

MEE-RI-THEER-EE-UM

This hippolike animal, which was named after the ancient Greek name (Moeris) for the lake in Egypt where it was found, was actually related to elephants. It had a low-slung, long body, with relatively short legs. Its nostrils were at the front of the skull, indicating that it did not have a trunk. The teeth were small, but two of the incisors formed small tusks. It was probably partly aquatic in its lifestyle, as is the modern hippopotamus.

• **DESCRIBED BY** Roy Chapman Andrews; 1923.
• **HABITAT** Rivers and swamps.

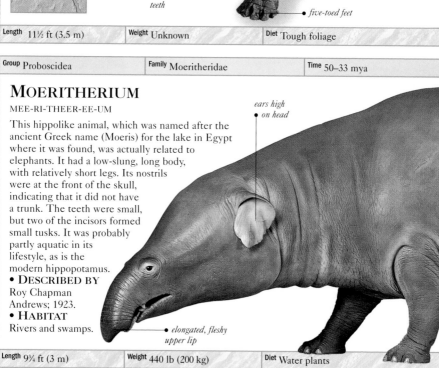

ears high on head

elongated, fleshy upper lip

Length 9¾ ft (3 m)	Weight 440 lb (200 kg)	Diet Water plants

Group Gruiformes	Family Gastornithidae	Time 56–41 mya

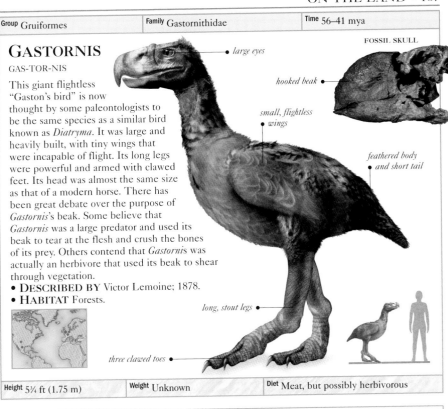

FOSSIL SKULL

GASTORNIS

GAS-TOR-NIS

This giant flightless "Gaston's bird" is now thought by some paleontologists to be the same species as a similar bird known as *Diatryma*. It was large and heavily built, with tiny wings that were incapable of flight. Its long legs were powerful and armed with clawed feet. Its head was almost the same size as that of a modern horse. There has been great debate over the purpose of *Gastornis*'s beak. Some believe that *Gastornis* was a large predator and used its beak to tear at the flesh and crush the bones of its prey. Others contend that *Gastornis* was actually an herbivore that used its beak to shear through vegetation.

- **DESCRIBED BY** Victor Lemoine; 1878.
- **HABITAT** Forests.

large eyes

hooked beak

small, flightless wings

feathered body and short tail

long, stout legs

three clawed toes

Height 5¾ ft (1.75 m)	Weight Unknown	Diet Meat, but possibly herbivorous

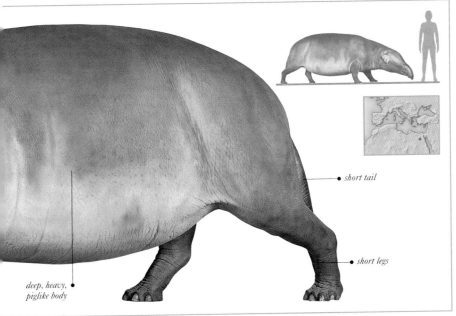

short tail

short legs

deep, heavy, piglike body

IN THE WATER

W ith the disappearance of the giant marine reptiles of the Mesozoic Period, more modern and recognizable forms of ocean life evolved during the early Tertiary Period. Fish took on more recognizable forms, and new groups of shellfish appeared. The first penguins also evolved at this time, including some giant forms.

At some point in the early Tertiary, mammals moved to fill the ecological niche left open by the absence of large, ocean-dwelling carnivores. The first whale is thought to have been an animal called *Pakicetus*. This mammal seems to have been closely related to the land-dwelling hoofed mammals. Only its skull has been discovered to date, and little is known of how it actually looked in life. Its claimed

relationship to cetaceans (whales) is due to certain peculiarities in its ear bones that are unique to whales. Its teeth are also ideal for a diet of fish. However, it is clear that this animal, as well as other early whales, had few adaptations for marine life.

The first whales had four walking limbs that could be used for swimming, perhaps with webbed toes. They probably spent most of their time on land, only entering the water to hunt. As they evolved, the front limbs gradually evolved into flippers, a tail fluke appeared, their bodies became more streamlined, and the hind limbs grew smaller. In later whales, the hind limbs are totally absent. Early whales did not have ears that were capable of detecting ultrasound. They therefore relied on sight for hunting.

Group Archaeoceti	Family Basilosauridae	Time 40–35 mya

BASILOSAURUS

BASS-IL-OH-SAW-RUS

Despite being a primitive whale, *Basilosaurus* ("king of the lizards") looked so much like a mythical sea monster that its bones were once used in a famous sea serpent hoax. It had a flexible, whalelike body, with forelimbs shaped like paddles. It had tiny hindlimbs that may have been used in mating. *Basilosaurus* probably swam by making undulating movements with its body. Its nostrils were high on its snout, but it did not have a blowhole. It was capable of hunting large fish and other marine mammals.
• **DESCRIBED BY** Richard Harlan; 1843.
• **HABITAT** Tropical oceans.

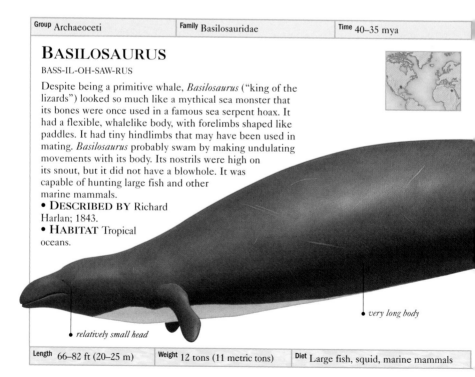

• *relatively small head*

• *very long body*

Length 66–82 ft (20–25 m)	Weight 12 tons (11 metric tons)	Diet Large fish, squid, marine mammals

Group Archaeoceti	Family Protocetidae	Time 50 mya

AMBULOCETUS

AM-BYU-LOH-SEE-TUS

Ambulocetus ("walking whale") is thought to be one of the most primitive cetaceans (whales). Its teeth, skull, and ear bones show features unique to this group. As its name suggests, it probably spent most of its time on land, although it may have been rather clumsy. Its feet and hands may have been webbed, and its powerful hind limbs would have made it a strong swimmer. It is thought to have hunted by ambushing its prey in water as modern crocodiles do.
• **DESCRIBED BY** Hans Thewissen; 1994.
• **HABITAT** Estuaries.

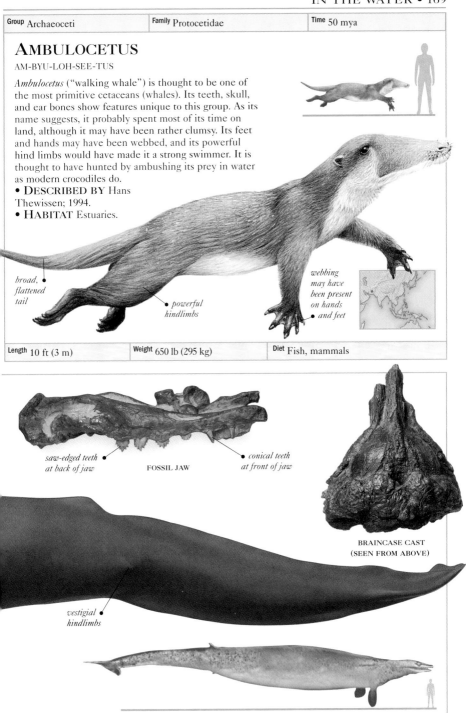

broad, flattened tail

powerful hindlimbs

webbing may have been present on hands and feet

Length 10 ft (3 m)	Weight 650 lb (295 kg)	Diet Fish, mammals

saw-edged teeth at back of jaw

FOSSIL JAW

conical teeth at front of jaw

BRAINCASE CAST
(SEEN FROM ABOVE)

vestigial hindlimbs

IN THE AIR

The timing of the first appearance of modern birds is still hotly debated. The standard view of avian evolution states that modern bird forms (Neornithes) first arose in the Paleocene. A new theory asserts that modern birds were already present at the end of the Cretaceous, and then closely paralleled mammals in an explosive evolution during the Paleocene and Eocene Epochs of the Early Tertiary.

Whichever view is correct, we know that within 10 million years of the start of the Paleocene, all of the major lineages of birds had evolved. All of the major bird orders had appeared by the early Eocene, including primitive herons, swifts, eagles, and owls. It seems likely that all of the bird lineages diverged from a common group fairly soon after the end-Cretaceous extinction.

The Early Tertiary also saw the appearance of the first flying mammals: bats. Some mammal teeth from the Paleocene found in France show characters of both bats and insectivores (the group including hedgehogs, moles, and shrews). However, it is not known whether these were primitive bats or not. The first undoubted bat fossils date from the Eocene and represent essentially modern-looking forms; by this time, bats had evolved all of their characteristic features, perhaps even an early type of echolocation. Their distribution was very different from that seen today, with fruit bats occurring in Europe, rather than in tropical areas, and vampire bats occurring as far north as California.

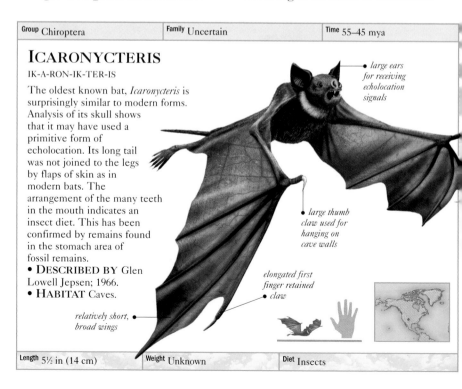

Group Chiroptera	Family Uncertain	Time 55–45 mya

ICARONYCTERIS

IK-A-RON-IK-TER-IS

The oldest known bat, *Icaronycteris* is surprisingly similar to modern forms. Analysis of its skull shows that it may have used a primitive form of echolocation. Its long tail was not joined to the legs by flaps of skin as in modern bats. The arrangement of the many teeth in the mouth indicates an insect diet. This has been confirmed by remains found in the stomach area of fossil remains.
• **DESCRIBED BY** Glen Lowell Jepsen; 1966.
• **HABITAT** Caves.

large ears for receiving echolocation signals

large thumb claw used for hanging on cave walls

elongated first finger retained claw

relatively short, broad wings

Length 5½ in (14 cm)	Weight Unknown	Diet Insects

Group Anseriformes	Family Presbyornithidae	Time 40–60 mya

PRESBYORNIS

PREZ-BEE-OAR-NIS

This primitive duck was so slenderly built that paleontologists first thought it was a type of flamingo. Unlike modern ducks, *Presbyornis* had very long legs and presumably was a wader, rather than a swimmer. The relative length of the neck and legs of *Presbyornis* are consistent with a wading, bottom-feeding style. However, the legs were set relatively far back, suggesting that it may also have been a diving bird. Its feet were large and webbed. *Presbyornis* was highly colonial, and seems to have gathered in large flocks to feed by the shores of lakes. Its principal diet was probably based on filter feeding, using the tongue to draw water in like a straw, extracting food by pressing the tongue against the roof of the mouth, and expelling the excess water out of the sides of the bill. Hundreds of *Presbyornis* fossils have been found, representing several species that range from 1½ ft (0.5 m) to 5 ft (1.5 m) tall.

• **DESCRIBED BY** Alexander Wetmore; 1926.

• **HABITAT** Lakeshores.

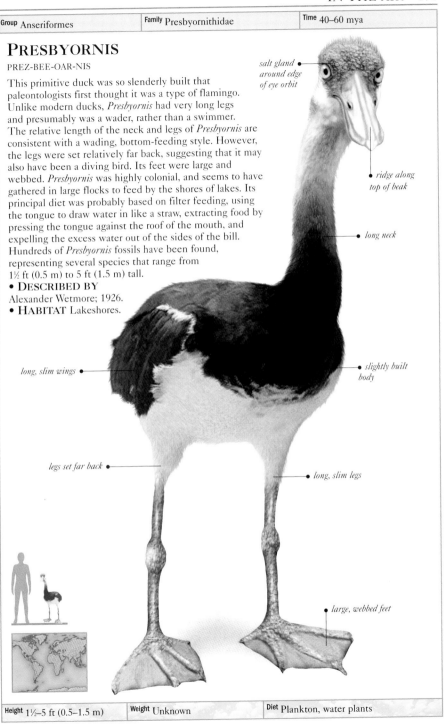

salt gland around edge of eye orbit

ridge along top of beak

long neck

long, slim wings

slightly built body

legs set far back

long, slim legs

large, webbed feet

Height 1½–5 ft (0.5–1.5 m)	Weight Unknown	Diet Plankton, water plants

LATE TERTIARY PERIOD
23.5–1.75 MILLION YEARS AGO

The Late Tertiary (the Miocene and Pliocene epochs) saw the continued evolution of mammals. The ice cap that had started to form at the South Pole in the Oligocene continued to expand. By the mid-Miocene, it covered the whole of Antarctica, further cooling the world's climate. These temperate conditions led to the development of huge expanses of grassland over Africa, Asia, Europe, and the Americas. The climate continued to cool into the Pliocene, when a large ice cap also formed at the North Pole. Most of the remaining forest areas had disappeared by the end of the Pliocene, but grasslands continued to spread.

LATE TERTIARY LIFE
The animals of the Miocene and Pliocene were very similar to modern forms. Grasslands were filled with herds of horses, camels, elephants, and antelopes. Large carnivores hunted across the plains, and the first humans evolved from primate ancestors. In the oceans, modern types of fish had appeared, and the primitive forms of whales had given way to more familiar, larger species.

sharp, hooked beak

reduced wings solely for display

TERRIBLE BIRDS
Large carnivorous birds were still some of the world's largest and most terrifying predators. The South American terror bird *Titanis* (left) hunted on open grassy plains. It moved into North America when the Panama Isthmus formed in the Miocene.

4,600 mya	4,000 mya	3,000 mya

LATE TERTIARY LANDMASSES

During the Miocene, Africa collided with Europe, forming the Alps, and India's collision with Asia caused the Himalayas to rise. The Rocky Mountains in North America and the Andes in South America formed. By the Pliocene, a land bridge linked North and South America. Australia continued to drift northward. By the end of the Pliocene, the continents had almost reached their modern positions.

BIG CATS
Many carnivores evolved large, stabbing canine teeth. *Thylacosmilus* (right) was a catlike marsupial found in Miocene and Pliocene South America.

large canine teeth

EARLY ELEPHANTS
By the beginning of the Miocene, primitive elephant forms, such as the horse-sized *Phiomia* (left) were dying out, and being replaced by more larger forms. These, such as the shovel-tusked *Platybelodon*, would give rise to the mammoths of the Pleistocene and to modern elephant species.

| 2,000 mya | 1,000 mya | 500 mya | 250 mya | 0 |

ON THE LAND

The grasslands that formed in huge expanses over the world during the Miocene and Pliocene Epochs provided new habitats for mammals to evolve. Exposed to predators on grasslands, animals developed mechanisms for faster running, such as longer, slimmer legs. By the end of the Tertiary, many mammal species closely resembled modern forms.

Hoofed mammals exploited the grassland environments. Camels and antelopes became more diverse, and many horselike animals appeared during the Miocene. One new type, called *Merychippus*, was far larger than earlier horses and was effectively single-hooved. By the end of the Pliocene, modern horses had evolved.

Also successful were the Deinotheres—a group within the elephant family. These strange-looking creatures had elephant-like bodies and a trunk, but no tusks in the upper jaw. Instead, they possessed a pair of long tusks in the shovel-like lower jaw, which seem to have been used for digging or for scraping bark from trees.

Other elephant groups included the mastodonts, such as *Gomphotherium*, which had large upper and lower tusks. By the start of the Pliocene, a variety of species of modern elephants and mammoths had evolved.

The most impressive carnivores of the Late Tertiary were the saber-tooth cats. These were larger than modern wild cats, and were armed with long, stabbing canine teeth.

Group Marsupialia	Family Borhyaenidae	Time 19 mya

CLADOSICTIS

CLAD-OH-SICK-TIS

This carnivorous marsupial species was short-lived. Some paleontologists have suggested that it may have had an otterlike lifestyle—hunting fish in rivers—but it may also have eaten the eggs and young of land-living creatures. *Cladosictis* had a long, lightly built body, short limbs, and a doglike skull. Its tail was long and thin. The teeth were similar to those of carnivorous placental mammals: there were sharp incisors at the front of the jaw, with pointed canines and shearing molars behind them.

• **DESCRIBED BY** Florentino Ameghino; 1887.
• **HABITAT** Woodland.

long body and thick neck

doglike snout

Length 2½ ft (80 cm)	Weight Unknown	Diet Small animals, perhaps fish and eggs

Group Marsupialia	Family Thylacosmilidae	Time 7–5 mya

THYLACOSMILUS

THIGH-LA-CO-SMILE-US

Thylacosmilus was a large, predatory marsupial. Like the saber-tooth cats, it sported long, stabbing upper canine teeth. However, in *Thylacosmilus*, these teeth grew continuously throughout life, and there were no incisor teeth in the lower jaw. Bony guards in the lower jaw protected the teeth when the jaws were closed. The neck and shoulders were strong and heavily muscled, allowing the teeth to be driven downward with great force.
• **DESCRIBED BY** Elmer Riggs; 1933.
• **HABITAT** Plains.

FOSSIL SKULL

large, deep skull

tooth guards in lower jaw to protect upper canine teeth

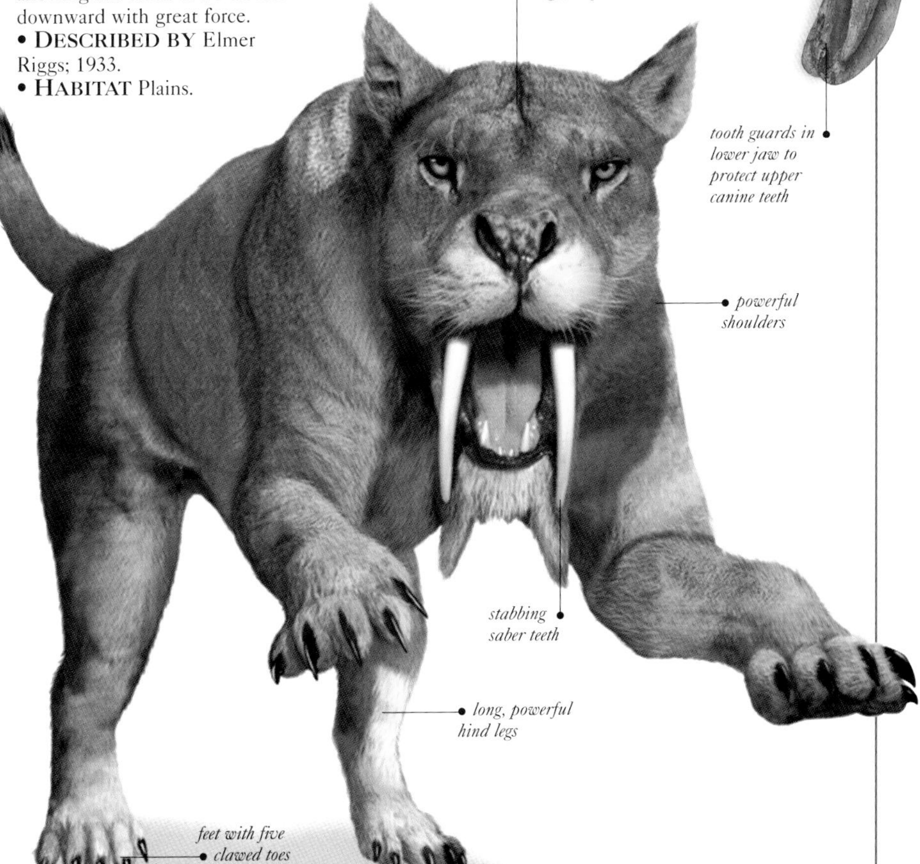

powerful shoulders

stabbing saber teeth

long, powerful hind legs

feet with five clawed toes

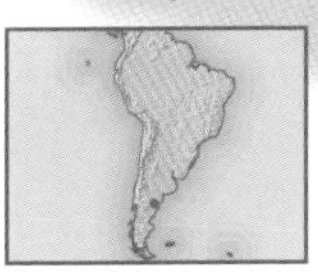

Length 4 ft (1.2 m)	Weight 250 lb (115 kg)	Diet Slow-moving, hoofed mammals

Group Carnivora	Family Amphicyonidae	Time 40–9 mya

AMPHICYON

AM-FIE-SIGH-ON

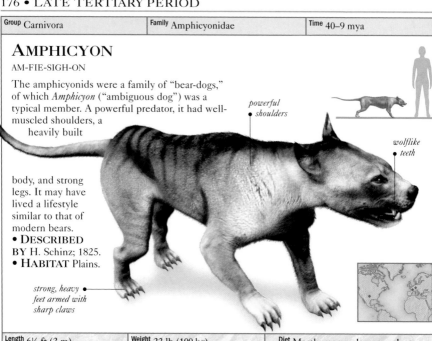

powerful
shoulders

wolflike
teeth

The amphicyonids were a family of "bear-dogs," of which *Amphicyon* ("ambiguous dog") was a typical member. A powerful predator, it had well-muscled shoulders, a heavily built body, and strong legs. It may have lived a lifestyle similar to that of modern bears.
• **DESCRIBED BY** H. Schinz; 1825.
• **HABITAT** Plains.

strong, heavy feet armed with sharp claws

Length 6½ ft (2 m)	Weight 22 lb (100 kg)	Diet Mostly mammals, some plants

Group Carnivora	Family Felidae	Time 40 mya

EUSMILUS

YOU-SMIL-US

short head

Eusmilus, a member of a family of "false saber-tooth cats," first arose in Europe, and then gradually spread into North America. It was a large, powerful hunting cat with a long, low body and relatively short legs. Its head and snout were short, with forward-facing eyes that probably allowed binocular vision and therefore accurate judgement of distances—an important attribute for a hunter. Its upper canine teeth were elongated into thick, stabbing "saber" teeth, just as in the true saber-tooth cats. These thick, curved teeth extended far below the level of the lower jaw, which was capable of opening to an angle of 90 degrees, enabling the cat to use the teeth to stab its prey. In comparison, the lower canines were very small. Many of the other teeth normally found in felines were not present—*Eusmilus* had only 26 teeth, compared to about 44 in a modern cat.
• **DESCRIBED BY** Henri Filhol; 1872.
• **HABITAT** Plains.

forward-facing eyes

long, curved saber teeth

Length 8 ft (2.5 m)	Weight Unknown	Diet Mammals

| Group Carnivora | Family Canidae | Time 20–15 mya |

CYNODESMUS

SY-NOH-DES-MUS

An early member of the dog family, *Cynodesmus* was a coyote-sized animal with a short snout and a long body. Its legs were similar to those of modern dogs, but were not as efficient for running. The feet had clawed toes, with the claws being partially retractable.
• **DESCRIBED BY** William Berryman Scott; 1893.
• **HABITAT** Plains.

long, lightly built body

long tail

short head and snout

| Length 3½ ft (1 m) | Weight 155 lb (70 kg) | Diet Smaller mammals, carrion |

long, heavy tail

relatively short yet powerful legs

retractable claws

Group Proboscidea	Family Gomphotheriidae	Time 38 mya

PHIOMIA

FI-OHM-EE-A

This primitive elephant had two pairs of tusks set in very long upper and lower jaws. The tusks on the lower jaw were flattened and formed a shovel-shaped projection that was probably used to collect food or to scrape bark off trees. The tusks in the upper jaw were shorter and were probably used for fighting or for display. The upper lip was likely to have been drawn out into a short trunk. To reduce the weight of the large skull, the bones were filled with air spaces. The rest of *Phiomia*'s body was very similar to that of a modern elephant—with column-like legs and a stocky body.

- **DESCRIBED BY** Henry F. Osborn; 1932.
- **HABITAT** Plains and woodland.

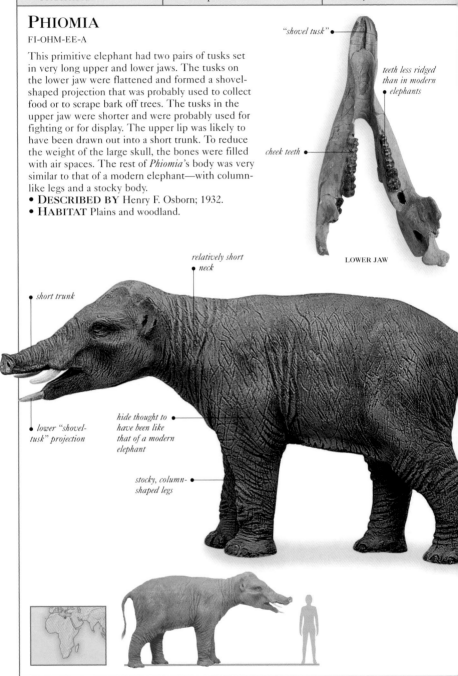

"shovel tusk"

teeth less ridged than in modern elephants

cheek teeth

LOWER JAW

relatively short neck

short trunk

lower "shovel-tusk" projection

hide thought to have been like that of a modern elephant

stocky, column-shaped legs

Length 16 ft (5 m)	Weight 3⅓ tons (3 metric tons)	Diet Plants

Group Proboscidea	Family Gomphotheriidae	Time 25–2 mya

GOMPHOTHERIUM

GOM-FO-THEER-EE-UM

Like *Phiomia*, *Gomphotherium* had a pair of upper jaw tusks for fighting and display, and long lower jaws that formed a food "shovel." It had a trunk as long as the lower tusks to help with feeding. Later species had fewer teeth, with more pronounced ridges for grinding.

• **DESCRIBED BY** Georges Cuvier; 1817.

• **HABITAT** Grassland, marsh, and forest.

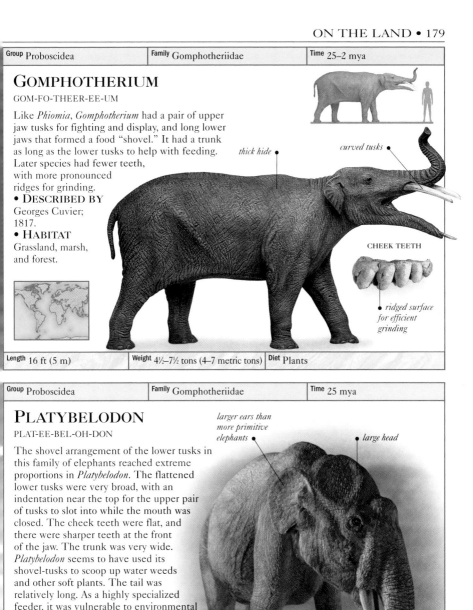

thick hide

curved tusks

CHEEK TEETH

ridged surface for efficient grinding

Length 16 ft (5 m)	Weight 4½–7½ tons (4–7 metric tons)	Diet Plants

Group Proboscidea	Family Gomphotheriidae	Time 25 mya

PLATYBELODON

PLAT-EE-BEL-OH-DON

larger ears than more primitive elephants

large head

The shovel arrangement of the lower tusks in this family of elephants reached extreme proportions in *Platybelodon*. The flattened lower tusks were very broad, with an indentation near the top for the upper pair of tusks to slot into while the mouth was closed. The cheek teeth were flat, and there were sharper teeth at the front of the jaw. The trunk was very wide. *Platybelodon* seems to have used its shovel-tusks to scoop up water weeds and other soft plants. The tail was relatively long. As a highly specialized feeder, it was vulnerable to environmental change, and was a short-lived genus.

• **DESCRIBED BY** William Granger; 1930.

• **HABITAT** Wet prairies.

Length 20 ft (6 m)	Weight 4½–5½ tons (4–5 metric tons)	Diet Soft water plants

Group Perissodactyla	Family Equidae	Time 25–40 mya

MESOHIPPUS

ME-ZO-HIP-PUS

Mesohippus ("middle horse") had features that seem to have been an evolutionary response to more open environments: its legs were longer than those of the earlier "dawn horse" *Eohippus*, and it had lost a toe. Of the three remaining toes, the middle bore most of the animal's weight. These features increased its speed. Its teeth grew larger, increasing their surface area for chewing. The jaw was shallow and the head was quite long and pointed. The eyes were set relatively far apart and far back on the head.

• **DESCRIBED BY** Joseph Leidy; 1870.
• **HABITAT** Open grassland.

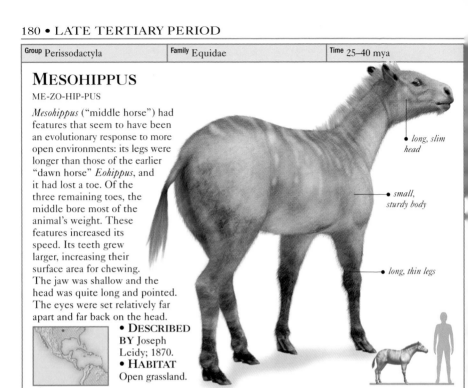

long, slim head

small, sturdy body

long, thin legs

Length 4 ft (1.2 m)	Weight 200 lb (90 kg)	Diet Foliage

Group Perissodactyla	Family Equidae	Time 17–11 mya

MERYCHIPPUS

MER-EE-CHIP-PUS

Merychippus ("ruminant horse") was the first horse to feed exclusively on grass, and the first one to have a head similar to that of modern horses. The muzzle was longer than in earlier horses, the jaw deeper, and the eyes farther apart. Its neck was also longer than in earlier horses, since it spent much of the time grazing. The middle toe on each foot had developed into a hoof that did not have a pad on the bottom. In some species the outer two toes only touched the ground when running; in others, they were larger.

• **DESCRIBED BY** Joseph Leidy; 1894.
• **HABITAT** Grassy plains.

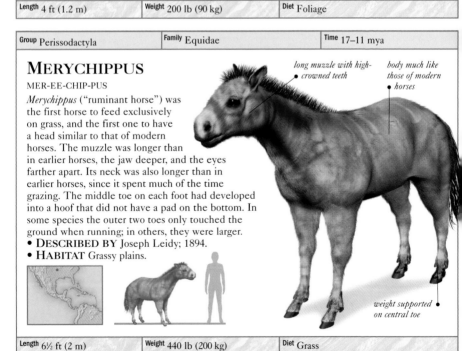

long muzzle with high-crowned teeth

body much like those of modern horses

weight supported on central toe

Length 6½ ft (2 m)	Weight 440 lb (200 kg)	Diet Grass

Group Perissodactyla	Family Equidae	Time 15–2 mya

HIPPARION

HIP-PAIR-EE-ON

Hipparion ("better horse") was one of several groups of grazing three-toed primitive horses that lived in the Miocene. It was a lightly built animal that greatly resembled a modern pony, with a long jaw and slim legs. The horse's full weight was borne on the enlarged central toe, which had developed a recognizable hoof. The two outer toes were much reduced in size and did not reach the ground. A tendon in the foot increased the springiness of the gait, giving the advantage of greater speeds. The teeth were large and high-crowned for grazing. *Hipparion* was a very successful genus of early horse, spreading over the world in large herds for millions of years.

• **DESCRIBED BY** de Cristol; 1832.
• **HABITAT** Plains.

UPPER JAW BONE

large premolars •

• high-crowned molars with many cusps

large eyes set far back along skull •

bony pocket • (antorbital fossa) larger in males

moderately • long tail

long, squarish • muzzle with large nostrils

BONES OF HIND FOOT

very slim, • light legs

elongated • foot bone

large central toe • forming a hoof

Length 5 ft (1.5 m)	Weight 250 lb (115 kg)	Diet Grass

| Group Ceratomorpha | Family Rhinocerotidae | Time 17–4.5 mya |

TELEOCERAS

TELL-EE-OH-SEA-RAS

This mammal was a member of the rhinoceros family. It had a long body and extremely short legs. In fact, the animal's belly must have sometimes dragged along the ground. It had a small, conical nose horn. It is thought to have had a lifestyle like that of a modern hippopotamus, wallowing in water during the day and moving onto land to feed at night.
• **DESCRIBED BY** Othniel C. Marsh; 1877.
• **HABITAT** Rivers.

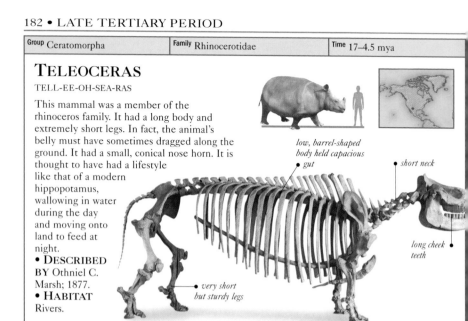

low, barrel-shaped body held capacious gut

short neck

long cheek teeth

very short but sturdy legs

| Length 13 ft (4 m) | Weight 3½ tons (3 metric tons) | Diet Shrubs and grass |

| Group Ceratomorpha | Family Rhinocerotidae | Time 30 mya |

PARACERATHERIUM

PAR-A-SER-A-THEER-EE-UM

This early rhinoceros was the largest land mammal known to have lived. Standing 18 ft (6 m) high at the shoulder, its head alone was over a yard (meter) long. Hollowed out vertebrae in the back kept the animal's weight down. The powerful legs were long and slim, and there were three toes on each foot. Despite its bulk, *Paraceratherium* was probably a fast runner. It seems to have had a flexible upper lip, allowing it to browse on leaves from trees as modern giraffes do.
• **DESCRIBED BY** Forster Cooper; 1911.
• **HABITAT** Open woodland.

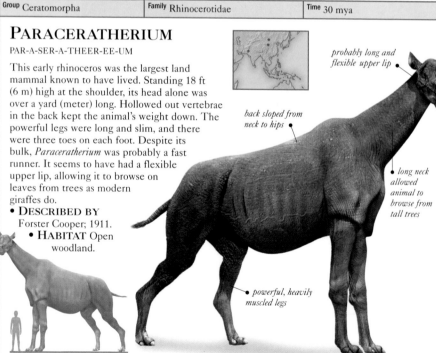

probably long and flexible upper lip

back sloped from neck to hips

long neck allowed animal to browse from tall trees

powerful, heavily muscled legs

| Length 30 ft (9 m) | Weight 16½ tons (15 metric tons) | Diet Leaves and twigs |

Group Gruiformes	Family Phorusrhacidae	Time 45–25 mya

PHORUSRHACUS

FOR-US-RAKE-US

Phorusrhacus was one of the dominant land predators in South America at the time it existed. It had very strong legs, allowing it to run at high speed, stubby, flightless wings, a long neck, and a proportionately large head. This ended in a huge, hooked beak that could have torn through flesh easily, or stabbed into prey. The lower jaw was smaller than the upper jaw. There were three toes on each of the feet, all of which were armed with sharp claws.

• **DESCRIBED BY** Florentino Ameghino; 1887.
• **HABITAT** Plains.

short skull

hooked beak

large upper mandible

Height 5 ft (1.5 m)	Weight 175 lb (80 kg)	Diet Small mammals, carrion

Group Gruiformes	Family Phorusrhacidae	Time 2–1 mya

TITANIS

TIE-TAN-IS

Titanis ("terror crane") was aptly named. This giant flightless bird was one of the most efficient predators of its time in North America. Its head was as large as that of a modern horse, and it had a huge, curved beak. Although it had no teeth, the sharp hook at the end of the beak was very efficient at tearing through flesh. Unusually among flightless birds, it had re-evolved fingers on its arm bones. There were two on each hand, and they were armed with sharp claws. Although short, these fingers could be used for grasping and holding prey. *Titanis* had a long neck, and males may have had an ornamental crest on the top of the head. It had long, agile legs, and three-toed feet with long talons. It could undoubtedly run at high speeds when hunting. This genus may be the same as *Phorusrhacus*, and there is some discussion about renaming it.

• **DESCRIBED BY** Robert Chandler; 1994.
• **HABITAT** Grassy plains.

nostrils high on top of beak

sharp hook on end of beak

two clawed fingers on each wing

short wings useless for flight

three long-clawed toes

powerful, heavily muscled legs

Height 8 ft (2.5 m)	Weight 330 lb (150 kg)	Diet Mammals

IN THE WATER

Climate change during the Late Tertiary greatly affected marine environments. The polar waters grew colder, and this led to the initiation of ocean currents. The movement of nutrients and marine species caused by these new ocean currents increased the productivity of seas worldwide, and new groups of animals arose to take advantage of these new resources.

Whales diversified from the primitive forms of the Early Tertiary into modern toothed forms. In the late Eocene, the first baleen whales also appeared. These had long sheets of keratin, known as baleen, hanging from their jaws. These enabled them to filter plankton, krill, and small animals and fish from the water. By the Miocene, baleen whales had reached the massive sizes of modern whales.

Other mammals returned to an aquatic lifestyle during the Miocene. Primitive seals, sea lions, walruses, and sea otters are thought to have evolved in the Mid Tertiary in the northern hemisphere. By the Miocene, they had spread south of the equator to dominate coastlines around the world. Current opinion among paleontologists is that all of these carnivorous groups evolved from an otterlike ancestor.

Whale vertebrae and flipper bones bearing large bite marks are testament to the success of nonmammalian marine animals during the Late Tertiary. The largest fish ever to have existed, the "megatooth" shark *Carcharodon* preyed on the large seal and whale populations in the Miocene oceans. This enormous shark is estimated to have been 50 ft (15 m) long.

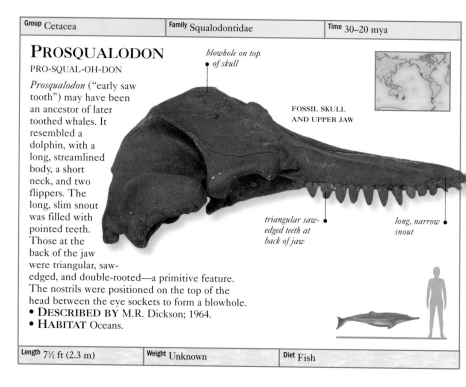

Group Cetacea	Family Squalodontidae	Time 30–20 mya

PROSQUALODON

PRO-SQUAL-OH-DON

blowhole on top of skull

Prosqualodon ("early saw tooth") may have been an ancestor of later toothed whales. It resembled a dolphin, with a long, streamlined body, a short neck, and two flippers. The long, slim snout was filled with pointed teeth. Those at the back of the jaw were triangular, saw-edged, and double-rooted—a primitive feature. The nostrils were positioned on the top of the head between the eye sockets to form a blowhole.
- **DESCRIBED BY** M.R. Dickson; 1964.
- **HABITAT** Oceans.

FOSSIL SKULL AND UPPER JAW

triangular saw-edged teeth at back of jaw

long, narrow snout

Length 7½ ft (2.3 m)	Weight Unknown	Diet Fish

Group Cetacea	Family Rhabdosteidea	Time 15–5 mya

EURHINODELPHIS

YOU-RHINE-OH-DEL-FIS

Eurhinodelphis ("true-nose dolphin") was one of the most common dolphins in the Miocene. Its most distinctive feature was its long snout, which may have been used to strike at its prey. The structure of the ear had become more complex than in earlier toothed whales, indicating that *Eurhinodelphis* had developed some form of echolocation system. The skull was slightly asymmetrical, as in modern toothed whales, with a blowhole at the top of the head.

• **DESCRIBED BY**
R. Kellogg; 1925.
• **HABITAT**
Oceans.

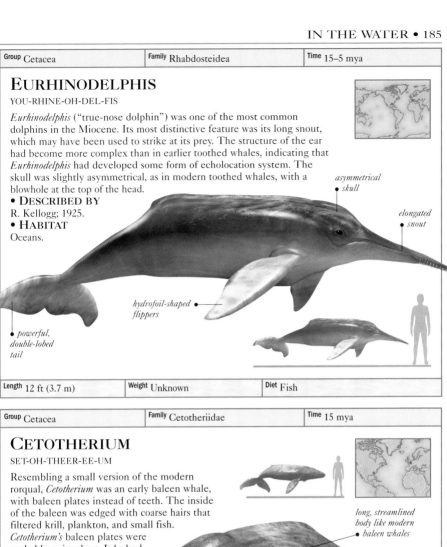

asymmetrical skull

elongated snout

hydrofoil-shaped flippers

powerful, double-lobed tail

Length 12 ft (3.7 m)	Weight Unknown	Diet Fish

Group Cetacea	Family Cetotheriidae	Time 15 mya

CETOTHERIUM

SET-OH-THEER-EE-UM

Resembling a small version of the modern rorqual, *Cetotherium* was an early baleen whale, with baleen plates instead of teeth. The inside of the baleen was edged with coarse hairs that filtered krill, plankton, and small fish. *Cetotherium's* baleen plates were probably quite short. It lacked echolocation. Its head was symmetrical and it probably had two blowholes.

• **DESCRIBED BY**
Lyddeker; 1894.
• **HABITAT**
Oceans.

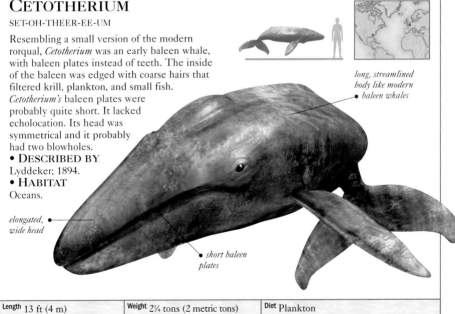

long, streamlined body like modern baleen whales

elongated, wide head

short baleen plates

Length 13 ft (4 m)	Weight 2¼ tons (2 metric tons)	Diet Plankton

IN THE AIR

By the Miocene, true birds were becoming common. The fossil remains of Late Tertiary birds appear much like birds that are alive now. They all had modern features: horny beaks with no teeth, light limb bones fused together, and a heart with four chambers for greater efficiency in pumping blood. By the end of the Pliocene, all but four of the orders of modern birds had evolved.

Due to the lifestyle and lighter bone structure of birds, bird fossils are less common than those of mammals, and evidence is patchy. Some of the best-known species from the Late Tertiary Period are seabirds, such as petrels, albatrosses, and cormorants. Many of these were far larger, often with a much heavier build than modern forms. Other bird groups that appeared at this time include hawks, storks, herons, parrots, and the modern budgerigars. There are also remains of flamingo-type birds. Birds of prey tended to be larger than their modern counterparts. For example, the massive, vulturelike *Argentavis* is the largest flying bird ever discovered.

An important step in the evolution of birds occurred during the Pliocene: songbirds appeared for the first time. However, the evolutionary pressures that led to the development of song for territorial and mating display are not yet fully understood.

Group Neornithes	Family Teratornithidae	Time 6–8 mya

ARGENTAVIS
AR-GEN-TAH-VIS

head possibly bald with neck fringe of feathers

Only a few bones of this large bird of prey have been discovered, but these indicate a wingspan of over 23 ft (7 m), which is twice the size of that of the largest living bird, the wandering albatross. In appearance, it was probably much like a modern vulture, and it may have been a scavenger. Its beak was large and hooked, and was used to grasp prey, since its clawed feet were not well adapted for this. There is discussion about whether *Argentavis* actively flew or glided on warm air currents called thermals. Given the size of the wingspan, the latter mechanism appears more likely.
• **DESCRIBED BY** K.E. Campbell and E. Tonni; 1980.
• **HABITAT** Inland and mountainous areas.

deep, hooked beak

large eyes

Height 5 ft (1.5 m)	Weight 175 lb (80 kg)	Diet Carrion, large herbivorous mammals

Group Osteodontornithidea	Family Pelagornithidae	Time 30–28 mya

OSTEODONTORNIS

OS-TEE-OH-DON-TOR-NIS

One of the largest birds ever to have flown, *Osteodontornis* was a bony-toothed seabird. It had a large, heavy body, and long, narrow wings designed for gliding long distances. The neck had a natural S-shaped curve, meaning that the head was held over the shoulders in flight. The beak was stout and rounded, with toothlike bony projections edging each jawbone.

- **DESCRIBED BY** Hildegarde Howard; 1962.
- **HABITAT** Seashores.

pelican-like head

large wingspan of up to 20 ft (6 m)

rounded bill with small hook at end

Length 4 ft (1.2 m)	Weight Unknown	Diet Fish

wing feathers up to 5 ft (1.5 m) long

long wings compared to body size

large feet with three forward-facing clawed toes

QUATERNARY PERIOD

1.75 MILLION YEARS AGO—PRESENT

The Quaternary Period includes the Pleistocene and Holocene Epochs. The Pleistocene was a time when the world was in the grip of the Great Ice Age, with enormous ice sheets covering most of the northern hemisphere. Glaciers also formed in the high mountain regions of the world, including the Andes and the Himalayas. Over the next one and a half million years, the Earth passed through at least four ice ages. Between ice ages, the climate was warmer. The most recent ice age ended about 10,000 years ago at the beginning of the Holocene, and saw mass extinctions of mammal species.

QUATERNARY LIFE
Animals responded to the colder conditions of the Pleistocene by migrating toward equatorial regions (for example, lizards) or evolving furry coats (for example, mammoths and the woolly rhino, *Coelodonta*). Truly modern humans, *Homo sapiens*, evolved during the Pleistocene, along with other, less successful human species, such as *Homo neanderthalensis*.

• *large canine teeth*

• *powerful hind limbs*

CANINE CARNIVORES
Many species of dogs lived during the Pleistocene. *Canis dirus* (left), was much like a modern wolf, but heavier. It survived into the Holocene. Fossil remains show that dire wolves and saber-tooth cats often fought over territory and food.

4,600 mya	4,000 mya		3,000 mya

QUATERNARY LANDMASSES

During the Pleistocene Epoch, huge ice sheets covered most of North America, Europe, and northern Asia. There were land bridges from North America to Eastern Asia and between Australia and New Guinea. At the start of the Holocene, rising sea levels caused by melting ice sheets covered these land bridges. Africa and Australia continued to move northward to occupy their present positions (see map).

LITOPTERNS
The Pleistocene grasslands were home to herds of strange hoofed animals called litopterns. These, such as the camel-sized *Macrauchenia* (right), were grazing animals, adapted for life on open plains.

GIANT MARSUPIALS
Herds of giant, grazing marsupials in Australia, such as *Diprotodon* (left), became rarer as the climate grew drier with the continent's continuing drift northward. They survived into the Holocene, but may have been hunted to extinction by humans.

2,000 mya		1,000 mya		500 mya	250 mya	0

ON THE LAND

A t the start of the Pleistocene, the first epoch of the Quaternary Period, land animals exhibited far greater diversity than those of today. The northern grasslands were filled with many different species of deer, antelope, horse, and cattle. Camels ranged all over North America, and had spread into South America and Asia across the Panama and Bering land bridges, respectively. Large cats were found worldwide, most of them armed with long canine teeth. Foxes and dogs continued to evolve and spread, and bears lived throughout Europe, Africa, and North America.

The Pleistocene saw two major evolutionary changes. There were at least four ice ages during the epoch, during each of which most of Europe, northern Asia, and North America

became covered in ice sheets. Many mammals adapted to the freezing conditions by growing to larger sizes and evolving thick fur.

Another major evolutionary advance was the appearance of new human species. *Homo erectus* appeared about 1.6 million years ago, and *Homo sapiens neanderthalensis* about 100,000 years ago, at about the same time as true modern man, *Homo sapiens sapiens*. Neanderthals died out about 35,000 years ago.

The last ice age ended about 10,000 years ago, at the start of the Holocene. This coincided with mass extinctions of many mammal species, especially in the Americas and Australia. These extinctions may have been due to a combination of rapid climate change and the activities of the expanding human population.

Group Carnivora	Family Canidae	Time 9,000 ya

CANIS DIRUS
KAN-ISS DIE-RUS

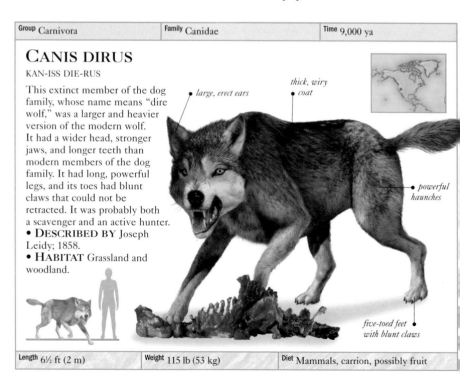

This extinct member of the dog family, whose name means "dire wolf," was a larger and heavier version of the modern wolf. It had a wider head, stronger jaws, and longer teeth than modern members of the dog family. It had long, powerful legs, and its toes had blunt claws that could not be retracted. It was probably both a scavenger and an active hunter.
• **DESCRIBED BY** Joseph Leidy; 1858.
• **HABITAT** Grassland and woodland.

thick, wiry coat

large, erect ears

powerful haunches

five-toed feet with blunt claws

Length 6½ ft (2 m)	Weight 115 lb (53 kg)	Diet Mammals, carrion, possibly fruit

Group Carnivora	Family Felidae	Time 5–1.5 mya

DINOFELIS

DIE-NOH-FEEL-IS

Dinofelis ("terrible cat") was a panther-sized cat. It had flattened canine teeth that were intermediate in length between those of the saber-tooth cats and those of biting cats, such as lions. It was probably an agile climber with long, strong legs, and sharp, retractable claws. Its tail was long and flexible and could be used to aid balance. The skull of *Dinofelis* was short and its eyes were forward-facing and positioned for binocular vision—essential for judging distances accurately when hunting or leaping. Its coat is likely to have had a pattern of camouflage similar to those of modern forest-dwelling cats.

• **DESCRIBED BY** Otto Zdansky; 1924.

• **HABITAT** Dense forest.

dappled coat for camouflage

flat head with forward-facing eyes

long canine teeth

retractable claws remained sharp

Length 7 ft (2.2 m)	Weight 350 lb (160 kg)	Diet Mammals

Group Carnivora	Family Felidae	Time 1 mya–4,000 ya

PANTHERA

PAN-THAIR-A

There were several subspecies of lion (*Panthera leo*) that are now extinct. *Panthera leo spelaea*, the European cave lion, was the largest cat ever to have lived. It is often seen in cave paintings. *Panthera leo atrox* lived in North America. Both subspecies killed prey by biting the neck with their canine teeth, and had sharp claws that could be retracted under a flap of skin.

• **DESCRIBED BY** Goldfuss; 1810.

• **HABITAT** Grassland.

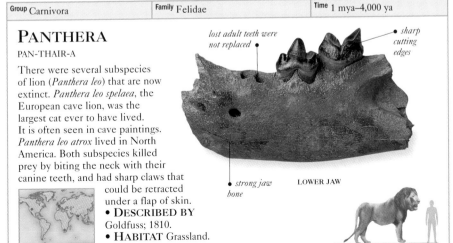

lost adult teeth were not replaced

sharp cutting edges

strong jaw bone

LOWER JAW

Length 11 ft (3.5 m)	Weight 520 lb (235 kg)	Diet Meat

Group Carnivora	Family Felidae	Time 2.5 mya–10,000 ya

SMILODON
SMILE-OH-DON

Smilodon was the cat popularly thought of as a saber-tooth tiger. Its sharp canine teeth were huge, and were serrated along their rear edges to increase their cutting ability. They were also oval in cross-section. This meant that they were strong while presenting minimum resistance when biting. Such long teeth meant that the cat's jaw had to open to an angle of more than 120 degrees to allow the teeth to be driven into its prey. However, it seems the teeth may have broken easily if they came into contact with bone. *Smilodon* therefore probably hunted by biting through an animal's neck. *Smilodon*'s arms and shoulders were very powerful, in order to produce a strong downward motion of the head. *Smilodon* appears to have hunted in packs, probably preying on large, slow, thick-skinned animals. Males may have had a mane similar to that of a modern lion.
- **DESCRIBED BY** Plieninger; 1846.
- **HABITAT** Grassy plains.

FOSSIL SKULL
Smilodon is very well known. More than 2,000 individuals have been excavated from the Rancho La Brea tar pits, a famous prehistoric predator trap, in Los Angeles, California.

jaw capable
of opening
120 degrees

short, sharp
molars

serrated rear
edge of "saber"
teeth

Length 5–8¼ ft (1.5–2.5 m)	Weight 710 lb (320 kg)	Diet Large mammals

large shoulder blades
provided attachment
sites for strong muscles

short, rounded skull

low-slung
hips

forward-facing eyes

extremely long
canines

front legs more
powerful than
hind legs

four toes on hind
feet with sharp,
retractable claws

short tail

Group Litopterna	Family Macraucheniidae	Time 7 mya—20,000 ya

MACRAUCHENIA

MAK-RAW-CHEN-EE-A

This curious animal (whose name means "great llama") had a number of camel-like features, such as its size, small head, and long neck. However, its three-toed feet were more like those of a rhinoceros. The unusual position of the nostrils, high on the skull between the eyes, suggests that this animal had a moderately long trunk. The legs were long and slim, but *Macrauchenia* was probably not a fast runner. The flexibility and strength of the ankles, however, suggest it was a relatively agile animal. The high-crowned cheek teeth, along with the presence of a trunk, indicate that *Macrauchenia* may have been a browser and a grazing animal.

- **DESCRIBED BY** Richard Owen; 1840.
- **HABITAT** Woodland.

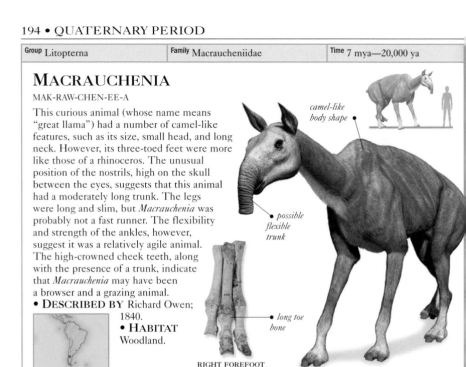

camel-like body shape

possible flexible trunk

long toe bone

RIGHT FOREFOOT BONES

Length 10 ft (3 m)	Weight 1,550 lb (700 kg)	Diet Plants

Group Rhinoceratoidea	Family Rhinocerotidae	Time 1.8 mya—10,000 ya

COELODONTA

SEEL-OH-DON-TA

The woolly rhinoceros, *Coelodonta* ("hollow tooth"), evolved to withstand cold conditions. Its fur was thick and shaggy, its body was massive with short legs, and its ears were small. It had a huge pair of horns on its snout, the front one of which grew to over 3 ft (1 m) in length in older males.

- **DESCRIBED BY** J.F. Blumenbach; 1799.
- **HABITAT** Tundra.

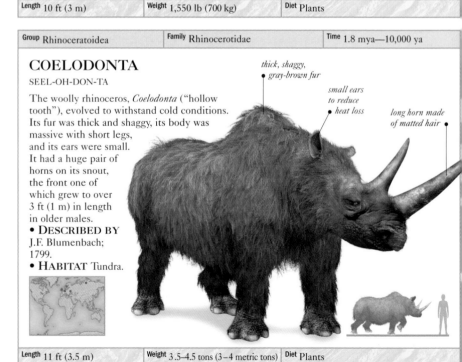

thick, shaggy, gray-brown fur

small ears to reduce heat loss

long horn made of matted hair

Length 11 ft (3.5 m)	Weight 3.5–4.5 tons (3–4 metric tons)	Diet Plants

Group Proboscidea	Family Elephantidae	Time 1.8 mya—9,000 ya

MAMMUTHUS IMPERATOR

MAM-UT-US IM-PER-A-TOR

The largest of all mammoth species, the imperial mammoth was probably the largest animal alive during the last ice age. Unlike the woolly mammoth, this mammoth was well-adapted to the warmer climates it lived in and did not have such thick fur. Besides its immense size, its most distinguishing feature was its tusks. These curled backward evenly and were up to 15 ft (4.8 m) long. They could weigh up to 185 lb (85 kg). Some paleontologists have suggested that the imperial mammoth is the same species as the Columbian mammoth, which was identical except for twisted tusks.
• **DESCRIBED BY** Joseph Leidy; 1870.
• **HABITAT** Plains.

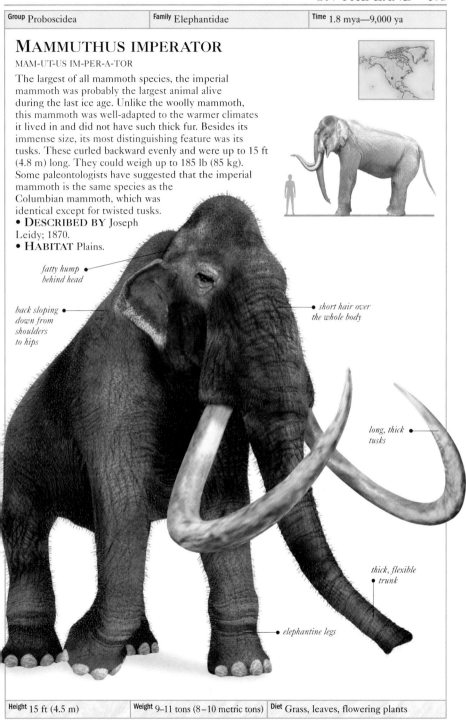

fatty hump behind head

back sloping down from shoulders to hips

short hair over the whole body

long, thick tusks

thick, flexible trunk

elephantine legs

Height 15 ft (4.5 m)	Weight 9–11 tons (8–10 metric tons)	Diet Grass, leaves, flowering plants

Group Proboscidea	Family Elephantidae	Time 120,000–6,000 ya

MAMMUTHUS PRIMIGENIUS

MAM-UT-US PRIM-EE-GEN-EE-US

Mammuthus primigenius, the woolly mammoth, was relatively small for a mammoth. It was adapted to living in the cold climates of northern tundras, with a thick coat of long dark hair overlying a downy undercoat. A thick layer of fat under the skin helped with insulation, and there was also a fatty hump behind the head used for food storage. Its ears were smaller than those of modern elephants, helping to reduce heat loss. The long, curved tusks appear to have been used to scrape away ice from the ground when feeding, as well as for protection and in dominance rituals. The woolly mammoth survived until relatively recent times, and paleontologists are therefore very familiar with its anatomy and appearance. Several well-preserved specimens have been found frozen in the permafrost of Siberia and Alaska, and cave paintings by early humans depict it clearly.

• **DESCRIBED BY** J.F. Blumenbach; 1799.
• **HABITAT** Frozen tundra.

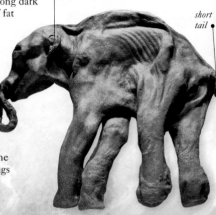

small, rounded ears

short tail

FROZEN REMAINS OF A
YOUNG MAMMOTH

long, curved tusks

Length 11½ ft (3.5 m)	Weight 3 tons (2.75 metric tons)	Diet Low-lying tundra vegetation

ridges for grinding
tough plant material

red hair color
due to chemical
reaction after
death

UPPER CHEEK TOOTH

PRESERVED HAIR

fatty hump used as
energy store

tall, domed head

hair up to 3 ft
(90 cm) long

Group Ratites	Family Dinornithidae	Time 2 mya–AD 1600

AEPYORNIS TITAN

APE-EE-OAR-NIS TIE-TAN

Aepyornis titan, commonly called the "elephant bird of Madagascar," was the heaviest bird species known to have existed. It was a wingless bird, with long, thick legs and feet ending in three widely spread toes. The thickness of the thigh bone indicates that *Aepyornis* was generally a slow-moving bird and could probably not run at high speeds. The small head had a toothless beak, and the only protection against predators was the bird's size and strength. Several eggs have been found fossilized in the mud of swampy areas near rivers.

• **DESCRIBED BY** Isidore Geoffroy-Saint-Hilaire; 1851.

• **HABITAT** Forests.

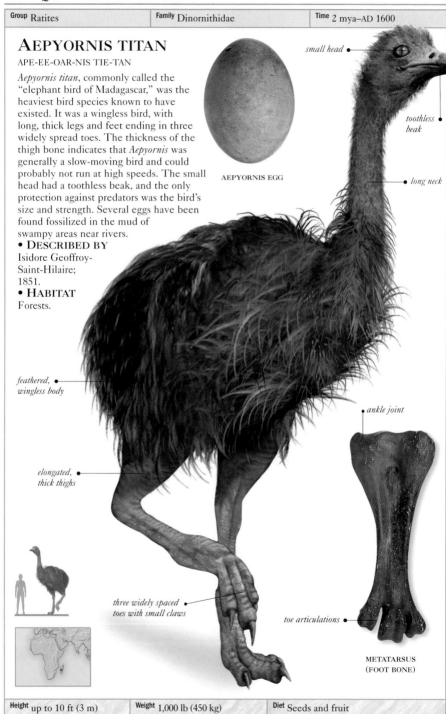

AEPYORNIS EGG

small head

toothless beak

long neck

feathered, wingless body

elongated, thick thighs

ankle joint

three widely spaced toes with small claws

toe articulations

METATARSUS (FOOT BONE)

Height up to 10 ft (3 m)	Weight 1,000 lb (450 kg)	Diet Seeds and fruit

Group Ratites	Family Dinornithidae	Time 2 mya–AD 1800

DINORNIS MAXIMUS
DIE-NOR-NIS MAX-EE-MUS

This was the tallest flightless bird ever to have existed, and was one of a dozen types of moa that survived in New Zealand until modern times. It was a slow-moving bird, with a bulky body, long, heavily built legs, and a long neck. Preserved feathers show that its plumage was mostly gray and fluffy. Its beak was short and sharp-edged, and was used to shear vegetation. Gizzard stones were used to help digest plant material. The numbers of *Dinornis* declined rapidly after the arrival of humans in New Zealand

short beak

heavy, wingless body

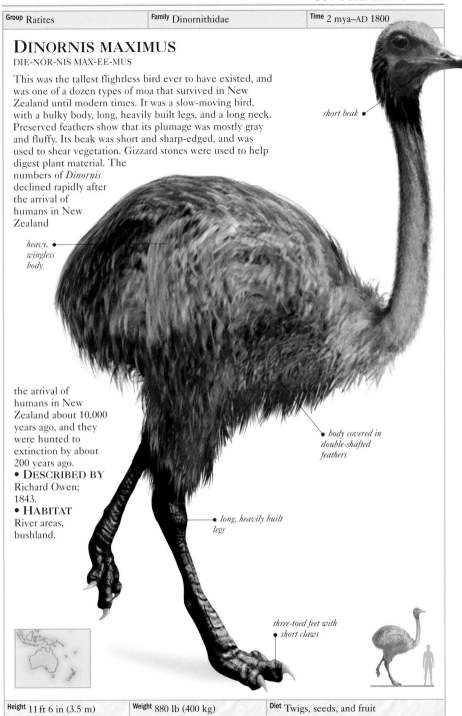

the arrival of humans in New Zealand about 10,000 years ago, and they were hunted to extinction by about 200 years ago.
• **DESCRIBED BY** Richard Owen; 1843.
• **HABITAT** River areas, bushland.

body covered in double-shafted feathers

long, heavily built legs

three-toed feet with short claws

Height 11 ft 6 in (3.5 m)	Weight 880 lb (400 kg)	Diet Twigs, seeds, and fruit

ADDITIONAL DINOSAURS

This section consists of a brief description of over 300 dinosaurs not included in the main body of the book. The entries are arranged alphabetically and each includes, wherever possible, its geological period and the country in which the principal fossil finds were made.

Abrictosaurus A small, early ornithopod dinosaur. May be a female *Heterodontosaurus*. Jurassic. South Africa.

Achelousaurus A ceratopsian that appears to be an intermediate form between *Einiosaurus* and *Pachyrhinosaurus*. Late Cretaceous. US.

Acrocanthosaurus An *Allosaurus*-like theropod with spines on the back supporting a sail or ridge. Early Cretaceous. US.

Adasaurus A lightly built dromaeosaur with long, sickle-shaped claws on each hind foot. Late Cretaceous. Mongolia.

Aegyptosaurus A sauropod known only from isolated bones. Late Cretaceous. North Africa.

Aeolosaurus A large sauropod. Late Cretaceous. Argentina.

Afrovenator A theropod. Cretaceous. Africa.

Agilisaurus A lightly built, herbivorous dinosaur. Possibly a hypsilophodontid. Mid-Jurassic. China.

Alamosaurus The last known sauropod and North America's only known titanosaur. Late Cretaceous. US.

Albertosaurus A *Tyrannosaurus*-like theropod. Late Cretaceous. North America.

Alectrosaurus A large theropod. Late Cretaceous. China and Mongolia.

Algoasaurus A small sauropod. Early Cretaceous. South Africa.

Alioramus A tyrannosaurid theropod with unusual crests running down the snout. Late Cretaceous. Mongolia.

Aliwalia An early theropod known only from a thigh bone. Late Triassic. South Africa.

Alocodon A small, ornithopod dinosaur known only from teeth. Late Jurassic. Portugal.

Altirhinus An iguanodontid with a beak on its snout and a spiked thumb on each hand. Early Cretaceous. Mongolia.

Alvarezsaurus A small, lightly built, theropod with an extremely long, thin, flat tail. Late Cretaceous. Argentina.

Alwalkeria A primitive theropod. Late Triassic. India.

Alxasaurus A large, primitive therizinosaur. Cretaceous. Mongolia.

Amargasaurus A sauropod with unusually long spines running along its back. Early Cretaceous. Argentina.

Ammosaurus A sauropod with large hands and thumb claws. Early Jurassic. US.

Ampelosaurus A large, titanosaurid sauropod dinosaur. Late Cretaceous. France.

Amtosaurus Possibly an ankylosaur, but identity and classification are doubtful. Late Cretaceous. Mongolia.

Amurosaurus A hadrosaur similar to *Lambeosaurus*. Not yet formally described. Cretaceous. Russia.

Amygdalon A large sauropod. Late Jurassic. Southern Argentina.

Anasazisaurus A hadrosaur known only from a skull. Late Cretaceous. US.

Anatosaurus Former name of *Edmontosaurus* and *Anatotitan*.

Anatotitan A hadrosaur. Late Cretaceous. US.

Anchiceratops A long-frilled ceratopsian. Late Cretaceous. Canada.

Andesaurus An enormous titanosaurid sauropod. Cretaceous. Argentina.

Angaturama A *Spinosaurus*-like theropod. Early Cretaceous. Brazil.

Anserimimus An *Ornithomimus*-like dinosaur. Late Cretaceous. Mongolia.

Antarctosaurus A very large, heavily built sauropod. Late Cretaceous. South America, India, and Russia.

Aragosaurus A huge sauropod. Early Cretaceous. Spain.

Aralosaurus A hadrosaur ornithopod known only from a skull. Late Cretaceous. Kazakhstan.

Araucanoraptor A theropod with a sickle claw on each foot. Late Cretaceous. Argentina.

Archaeornithoides A theropod with unserrated teeth. Late Cretaceous. Mongolia.

Archaeornithomimus An *Ornithomimus*-like dinosaur with primitive clawed fingers. Late Cretaceous. North America and China.

Achillobator A large deinonychosaur with a sickle-shaped claw on each foot. Late Cretaceous. Mongolia.

Argyrosaurus A large sauropod. Late Cretaceous. South America.

Arkansaurus A theropod, perhaps an ornithomimid. Late Cretaceous. US.

Arrhinoceratops A horned ceratopsian with a short nose horn. Late Cretaceous. Canada.

Arstanosaurus A hadrosaur with a flat head. Late Cretaceous. Kazakhstan.

Asiaceratops Primitive ceratopsian. Fragmentary remains only. Late Cretaceous. Russia.

Astrodon A brachiosaurid sauropod mainly known from teeth. Early Cretaceous. US.

Atlantosaurus A *Diplodocus*-like sauropod. Late Jurassic. US.

Atlascopcosaurus A *Hypsilophodon*-like dinosaur. Early Cretaceous. Australia.

Aublysodon Small *Tyrannosaurus*-like theropod with smooth teeth. Late Cretaceous. North America.

Austrosaurus A primitive sauropod dinosaur. Cretaceous. Australia.

Avaceratops A small ceratopsian dinosaur, possibly a juvenile. Late Cretaceous. US.

Avimimus An *Oviraptor*-like theropod. The most bird-like dinosaur known. May have had feathered wings. Late Cretaceous. Mongolia and China.

Avipes A small theropod or *Lagosuchus*-like dinosaur with birdlike feet. Triassic. Germany.

Azendohsaurus A primitive prosauropod. One of the earliest dinosaurs known. Fossil remains comprise teeth and part of jaw. Late Triassic. Morocco.

Bactrosaurus A duckbilled ornithopod with a flat head and high-spined vertebrae. Late Cretaceous. China and Uzbekstan.

Bagaceratops A very small ceratopsian. Late Cretaceous. Mongolia.

Bagaraatan A primitive theropod. Late Cretaceous. Mongolia.

Bahariasaurus A tetanuran theropod. Full classification uncertain. Late Cretaceous. Egypt and Niger.

Bambiraptor A juvenile theropod with a sickle-shaped claw on the second toe. Originally thought to be a juvenile *Velociraptor* or *Saurornitholestes*. Late Cretaceous. US.

Barsboldia A large duck-billed ornithopod. Late Cretaceous. Mongolia.

Becklespinax A theropod with long spines along its back. Early Cretaceous. England.

Beipiaosaurus A herbivorous theropod with primitive feathers. Cretaceous. China.

Bellusaurus A small sauropod. May be young of another genus. Jurassic. China.

Bienosaurus An early thyreophoran. Cretaceous. China.

Bihariosaurus An *Iguanodon*-like ornithopod known only from fossil teeth and bone fragments. Late Cretaceous. Romania.

Blikanosaurus Bulky sauropodomorph. Late Triassic. South Africa and Lesotho.

Borogovia A *Troodon*-like theropod with a sickle-shaped claw on each foot. Late Cretaceous. Mongolia.

Brachyceratops A ceratopsian with nose horn and two brow horns. Late Cretaceous. US.

Brachylophosaurus Primitive hadrosaurid ornithopod with a flat crest on the top of its head. Late Cretaceous. North America.

Breviceratops A ceratopsian. Late Cretaceous. Mongolia.

Brontosaurus Former name of *Apatosaurus*.

Bugenasaura An ornithopod. Late Cretaceous. US.

Byronosaurus A *Troodon*-like theropod. The first of its family with unserrated teeth. Late Cretaceous. Mongolia.

Caenagnathus A lightly built tetanuran theropod, originally thought to be a bird. Late Cretaceous. North America.

Callovosaurus An ornithopod. Mid-Jurassic. England.

Camelotia A large prosauropod. Late Triassic. England.

Campylodoniscus A long-necked titanosaur sauropod known from scanty remains. Late Cretaceous. Argentina.

Carcharodontosaurus A large carnosaur. Cretaceous. Africa.

Cathetosaurus A sauropod known only from scanty fossils. May be the same as *Camarasaurus*. Late Jurassic. US.

Cedarosaurus A *Brachiosaurus*-like sauropod. Late Cretaceous. US.

Ceratops A ceratopsian known from two horn cores and a single skull bone. Late Cretaceous. US.

Cetiosauriscus A diplodocid sauropod. Jurassic. England.

Changdusaurus A stegosaurid ornithischian. Jurassic. China

Chaoyoungosaurus A small, bipedal ornithischian, probably a pachycephalosaur. Late Jurassic. China.

Craspedodon An ornithischian known from teeth. Late Cretaceous. Belgium.

Chassternbergia A large nodosaur. May be the same genus as *Edmontonia*. Late Cretaceous. North America.

Chialingosaurus A stegosaur with two rows of small plates down its back. Mid-Jurassic. China.

Chilantaisaurus A large *Allosaurus*-like carnosaur. Late Cretaceous. China and Russia.

Chindesaurus A lightly built theropod. One of the earliest known dinosaurs. Late Triassic. North America.

Chirostenotes An oviraptorid theropod with a parrotlike head and toothless beak. Late Cretaceous. Canada.

Chubutisaurus An unusual sauropod with heavily hollowed vertebrae. Late Cretaceous. Argentina.

Chungkingosaurus A stegosaurid. Late Jurassic. China.

Claosaurus A primitive hadrosaur. Late Cretaceous. US.

Coloradisaurus A plateosaurid sauropod. Late Triassic. Argentina.

Conchoraptor A small oviraptorid theropod. Late Cretaceous. Mongolia.

Cryolophosaurus. A theropod. Early Jurassic. Antarctica.

Dacenturus An early stegosaurid with two rows of asymmetrical plates along its back and large spines along its tail. Late Jurassic. England, France, Portugal, and Spain.

Daspletosaurus A heavily built tyrannosaurid theropod with brow horns. Late Cretaceous. Canada.

Datousaurus A *Cetiosaurus*-like sauropod with a long neck and a very solid skull. Mid-Jurassic. China.

Deltadromeus A long-limbed and fast-running tetanuran theropod. Late Cretaceous. Morocco.

Diceratops A large, two-horned ceratopsian. Late Cretaceous. US.

Dicraeosaurus A diplodocid sauropod with a long neck and a whiplike tail. Jurassic. Tanzania.

Dinotyrannus A large tyrannosaurid. Late Cretaceous. North America.

Draconyx An *Iguanodon*-like dinosaur. Late Jurassic. Portugal.

Dracopelta A nodosaur. Late Jurassic. Portugal.

Dromiceiomimus An *Ornithmimus*-like dinosaur. Cretaceous. Canada.

Dryptosauroides A large theropod known from only a few vertebrae. Late Cretaceous. India.

Dryptosaurus The first theropod to be discovered in North America. Late Cretaceous. US.

Dystylosaurus A large, either brachiosaurid or diplodocid sauropod. Late Jurassic. US.

Echinodon A small, early ornithischian. Late Jurassic. England.

Edmarka A large theropod known only from a few bones. May be the same as *Torvosaurus*. Late Jurassic. US.

Efraasia A lightly built prosauropod that some paleontologists believe to be the same genus as *Sellosaurus*. Late Triassic. Germany.

Einiosaurus A ceratopsian. Cretaceous. US.

Elaphrosaurus A lightly built theropod. Previously classed as an ornithomimid, now usually considered a ceratosaur. Cretaceous. Tanzania.

Elmisaurus A theropod known from hands and feet. Late Cretaceous. Mongolia.

Elvisaurus Informal name for *Cryolophosaurus*.

Emausaurus An ornithischian with skin covered with cone-shaped and flat armor plates. Jurassic. Germany.

Enigmosaurus A large therizinosaur. Cretaceous. Mongolia.

Eobrontosaurus A diplodocid sauropod. Jurassic. US.

Eoceratops A primitive ceratopsian with a short frill and three short facial horns. Late Cretaceous. North America.

Eolambia An early hadrosaur-like ormithopod. Cretaceous. US.

Eotyrannus A theropod. Cretaceous. England.

Epachthosaurus A very large armored sauropod. Cretaceous. Argentina.

Epanterias A huge *Allosaurus*-like theropod known from fragmentary remains. Late Jurassic. US.

Erectopus A therizinosaur. Cretaceous. France and Egypt.

Erlikosaurus A large theropod. Late Cretaceous. Mongolia.

Eucoelophysis A theropod. Triassic. US.

Euhelopus A large sauropod with a very long neck and bulky body. Jurassic. China.

Euronychodon A tetanuran theropod. Cretaceous. Portugal and Uzbekistan.

Euskelosaurus A large prosauropod. Early Jurassic. Lesotho, South Africa, and Zimbabwe.

Eustreptospondylus A large tetanuran theropod with a primitive hip structure. Jurassic. England.

Fabrosaurus An ornithiscian that may be the same genus as *Lesothosaurus*. Early Jurassic. Lesotho and South Africa.

Frenguellisaurus A primitive carnivorous dinosaur that may be the same as *Herrerasaurus*. Triassic. Argentina.

Fulgurotherium An ornithopod. Very fragmentary remains. Early Cretaceous. Australia.

Futabasaurus A tyrannosaurid theropod. Cretaceous. Japan.

Garudimimus An *Ornithomimus*-like dinosaur. A small crest near its eyes distinguishes it from other similar dinosaurs. Cretaceous. Mongolia.

Gasparinisaura A very small ornithopod, probably a juvenile. Cretaceous. Argentina.

Genyodectes A large theropod. Cretaceous. Argentina.

Geranosaurus An ornithischian with fangs and a beak. Jurassic. South Africa.

Gilmoreosaurus A primitive ornithischian hadrosaur. Cretaceous. China.

Giraffatitan An enormous, lightly built, *Brachiosaurus*-like sauropod. Jurassic. Tanzania.

Gojirasaurus A large theropod. Late Triassic. US.

Gongbusaurus An ornithischian. Jurassic. China.

Gorgosaurus A tyrannosaurid, once thought to be *Albertosaurus*. Cretaceous. North America.

Goyocephale A pachycephalosaur with a thick-skull, flat-head, knobs and spikes on the skull, and large teeth. Cretaceous. Mongolia.

Gryposaurus A hadrosaurid. Cretaceous. Canada.

Haplocanthosaurus A sauropod. Late Jurassic. US.

Harpymimus A primitive *Ornithomimus*-like tetanuran. Early Cretaceous. Mongolia.

Hesperosaurus A primitive stegosaurid with a single row of rounded plates along its back. Originally called *Hesperisaurus*. Jurassic. US.

Histriasaurus A large sauropod that may have had a sail along the back. Early Cretaceous. Croatia.

Homalocephale A pachycephalosaur with a flat skull bordered by bony knobs. Late Cretaceous. Mongolia.

Hoplitosaurus An ankylosaur. Early Cretaceous. US.

Hulsanpes A small theropod known only from foot bones. Late Cretaceous. Mongolia

Hypacrosaurus A large hadrosaur with a small fin along its back. Cretaceous. North America.

Hypselosaurus A titanosaurid sauropod, whose eggs were the first dinosaur eggs discovered. Cretaceous. France and Spain.

Kritosaurus A hadrosaurid. Late Cretaceous. Argentina.

Labocania A tetanuran theropod. Late Cretaceous. Mexico.

Laosaurus An ornithischian known only from fragmentary fossils. Jurassic. North America.

Laplatasaurus An armored sauropod that had a very long neck with grooved vertebrae. Late Cretaceous. Argentina and Uruguay.

Leaellynasaura A small hypsilophodontid with large eyes. Early Cretaceous. Australia.

Leptoceratops A primitive ceratopsian from Cretaceous. North America.

Lexovisaurus A *Stegosaur*-like dinosaur with thin plates along its back and two long shoulder spikes. Jurassic. England and France.

Lophorhothon A hadrosaurid. Cretaceous. US.

Loricosaurus A sauropod known only from bony plates embedded in its skin. Cretaceous. Argentina.

Losillasaurus An enormous diplodocid sauropod. Jurassic and Cretaceous. Spain.

Lycorhinus An early ornithopod. Jurassic. South Africa.

Magyarosaurus A small titanosaurid sauropod. Late Cretaceous. Romania.

Majungatholus A large theropod with a small horn over the eyes. Late Cretaceous. Madagascar.

Malawisaurus A sauropod, perhaps with armored plates on the back. Early Cretaceous. Malawi.

Maleevus An ankylosaur known only from partial skull remains. Late Cretaceous. Mongolia.

Marshosaurus A large theropod. Late Jurassic. US.

Masiakasaurus A theropod. Cretaceous. Madagascar.

Megaraptor A theropod known from an incomplete skeleton (including a sickle-shaped claw, metatarsal, ulna, and finger bone). Cretaceous. Argentina.

Melanorosaurus A large sauropod. Late Triassic and Early Jurassic. Lesotho and South Africa.

Metriacanthosaurus A theropod with high dorsal spines. Cretaceous. England.

Microceratops A small ceratopsian similar to *Protoceratops*. Late Cretaceous. China and Mongolia.

Micropachycephalosaurus A tiny pachycephalosaur, one of the smallest dinosaurs known. Late Cretaceous. China.

Microraptor A birdlike theropod whose feet were adapted for climbing. The arms and legs were covered with feathers. Cretaceous. China.

Microvenator A bipedal herbivorous or carnivorous oviraptorid dinosaur. Early Cretaceous. China and US.

Mussaurus A *Plateosaurus*-like prosauropod known only from remains of hatchlings—the smallest dinosaur skeletons yet discovered. Triassic. Argentina.

Muttaburrasaurus An *Iguanodon*-like ornithopod. Early Cretaceous. Australia.

Mymoorapelta An ankylosaurid. Cretaceous. Australia.

Naashoibitosaurus A hadrosaur known only from a skull. May be a species of *Kritosaurus*. Cretaceous. US.

Nanosaurus A small ornithischian. Jurassic. North America.

Nanotyrannus A theropod known only from a small skull. Many paleontologists think *Nanatyrannus* is a juvenile *Tyrannosaurus*. Cretaceous. US.

Nanyangosaurus An ornithopod dinosaur. Cretaceous. China.

Nedcolbertia A small theropod known from three partial skeletons. Early Cretaceous. US.

Nemegtosaurus A sauropod known only from a skull. Late Cretaceous. Mongolia and China.

Neovenator An *Allosaurus*-like theropod, with a "puffinlike" skull profile. Early Cretaceous. England.

Ngexisaurus A lightly built theropod. Mid-Jurassic. China.

Nigersaurus A primitive diplodocid sauropod. Early Cretaceous. Niger.

Nipponosaurus A small hadrosaur with a bony head crest. Cretaceous. Russia.

Noasaurus A small theropod with a sickle-shaped claw on each foot, which was similar to that of dromaeosaurs, but had a unique retractor tendon. Cretaceous. Argentina.

Nothronychus The first therizinosaur found outside Asia. It may have been feathered. Cretaceous. US.

Notoceratops A ceratopsian known only from a jaw bone. Cretaceous. Argentina.

Nqwebasaurus A theropod with a very large claw on the first finger. Cretaceous. South Africa.

Nyasasaurus A very early prosauropod of uncertain classification. Triassic. East Africa.

Ohmdenosaurus A sauropod known from one complete shin bone. Early Jurassic. Germany.

Omeisaurus A large *Cetiosaurus*-like sauropod with a very long neck. Jurassic. China.

Opisthocoelicaudia A large, short-tailed *Camarasaurus*-like sauropod. Cretaceous. Mongolia.

Orcomimus An *Ornithomimus*-like theropod. Cretaceous. US.

Ornatotholus A pachycephalosaur once thought to be female *Stegoceras*. Cretaceous. North America.

Orodromeus An ornithopod found with unhatched eggs and young. Its young are thought to have been able to fend for themselves after hatching. Cretaceous. US.

Orthomerus A hadrosaur named for its straight thigh bone. Cretaceous. Netherlands.

Oshanosaurus An early sauropod. Early Jurassic. China.

Othnielia Small ornithopod with very long legs, five-fingered hands, long tail, and horny beak. Jurassic. US.

Ozraptor A tetanuran theropod with three-fingered hands and a stiff tail. Jurassic. Australia.

Pachyrhinosaurus A short-frilled ceratopsian that may have had a snout horn. Cretaceous. North America.

Panoplosaurus A nodosaurid ankylosaur with no tail club. Cretaceous. North America.

Paranthodon A stegosaur known from a jaw bone with teeth. Cretaceous. South Africa.

Parksosaurus An ornithopod. Cretaceous. North America.

Patagonykus A dromaeosaur or a primitive bird, with long legs and tail and short arms. Late Cretaceous. Argentina.

Patagosaurus A primitive *Cetiosaurus*-like sauropod. Mid-Jurassic. Argentina.

Pawpawsaurus A large nodosaur with armor over most of its body but no tail club. Cretaceous. US.

Pelecanimimus The first ornithomimosaur discovered in Europe. It had about 220 teeth, more than any other known theropod, and fossil remains show evidence of feathers. Cretaceous. Spain.

Pelorosaurus A sauropod known from incomplete skeletons and fossilized skin impressions. Early Cretaceous. England and France.

Phyllodon A small *Hypsilophodon*-like dinosaur. Jurassic. Portugal.

Pinacosaurus An ankylosaur. Cretaceous. Mongolia.

Pisanosaurus A small, possibly ornithopod, early ornithischian known only from fragmentary fossils. Late Triassic. Argentina.

Piveteausaurus A theropod of indeterminate size known from scanty remains. Jurassic. France.

Planicoxa Recently discovered ornithopod. Cretaceous. US.

Pleurocoelus A small *Brachiosaurus*-like sauropod, whose vertebrae had deep hollows. Cretaceous. US.

Poekilopleuron A *Megalosaurus*-like theropod. Jurassic. France.

Polacanthus A primitive ankylosaur with spines. Cretaceous. England.

Prenocephale A *Stegoceras*-like pachycephalosaur. Cretaceous. Mongolia and North America.

Probactrosaurus An *Iguanodon*-like ornithopod dinosaur. Early Cretaceous. China.

Proceratosaurus A crested theropod. Jurassic. England.

Prosaurolophus A hadrosaur. Late Cretaceous. North America.

Protarchaeopteryx A birdlike, non-flying theropod with feathers on the arms, most of the body, and on the short tail. Early Cretaceous. China.

Protoavis A primitive bird or theropod dinosaur. Its partly toothless jaw and breastbone were birdlike. Late Triassic. US.

Protohadros The oldest known hadrosaur. Late Cretaceous. US.

Pyroraptor A *Deinonychus*-like dinosaur. May be the same as *Variraptor*. Late Cretaceous. France.

Qantassaurus A kangaroo-sized ornithopod. Cretaceous. Australia.

Quaesitosaurus Large, diplodocid sauropod known only from a partial skull. Cretaceous. Mongolia.

Quilmesaurus A medium-sized theropod. Late Cretaceous. Argentina.

Rahonavis A dinosaur or primitive bird with sickle-shaped toe claws and a long, bony tail. Late Cretaceous. Madagascar.

Rapetosaurus A recently discovered *Titanosaurus*-like sauropod. Late Cretaceous. Madagascar.

Rebbachisaurus A diplodocid sauropod dinosaur that may have had a sail on its back. Cretaceous. Morocco and Niger.

Revueltosaurus A poorly known ornithischian. Late Triassic. US.

Rhabdodon An *Iguanodon*-like ornithopod. Late Cretaceous. Austria, France, Romania, and Spain.

Rhoetosaurus A *Cetiosaurus*-like sauropod. Mid-Jurassic. Australia.

Ricardoestesia A small theropod. Cretaceous. North America.

Rioarribasaurus A small theropod. Late Triassic. US.

Riojasaurus A heavily built prosauropod. Late Triassic and Early Jurassic. Argentina.

Ruehleia A recently discovered primitive *Plateosaurus*-like prosauropod. Triassic. Germany.

Saichania An ankylosaur with a clubbed-tail, and bony spikes and knobs running along its sides. Both body armor and belly armor have been found. Cretaceous. Mongolia.

Saltopus A tiny, primitive theropod. Late Triassic. Scotland.

Santanaraptor A theropod known from partial skeleton and skin impressions. Early Cretaceous. Brazil.

Sarcolestes An early nodosaur or ankylosaur known only from a partial lower jaw. Jurassic. England.

Saurophaganax A large carnosaur. May be *Allosaurus*. Jurassic. US.

Sauroposeidon A *Brachiosaurus*-like sauropod. Cretaceous. US.

Saurornitholestes A *Velociraptor*-like theropod. Cretaceous. Canada.

Scipionyx A theropod, perhaps a maniraptor, known from a single hatchling that includes soft tissues. Cretaceous. US.

Secernosaurus A hadrosaur, the first to be found in South America. Cretaceous. Argentina.

Segisaurus A goose-sized, birdlike theropod whose collar bone was similar in structure to that of true birds. Jurassic. US.

Segnosaurus A strange theropod of uncertain size. May have been a plant eater. Cretaceous. Mongolia.

Shamosaurus An ankylosaur. Cretaceous. Mongolia.

Shanshanosaurus A lightly built theropod. Cretaceous. China.

Shantungosaurus The largest known hadrosaur. Late Cretaceous. China.

Shanxia An ankylosaur. Late Cretaceous. China.

Siamosaurus A large, sail-backed, *Spinosaurus*-like theropod. Cretaceous. Thailand.

Siamotyrannus A tyrannosaurid theropod. Cretaceous. Thailand.

Silvisaurus A nodosaur with a relatively long neck, and spines jutting out from the back, and perhaps the tail. Cretaceous. US.

Sinornithosaurus A recently found dromaeosaurid. The fossil had traces of downy fibres on its skin. Jurassic. China.

Sinosauropteryx A feathered theropod. Jurassic. China.

Sinraptor A large theropod. Late Jurassic. China.

Sonorasaurus A *Brachiosaurus*-like sauropod. Cretaceous. US.

Stenopelix A ceratopsian, perhaps similar to *Psittacosaurus*, known from hip and leg bones. Early Cretaceous. Germany.

Stokesosaurus A theropod that may have been the earliest tyrannosaurid. Jurassic. US.

Struthiosaurus An ankylosaur. Late Cretaceous. Europe.

Stygimoloch A pachycephalosaur with strange spikes and bumps on the skull. Cretaceous. US.

Stygivenator A tyrannosaurid theropod. Cretaceous. US.

Supersaurus A diplodocid sauropod. One of the longest dinosaurs yet discovered. Late Jurassic. US.

Syntarsus A lightly built theropod with fused foot bones. Triassic. South Africa, US, and Zimbabwe.

Szechuanosaurus An *Allosaurus*-like theropod. Jurassic. China.

Tangvayosaurus A titanosaurid sauropod. Cretaceous. Asia.

Talarurus An ankylosaur. Cretaceous. Mongolia.

Tarchia An ankylosaur with a very large tail club and large braincase. Cretaceous. Mongolia.

Telmatosaurus A hadrosaur. Cretaceous. France, Romania, and Spain.

Tendaguria A recently discovered sauropod. Jurassic. Tanzania.

Tenontosaurus A large ornithopod with relatively long arms. Cretaceous. North America.

Texasetes An ankylosaur. Cretaceous. US.

Teyuwasu A recently discovered theropod. Known from leg bones. Triassic. Brazil.

Thescelosaurus An ornithopod dinosaur, whose fossilized four-chambered heart was found. Cretaceous. North America.

Timimus A theropod known from leg bones. Cretaceous. Australia.

Torvosaurus A large theropod. Late Jurassic. US.

Tsintaosaurus A poorly known hadrosaur that may have had a bony crest on the head. Cretaceous. China.

Tylocephale A small pachycephalosaur known only from incomplete skull. Cretaceous. Mongolia.

Ultrasaurus A sauropod. Cretaceous. South Korea.

Unenlagia A birdlike theropod. Cretaceous. Argentina.

Utahraptor A large dromaeosaurid. Cretaceous. US.

Valdoraptor A tetanuran theropod known from footbones. Early Cretaceous. England.

Variraptor A recently discovered dromaeosaurid theropod. Late Cretaceous. France.

Venenosaurus A titanosaurid sauropod. Cretaceous. US.

Walkeria A primitive theropod. Late Triassic. India.

Wannanosaurus A tiny, primitive pachycephalosaur. Cretaceous. China.

Wuerhosaurus A stegosaur with smaller plates than *Stegosaurus*. Early Cretaceous. Mongolia.

Xenotarsosaurus A theropod known from a few vertebrae and hind-leg bones. Cretaceous. Argentina.

Xiaosaurus A small ornithischian. Jurassic. China.

Xuanhanosaurus A tetanuran theropod. Mid-Jurassic. China.

Xuanhuasaurus An ornithischian. Cretaceous. China.

Yandusaurus Ornithopod ornithischian. Jurassic. China.

Yaverlandia An early pachycephalosaur. Cretaceous. England.

Yunnanosaurus A large prosauropod, the only one known with self-sharpening, chisel-shaped teeth. Jurassic. China.

Zephyrosaurus A *Hypsilophodon*-like dinosaur known from a partial skull and vertebrae. Cretaceous. US.

Zigongosaurus Probably the same dinosaur as *Omeisaurus*. Jurassic. China.

Zizhongosaurus A primitive sauropod. Jurassic. China.

Zuniceratops An early ceratopsian with brow horns. Cretaceous. US.

GLOSSARY

This glossary is an easy-reference guide to the technical terms that are used in this book. It focuses mainly on the terms used to describe different groups of dinosaurs and other forms of prehistoric life. It also includes scientific names used to describe anatomical features. If you cannot find the term you are looking for here, check the general index, since the information you require may be found elsewhere in the book. Words in bold type within the entries have their own glossary entry.

• ACANTHODIANS
The earliest jawed vertebrates. Primitive fish, also known as spiny sharks, that lived from the Ordovician to the Carboniferous.

• ACETABULUM
The hip socket.

• AËTOSAURS
A group of early thecodonts that superficially resembled crocodiles, with bulky bodies and leaf-shaped teeth.

• AGNATHANS
"Jawless fish"—primitive vertebrates that flourished in Early Paleozoic times.

• AIRFOIL
The curved surface of a wing that aids flight by creating an upward force.

• ALGAE
Primitive plants and plantlike organisms.

• ALLOSAURS
Large, fairly primitive tetanuran (stiff-tailed) theropods.

• AMMONITES
Extinct, predatory, marine invertebrates (cephalopods). These animals had a shell (usually spiral-coiled) containing air-filled chambers; the animal lived only in the outer chamber.

• AMNIOTES
Animals whose eggs contain an amnion, a membrane that surrounds the embryo. Mammals, birds, and reptiles are amniotes.

• AMPHIBIANS
Vertebrates whose young live in the water (breathing through gills), but usually live on land as adults (breathing with lungs). The living amphibians include newts, salamanders, frogs, and toads.

• ANAPSIDS
Primitive reptiles with no hole in the skull behind the eye. Anapsids include the turtles and their extinct kin.

• ANCHIASAURIDS
A group of small, lightly built early sauropodomorphs of the Late Triassic Period.

• ANGIOSPERMS
Flowering plants, which produce seeds enclosed in fruit (an ovary).

• ANKYLOSAURS
A family of heavily armored, plant-eating, quadrupedal ornithischian dinosaurs that lived from the Mid-Jurassic to the Late Cretaceous Period.

• ARBOREAL
An organism that spends most of its life in trees, off the ground.

• ARCHAEOCYTES
Primitive whales that lived during the Eocene Epoch. Some had hind limbs.

• ARCHOSAURS
A major group of reptiles that includes the crocodilians, pterosaurs, dinosaurs, and aves (birds).

• ARTHROPODS
A group of invertebrates with exoskeletons made of chitin, segmented bodies, and jointed limbs. Insects, spiders and scorpions, trilobites, and crustaceans are members of this group.

• ARTIODACTYLS
Ungulates (hoofed mammals) with an even number of toes. Pigs, camels, deer, giraffes, and cattle are modern animals in this group.

• AVES
The scientific name for birds.

• BALTICA
An ancient continent of the Paleozoic Era.

• BIPEDAL
Walking on the hind limbs rather than on all four legs. See also Quadrupedal.

• BIVALVES
Aquatic mollusks enclosed by a two-part, hinged shell.

• BRACHIOPODS
Marine invertebrates with two joined, valved shells.

• BRACHIOSAURIDS
A group of huge sauropods with spoon-shaped teeth and long forelimbs. They lived in the Late Jurassic and Early Cretaceous Periods.

• BRAINCASE
The bones of the skull that contain and protect the brain.

• BRONTOTHERES
Also known as titanotheres. An extinct family of large, rhinoceros-like mammals.

• BROWSER
An animal that eats tall foliage (leaves, trees, or shrubs).

• CAMARASAURIDS
A group of relatively short-necked sauropods of the Jurassic and Cretaceous Periods.

• CARINATES
A group of birds with deep-keeled breastbones.

• **CARNIVORA**
A group of sharp-toothed, meat-eating mammals, including cats and dogs.

• **CARNOSAUR**
A group of large theropods that lived during the Jurassic and Cretaceous Periods.

• **CENTROSAURINES**
A group of rhinoceros-like **ceratopsian** dinosaurs—most had long horns on the snout and a short neck frill.

• **CEPHALOPODS**
Mollusks with tentacles surrounding a large head. These soft-bodied invertebrates include squid, octopuses, cuttlefish, and **ammonites**.

• **CERAPODS**
A group of **ornithischian** dinosaurs that included the **ornithopods** and the **marginocephalians**.

• **CERATOPSIANS**
A group of plant-eating **ornithischian** dinosaurs with beaks and bony head frills along the back of the skull.

• **CERATOSAURS**
A major group of **theropod** dinosaurs—those in which the three hip bones (**ilium, ischium,** and **pubis**) are fused.

• **CETACEANS**
Marine mammals with a streamlined body and flippers for limbs. The group includes whales and dolphins.

• **CETIOSAURIDS**
A group of early **sauropods** of the Jurassic Period.

• **CHORISTODERES**
A group of crocodile-like **diapsid** reptiles, also known as champsosaurs.

• **CLADE**
A grouping of animals (or other organisms) that share anatomical features derived from the same ancestor.

• **COELUROSAURS**
A group of **tetanuran**

theropods that includes the **maniraptorans, ornithomimids,** and **tyrannosaurids.**

• **COLD-BLOODED**
See **ectotherms.**

• **CONDYLARTHS**
A group of herbivorous mammals that arose in the Early Tertiary. Some had clawed feet, others had blunt hooves.

• **CONFUCIORNITHIDS**
A family of early birds similar to *Confuciornis.*

• **CREODONTS**
A group of meat-eating mammals with clawed feet, a small brain, large jaws, and many sharp teeth that were the dominant carnivorous mammals during the Tertiary Period.

• **CROCODILIANS**
A group of **archosaurs** that includes alligators, crocodiles, and gavials. They evolved during the Late Triassic Period.

• **CRINOIDS**
Plant-shaped echinoderms (sea lilies).

• **CRUSTACEANS**
A class of invertebrates with a hard **exoskeleton**, jointed legs, and a bilaterally symmetrical segmented body.

• **CYCADS**
Primitive seed plants that dominated Jurassic habitats. They are palmlike trees, with separate male and female plants.

• **CYNODONTS**
A group of herbivorous and carnivorous **synapsids** that appeared late in the Permian Period and were the ancestors of mammals.

• **DEINONYCHOSAURS**
A group of advanced **theropod** dinosaurs with a long, sharp, sickle-shaped claw on the second toe of each hind foot.

• **DIAPSIDS**
A **clade** of animals, distinguished by two temporal **fenestrae**, that includes **archosaurs** and **lepidosaurs.**

• **DICYNODONTS**
Piglike, herbivorous **therapsids** with two large tusks in the upper jaw.

• **DIMORPHISM**
Having two forms—for example, sexual dimorphism between males and females of the same species.

• **DINOCEPHALIANS**
Late Permian **therapsids**. Some were meat-eating, others were plant-eating or omnivorous.

• **DINOSAURS**
A **clade** of reptiles, partly distinguished by a largely to fully open **acetabulum** and erect limbs. They were wholly terrestrial. Only one major group of dinosaurs, **aves** (birds), survived after the end of the Cretaceous.

• **DIPLODOCIDS**
A family of huge sauropods characterized by a small head with peglike teeth and nostrils opening at the top of the head.

• **DOCODONTS**
A group of primitive mammals.

• **DROMAEOSAURIDS**
A family of small, fast **theropods**, with large, retractable, sickle-shaped toe claws and large eyes.

• **ECHINODERMS**
Salt-water invertebrates whose living members have five arms or divisions of the body (or multiples of five).

• **ECTOTHERMS**
Animals, often called "cold-blooded," whose internal temperature changes with the surrounding environment.

• **ELASMOSAURS**
A family of long-necked **plesiosaurs.**

• **ENANTIORNITHES**
A group of toothless birds that lived during the Cretaceous. Their shoulder blade (scapula) and coracoid (a small bone connected to the scapula) are oriented in the opposite way of that of modern birds.

• **ENDOTHERMS**
Animals, often called "warm-blooded," that maintain a relatively constant internal temperature by generating their own body heat.

• **EUORNITHES**
Modern "true" birds.

• **EOSUCHIANS**
A now-redundant term used to describe lizardlike **diapsids** that probably gave rise to lizards and snakes.

• **EURASIA**
The continent formed by the combined land masses of Europe and Asia.

• **EURYAPSIDS**
A group of extinct marine reptiles with a single opening in the skull behind the eye socket. They included **plesiosaurs, nothosaurs, placodonts**, and **ichthyosaurs**.

• **EVOLUTION**
The theoretical process by which the gene pool of a population changes in response to environmental pressures, natural selection, and genetic mutations.

• **EXOSKELETON**
A tough, outer body covering made of chitin (a type of protein) or calcium carbonate.

• **FAMILY**
A group of related or similar organisms. A family contains one or more **genera**.

• **FEMUR**
The thigh bone.

• **FENESTRA (pl. fenestrae)**
A natural, windowlike hole or opening in a bone. The skull has many fenestrae.

• **FIBULA**
The smaller of the two bones of the lower leg.

• **FOSSIL**
Mineralized skeletons or casts of ancient plants and animals (or their traces, such as footprints).

• **FURCULA**
The "wishbone" in birds.

• **GASTRALIA**
Thin ribs in the belly area not attached to the backbone.

• **GASTROPODS**
A class of **mollusks** with a suckerlike foot and often a spiral shell.

• **GENUS (pl. genera)**
A group of related or similar organisms. A genus contains one or more **species**. A group of similar genera comprise a **family**.

• **GONDWANA**
The southern supercontinent formed after the breakup of the supercontinent **Pangaea**. It included present-day South America, Africa, India, Australia, and Antarctica.

• **GRACILE**
Small and slender. Some species have both gracile and **robust** forms, possibly representing differences between males and females.

• **GRAPTOLITE**
Extinct, tiny marine colonial animals, with a soft body and a hard outer covering.

• **GRAZER**
An animal that eats low-lying vegetation, such as grasses.

• **GYMNOSPERMS**
Seed-bearing plants that do not produce flowers.

• **HADROSAURS**
A group of "duckbilled" Cretaceous **quadrupedal ornithopods**.

• **HERBIVORE**
An animal that eats plants.

• **HESPERORNITHIFORMS**
A family of early birds similar to *Hesperornis*.

• **HOMEOTHERMIC**
An animal that keeps a fairly constant body temperature.

• **HORSETAIL**
A primitive, spore-bearing plant with rhizomes that was common during the Paleozoic and Mesozoic Eras.

• **HYPSILPHODONTIDS**
A group of small, herbivorous **ornithopod ornithischians** that were widespread in the Jurassic and Cretaceous Periods.

• **IAPETUS OCEAN**
The precursor of the Atlantic Ocean, between the ancient continents of **Laurentia** and **Baltica**.

• **ICHTHYORNITHIFORMS**
A family of early birds similar to *Ichthyornis*.

• **IGUANODONTIDS**
A group of herbivorous **ornithopod ornithischians** that were widespread in the Cretaceous Period.

• **ILIUM**
One of the three (paired) bones of the pelvis.

• **INSECTIVORE**
An organism (animal or plant) that eats insects.

• **INVERTEBRATES**
Animals without a backbone.

• **ISCHIUM**
One of the three (paired) bones of the pelvis.

• **JUVENILE**
A young or immature individual.

• **K-T EXTINCTION**
The mass extinction that occurred at the boundary of the Cretaceous and Tertiary Periods.

• **LAGOMORPHS**
A group of mammals that became widespread in the Tertiary Period and includes modern rabbits and hares.

• **LAGOSUCHIANS**
A group of early **archosaurs** that were probably ancestors of the **dinosaurs**.

- **LAURASIA**
The northern supercontinent formed after the breakup of **Pangaea.**
- **LAURENTIA**
An ancient continent of the Paleozoic Era.
- **LEPIDOSAURS**
The group of reptiles that includes snakes and lizards.
- **LEPOSPONDYLS**
Small, extinct **amphibians** that resembled salamanders or snakes. They lived through the Carboniferous and Permian Periods.
- **LITOPTERNS**
A group of extinct hoofed mammals that resembled camels and horses.
- **LOBE-FINNED FISH**
A group of fish whose fins are supported on fleshy lobes. Lobe-finned fish appeared during the Silurian Period.
- **LYCOPODS**
A group of **lycopsid** plants, also known as club mosses. They were at their peak in the Carboniferous Period.
- **LYCOPSIDS**
Primitive **vascular** plants that evolved during the Devonian Period.
- **MANIRAPTORANS**
A group of advanced **theropods** with birdlike characteristics. It included **dromaeosaurs, oviraptorids, troodontids, therizinosaurs,** and **aves.**
- **MARGINOCEPHALIANS**
A group of **ornithischian** dinosaurs with a bony frill or shelf on the back of the skull. This group includes the **ceratopsians** and **pachycephalosaurs.**
- **MARSUPIALS**
Mammals, including modern-day kangaroos, that give birth to small, undeveloped young that grow and mature in a pouch on the mother's abdomen.

- **MASTODONS**
An extinct group of mammals closely related to elephants.
- **MEGALOSAURS**
A group of large **theropods,** less advanced than **allosaurs.**
- **MESOSAURS**
Extinct, lizardlike aquatic reptiles.
- **MOLLUSKS**
A group of invertebrates including **gastropods** and **cephalopods.**
- **MONOTREMES**
Primitive egg-laying mammals. The platypus and echidnas are the only living representatives of this group.
- **MOSASAURS**
Large marine reptiles that lived during the Cretaceous Period.
- **MULTITUBERCULATES**
Rodentlike mammals of the Late Jurassic to Early Tertiary Periods. All were very small.
- **MYRIAPODS**
A group of many-legged **arthropods** that includes centipedes and millipedes.
- **NAUTILOIDS**
Primitive **cephalopods** with thick shells. Only a single genus survives.
- **NEOGNATHAE**
A group of birds that evolved during the Late Cretaceous. They include most flying birds, plus swimming and diving birds such as modern penguins.
- **NEORNITHES**
The **clade** of modern birds that have feathers, a beak covered in horn, and a four-chambered heart.
- **NODOSAURS**
A group of **quadrupedal ornithiscian** armored dinosaurs.
- **NOTHOSAURS**
Extinct marine reptiles with four paddlelike limbs that lived during the Triassic Period.

- **ODONTORNITHES**
A group of Cretaceous birds with conical teeth in both jaws.
- **ORBIT**
The eye socket.
- **ORNITHISCHIANS**
"Bird-hipped" dinosaurs—one of the two main dinosaur groups. They were **herbivores** and had hooflike claws. See also **Saurischians.**
- **ORNITHODIRANS**
The **archosaur clade** that includes **dinosaurs,** their early ancestors the **lagosuchians,** and **pterosaurs.**
- **ORNITHOMIMIDS**
A group of **theropod** dinosaurs whose name means "bird-mimic." They outwardly resembled flightless birds.
- **ORNITHOPODS**
A group of **ornithischian dinosaurs** that have no hole in the outer, lower jaw, and a long pubis that extends farther forward than the **ilium.** They were beaked, mostly **bipedal herbivores.**
- **ORNITHOTHORACES**
A clade of birds that had evolved the alula—a feather that directs air over the upper surface of the wing.
- **OVIPAROUS**
A term used to describe animals that hatch from eggs.
- **OVIRAPTORIDS**
A family of toothless **maniraptoran theropods.**
- **PACHYCEPHALOSAURS**
A group of **bipedal ornithischian** dinosaurs with immensely thick skulls.
- **PALEONTOLOGY**
The branch of biology that studies the forms of life that existed in former geologic periods.
- **PALEONTOLOGIST**
A scientist who studies paleontology.

• **PANGAEA**
A supercontinent consisting of all of Earth's landmasses that formed at the end of the Paleozoic Era.

• **PAREIASAURS**
A group of early **anapsid** reptiles with massive, heavy bodies and sturdy limbs. Close relatives of turtles.

• **PELYCOSAURS**
The earliest **synapsids**, pelycosaurs evolved during the Carboniferous and became extinct during the Permian Period.

• **PERMINERALIZATION**
The process in which minerals are deposited within the fabric of a bony fossil.

• **PERISSODACTYLS**
A group of hoofed mammals that includes horses, rhinoceroses, and tapirs.

• **PETRIFICATION**
The process by which organic tissue turns to stone.

• **PHYTOSAURS**
A group of extinct semiaquatic **archosaurs** superficially resembling crocodiles.

• **PLACENTALS**
Mammals whose unborn young are nourished by an organ called a placenta.

• **PLACODERMS**
A class of jawed fish protected by armor plates.

• **PLACODONTS**
Aquatic reptiles that lived in shallow seas during the Triassic, becoming extinct at the end of the period. Many had turtlelike shells.

• **PLESIOSAURS**
Large marine reptiles of the Mesozoic Era with pairs of flipper-shaped limbs.

• **PLIOSAURS**
Large, short-necked **plesiosaurs.**

• **PREDATOR**
An animal that preys on other animals for food.

• **PREHENSILE**
Able to grasp something by wrapping around it. An animal with a prehensile tail is able to grasp branches with it, for example.

• **PRIMITIVE**
Having characteristics similar to those of earlier forms.

• **PROBOSCIDEANS**
A group of mammals with trunks that includes modern elephants as well as the now-extinct mammoths.

• **PROCOLOPHONIDS**
A group of early herbivorous **Anapsids** of the Triassic Period.

• **PROSAUROPODS**
A group of early sauropodomorph dinosaurs that lived in the Late Triassic and Early Jurassic Periods.

• **PROTOZOANS**
General term for single-celled animals.

• **PSITTACOSAURS**
A group of **bipedal,** herbivorous **ceratopsians** with a parrotlike beak.

• **PTERODACTYLOIDS**
Short-tailed **pterosaurs** that replaced earlier long-tailed forms.

• **PTEROSAURS**
Flying **archosaurs** closely related to the dinosaurs.

• **PUBIS**
A bone that is part of the pelvic girdle. It points downward and slightly toward the front in **saurischians** and downward and toward the tail in **ornithischians.**

• **PYGOSTYLE**
The short tailbone of a bird, formed from fused tail **vertebrae.**

• **QUADRUPEDAL**
Walking on four legs. See also **Bipedal.**

• **RADIUS**
One of the two lower arm bones.

• **RATITES**
Flightless birds.

• **REPTILES**
The common name for a group of animals characterized by having scales (or modified scales), being cold-blooded, and laying eggs with shells.

• **RHYNCHOSAURS**
Herbivorous, land-dwelling **diapsid** reptiles from the Late Triassic Period.

• **ROBUST**
Large form of a species. See also **Gracile.**

• **SACRUM**
The **vertebrae** of the lower back fused to the pelvis.

• **SARCOPTERYGIANS**
A group of bony fish with fleshy fins, including lungfish, coelacanths, and many extinct forms.

• **SAURISCHIANS**
"Lizard-hipped" dinosaurs—one of the two main dinosaur groups. Saurischians are divided into the **theropods** and **sauropodomorphs.** See also **Ornithischians.**

• **SAUROPODOMORPHS**
Large, four-legged, long-necked herbivorous **saurischian** dinosaurs. They are commonly divided into the **prosauropods** and the **sauropods.**

• **SAUROPODS**
Huge, **quadrupedal,** herbivorous dinosaurs with long necks, small heads, and long tails.

• **SAUROPTERYGIANS**
An group of extinct aquatic reptiles from the Mesozoic Era. They include **plesiosaurs, nothosaurs,** and **placodonts.**

• **SCLEROTIC RING**
A ring of bones that supports the structure of the eye.

• **SCUTE**
A bony plate with a horny outer covering embedded in the skin.

- **SEED FERNS**
Primitive seed plants (pteridosperms) that grew in swampy areas through the Paleozoic and Mesozoic Eras.
- **SIRENIANS**
A group of mammals that includes modern sea cows (manatees).
- **SPECIES**
In Linnaean classification, the level below a **genus**. Only individuals within the same species can breed and produce viable, fertile young.
- **STEGOSAURS**
Four-legged **ornithischian** dinosaurs with bony plates and/or spikes down the neck, back, and tail.
- **STERNUM**
The breastbone.
- **SYNAPSIDS**
A group of **tetrapod vertebrates** distinguished by having a skull with a low opening behind the eyes. Synapsids include the **mammals, pelycosaurs**, and many other Permian and Triassic forms.
- **TARSAL**
Ankle bone.
- **TELEOSTS**
A group of advanced bony fish.
- **TEMNOSPONDYLS**
A group of early **tetrapods**.
- **TETANURANS**
One of the major groups of **theropod** dinosaurs. The rear part of the tails of tetanurans were stiffened by interlocking bony ligaments on the **vertebrae**.
- **TETHYS SEA**
A shallow sea that existed during the early Mesozoic Era, separating the northern landmass of **Laurasia** from **Gondwana** in the south.
- **TETRAPODS**
Four-legged **vertebrates** and the vertebrates descended from them.

- **THALATTOSAURS**
Large, lizardlike marine reptiles that lived in the Triassic Period.
- **THECODONTS**
A group of socket-toothed **archosaurs** that lived during the Triassic Period.
- **THERAPSIDS**
A general term used to describe **synapsids** in the Permian and Triassic Periods.
- **THERIZINOSAURS**
A group of strange **theropod** dinosaurs that had a toothless beak and four toes on each foot.
- **THEROPODS**
A suborder of **saurischian** dinosaurs. They were **bipedal carnivores**.
- **THYREOPHORANS**
A group of armored, plated, and/or spiked **ornithischian** dinosaurs. They included the **ankylosaurs, nodosaurs**, and **stegosaurs**.
- **TIBIA**
The shin bone.
- **TRICONODONTS**
An extinct group of small, early mammals that lived from the Triassic until the Cretaceous Period.
- **TRILOBITES**
Early **arthropods** with external skeletons divided into three lobes.
- **TROODONTIDS**
A group of small, lightly built, long-legged **tetanuran theropods** with unusually large **braincases**.
- **TYRANNOSAURIDS**
A family of very large **tetanuran theropods** with two-fingered hands, small arms, a large head, sharp teeth, and powerful hind legs.
- **ULNA**
One of the two bones of the lower arm.
- **UNGULATES**
Hoofed mammals, such as horses.

- **VASCULAR PLANTS**
Land-living plants with a specialized system of tubes that carry water and nutrients.
- **VERTEBRAE (sing. vertebra)**
The linked bones that form the backbone in **vertebrates**.
- **VERTEBRATES**
Animals with a backbone and a skull made of bone or cartilage.
- **WARM-BLOODED**
See **Endotherms**.

INDEX

ACKNOWLEDGMENTS

Dorling Kindersley would like to thank Alison Woodhouse for proofreading the text and Jane Parker for compiling the index.

The publisher would like to thank the following for their kind permission to reproduce their photographs:
(Abbreviations key: b=bottom, c=centre, l=left, r=right, t=top, b/g=background)

10: Queensland Museum; 11br, cr: Royal Tyrrell Museum, Canada; 13tr: Corbis; 20/21b/g: Corbis/Roger Ressmeyer; 22/23: Corbis /ML Sinibaldi; 24/25b/g: Corbis/Yann Arthus-Bertrand; 26/27b/g: Corbis/David Muench 27cl: Natural History Museum; 28/29b/g: Corbis /Geoffrey L. Rotman; 30/31b/g: Corbis/Michael & Patricia Fogden; 30cl: Natural History Museum; 32/33b/g: Getty Images/William J. Hebert; 34/35b, c: Corbis/Michael & Patricia Fogden; 34/35t Getty Images/Harvey Lloyd; 36/37b/g: Getty Images/Harvey Lloyd; 37br: Natural History Museum, London; 38br: Corbis; 38tc: Natural History Museum; 44b: State Museum of Nature; 45tr: Carnegie Museum of Art, Pittsburgh; 48t: American Museum of Natural History; 49b:Yorkshire Museum; 51b: Natural History Museum, London; 58/59b/g: Corbis:/Michael & Patricia Fogden; 63tr: Science Photo Library; 65tc: State Museum of Nature; 65tr: Smithsonian Institution; 66/67: Royal Tyrrell Museum, Canada; 67br: Carnegie Museum of Art, Pittsburgh; 68/69b/g: Corbis; 74cr: Natural History Museum; 75tr: Carnegie Museum of Art, Pittsburgh; 75cr: The Institute of Archaeology, Beijing; 76b: American Museum of Natural History; 78/79b/g: Corbis; 80tc: Natural History Museum, London; 82c: Royal Tyrrell Museum, Canada; 82/83b/g: Getty Images; 83t: Senekenberg Nature Museum; 84b: Leicester Museum; 86b: Royal Tyrrell Museum, Canada; 89b: Natural History Museum, London; 94/95b/g: Natural History Museum, London; 96: Hunterian Museum; 97: Natural History Museum, London; 99bl: Natural History Museum, London; 101b: Natural History Museum, London; 102/103b/g: Corbis; 104/105b/g: Corbis; 111c: Natural History Museum, London; 112b: Getty Images; 114tr: American Museum of Natural History; 115b: American Museum of Natural History; 116: Senekenberg Nature Museum; 118: American Museum of Natural History; 123tr: Science Photo Library; 124t: Museo Argentino de Cirendas Naturales, Buenos Aires; 127c: Natural History Museum, London; 129tr: American Museum of Natural History; 130t: Natural History Museum, London; 130/131b/g: Getty Images; 131br: Royal Tyrrell Museum, Canada; 133t: Queensland Museum; 134cl: Natural History Museum, London; 135tr: Witmer Laboratories; 135cr: Natural History Museum, London; 136b: Auscape; 136tr, cl: Royal Tyrrell Museum, Canada; 137b: Natural History Museum, London; 137tr: Science Photo Library; 138/139b/g: Corbis; 139tc, cr: Natural History Museum, London. 140cl: Ligabue Study and Research Centre, Italy; 140c: Royal Tyrrell Museum, Canada; 143cr: Smithsonian Institution; 144b: Natural History Museum, London; 144t: Royal Tyrrell Museum, Canada; 145c: Royal Tyrrell Museum, Canada; 146t: Natural History Museum, London; 152/153b/g: Getty Images; 155b: Aero Vironment Inc; 155c: Science Photo Library; 158/159b/g: Corbis; 160/161b/g: Corbis; 162b: American Museum of Natural History. 163tr: Natural History Museum, London; 165b: Natural History Museum, London; 166t: Natural History Museum, London; 167tr: Natural History Museum, London; 172/173b/g: Corbis; 179b: Corbis; 182t: American Museum of Natural History; 183b: Natural History Museum, London; 188/189b/g: Corbis; 192/193b/g: Corbis; 197tl, tr: Natural History Museum; 198b: Natural History Museum, London.

All other images © Dorling Kindersley. For further information, see www.dkimages.com